WHAT DROVE SASHA BRUCE
to take a succession of married black lovers from
a Boston ghetto while making the sex and drug scene
at Radcliffe in the sixties?

WHAT DROVE SASHA BRUCE
to become both the accomplice and victim of a
notorious swindler and insatiable womanizer in
ultra-sophisticated swinging London?

WHAT DROVE SASHA BRUCE
to be the adoring puppet of a Greek gigolo who
leeched away her fortune while savagely punishing
her?

WHAT DROVE SASHA BRUCE
into the compulsive downward spiral of degradation
that ended only with her shocking death at
twenty-nine?

PRIVILEGE

*"A poor little rich girl who slummed through a nether
world of perverse love."*—WASHINGTON POST

*"Thought-provoking . . . the tragic biography of a
woman with a superb mind."*—Kurt Vonnegut

Gripping Reading from SIGNET

PRIVILEGE

THE ENIGMA OF SASHA BRUCE

BY JOAN MELLEN

A SIGNET BOOK

NEW AMERICAN LIBRARY

TIMES MIRROR

Photograph of the Bruce family by Alfred Eisenstaedt, used with permission of
Life magazine, © 1979 Time Inc.

Aerial view of Staunton Hill by Stanley Tretick, used with permission of *Life*
magazine, © 1979 Time Inc.

Photograph of Marios Michaelides used with permission of Enrico Ferorelli/Wheeler
Pictures.

Photograph of Mrs. Bruce and Hans Gleisner used with permission of Tim
Jenkins/WWD.

Photographs of Staunton Hill and its environs used with permission of Lynda Jones.

After great pain, a formal feeling comes—
The Nerves sit ceremonious, like Tombs—
The stiff Heart questions was it He, that bore,
And Yesterday, or Centuries before?

The Feet, mechanical, go round—
Of Ground, or Air, or Ought—
A wooden way
Regardless grown,
A Quartz contentment, like a stone—

This is the Hour of Lead—
Remembered, if outlived,
As Freezing persons, recollect the Snow—
First—Chill—then Stupor—then the letting go—

Emily Dickinson

Acknowledgments

I am grateful first to all those of Sasha's friends who discussed her life with me despite the pain of remembering the brief time they shared together: Bear Barnes, Geoff Beane, Celestine Bolen, Loraine Bolen, Anne Borland, Steve Blodgett, Julia Clark Boak, Judy Bruce, Rosalie Hornblower Catlin, Susan Colgate, Tom Dolembo, Wendy Wisner Hazard, David Irons, Maeve Kinkead, Peter Lubin, Peter McCaffery, Sarah Clark McIntyre, Susan Mullin, Mark Nye, Barbara Hanson Pierce, Wesley Profit, and Terry Graham Smith.

My special gratitude goes as well to Dr. Stanley N. Frye and to Mary and Jessica Frye for their generosity.

I wish to thank too all those in Southside Virginia who talked with me of the last year and a half of Sasha's life, and of the aftermath of her death: Edwin B. Baker; John Clement; Ethel Clowdis; Emma Elam; Stuart B. Fallen; Herman Ginther; Marie Harper; Mack Harper; Cleo and Carroll Holt; John and Mary LeGrand; Bill McKelway; Fred Mills; Diane, Mary, and John Morris; Dr. David Oxley; Reginald Pettus; and Meg Tibbs.

For their frankness and time I wish to thank all those who knew Sasha during her years in London: Maria Andipa, Claudio Astrologo, Eric Bradley, Elvira Cooper, Michael and Loula Kailas, Maria Karantinou, Yannis Petsopoulos, John Stuart, Dick Temple, Maria and Beresford Willcox, and George Yemanakis.

I am appreciative of the courtesy of Professors John Rosenfield and Seymour Slive of Harvard University, of Linda Seidel of the University of Chicago, and of Christa Hollman of St. Timothy's School.

I would also like to thank particularly Alan Z. Feuer, Stephen Massey, and Oliver Twigg.

Many contributed to this study in small ways and large. I

would like to thank George Agree, Norbert L. Anschuetz, Mrs. Gregory Arzoglou, Isabel Bass, Cyril Black, John Goodall Bruce, Louise Bruce, David Surtees Bruce, Jane Lee Eddy, Harold Fleming, Lloyd K. Garrison, Lauder Greenway (in memoriam), Frank Greve, Frederick T. Gray, Jr., Professor Henry Horn, Sir Anthony Hooper, Lucy Hummer, Robert Kimball, J. Ray Knopf, John Lowe, Helen Mark, Carl McCall, Cheryl McCall, Paul Mellon, Mary Lewis Michaelides, Marios Michaelides, Harold Newman, McKim Norton, John Oliver, Paul O'Neil, Tim Randall, Mrs. Downey Rice, Yannis Roubatis, Paul Schlamm, Arthur Schlesinger, Jr., John Simon, Duncan Spencer, Patrick Swafler, Sigourney Thayer, Dan Tomkins, Elias Vlanton, Harold Weisberg, Theodore H. White, Dr. Evan Wolarsky, and Professor Athanasios Yannopoulos.

I would also like to thank John Taylor, custodian of the OSS collection at the National Archives Records Service in Washington, and the librarians at the Virginia Historical Society in Richmond for graciously making available Bruce family papers.

For their suggestions and encouragement I am grateful to Jim Ambandos, Richard A. Falk, Ralph Schoenman, and Francine Toll, and to Lynda Jones for the enthusiasm and intelligence with which she assisted me during the early stages of this project.

I wish to thank as well my agent Berenice Hoffman.

The guiding spirit behind this project has been Michael Pakenham, whom I thank for his wisdom and for his very special and sustaining friendship and encouragement.

Finally, my deepest appreciation belongs to my editor, Joyce Johnson, for the creativity, professionalism, tact, and superb good sense with which she worked with me on this book.

A Rainy Afternoon:
November, 7, 1975

Staunton Hill sits on the crest of a hill, a neo-Gothic castle rising up suddenly out of the flat pastureland and wild forests of Charlotte County, a poverty-stricken corner of Southside Virginia. Diseased and ravaged magnolia trees line the driveway leading to the fortresslike Mansion House with its crenellated roofline, turrets, and battlements.

Charlotte County is tobacco and timber country. To the plain and simple folk of the area, Staunton Hill has always seemed awesome, mysterious, haunted. Legend has it that an armed sentry sits on one of the roof's towers, perpetually poised, shotgun in hand, to shot any intruder foolish enough to venture onto these forbidden grounds.

Four generations of the Bruce family had owned Staunton Hill since 1850. In November 1975 the occupant of the sprawling house was Sasha Bruce, the twenty-nine-year-old daughter of David K. E. Bruce, former ambassador to France, Germany, and England and first American emissary to the People's Republic of China. Old-timers in Charlotte County remembered Sasha as a pretty little girl touring the countryside with her father on Christmas vacations and later as a lively teen-ager home on holidays from boarding school. They had expected her to grow up into an uppity heiress like her aunt, Mrs. James Cabell Bruce, who had been much resented for her snobbishness. In the late twenties local gossips had taken pleasure when Staunton Hill was briefly lost to the Bruce family. "Think how seclusive and exclusive Mrs. Bruce was! I was glad to see the desecration!" wrote one Charlotte County resident to another.

Sasha surprised everyone by being natural, friendly, and down-to-earth. She insisted on being called only "Sasha" and would not allow anyone to introduce her as "David Bruce's daughter," let alone as "the ambassador's daughter."

She raised chickens and drove around in a Ford—not what people expected at all.

And so they were even more surprised when a Greek named Marios Michaelides began to be seen at Staunton Hill. He seemed to turn up out of nowhere and was aloof and arrogant, ostentatiously disapproving of Sasha's efforts to be friendly. And she shriveled in his presence, becoming silent and withdrawn. Dark and moody, a small, unprepossessing man with a pencil-line mustache, Marios revealed little of himself to the residents of Charlotte County and no one liked him. He seemed an unlikely partner for Sasha, who was so cheerful and joyous.

Yet the previous August, three months ago, she had married him in Charlotte Courthouse at a wedding attended by neither her parents nor her two brothers, David and Nicky. She told people she'd be on her honeymoon in Greece until Christmas, but she came home abruptly in the middle of October. Since the advent of Marios, Sasha's old friends had been kept away. Still they continued to call and for the weekend of the seventh of November, without telling Marios, Sasha had invited Wes Profit, a Harvard classmate, to come to Staunton Hill. Early in that first week of November, Sasha had to cancel the visit.

"Things are bad," Sasha told Wes. She would have left it at that, but he pressed her for more detail.

"There's some trouble, a continual series of difficulties since we got back from Greece," she said. "I'm having arguments with my husband."

On Monday or Tuesday of that first week of November her neighbor Meg Tibbs noticed that Sasha had a black eye.

"How'd you get that shiner?" she asked.

Sasha gave her an elaborate explanation of the large black bruise.

"Target practice," she said, and went on to detail how the rifle had a scope and the scope had been next to her eye. As she shot the rifle, it had kicked back, forcing the scope into her left eye and bruising it.

Later Meg had cause to wonder: Wouldn't you sight with your right eye if you were left-handed?

With her husband and two small children, Meg Tibbs, a teacher in her mid-twenties, had been renting the ivy-covered caretaker's cottage next to the Mansion House since March.

In the lonely isolation of Staunton Hill, deeply set back from the two roads on which it gave entry, with signs warning trespassers to beware, Meg had attempted to become friendly with Sasha. But if Sasha wasn't snobbish, Marios had seemed to be; he had objected very strongly to the Tibbses using the tennis courts and swimming pool, although Sasha had very cordially invited them to do so. Marios looked sulky and nervous every time Meg had seen him and he had never been inside her house.

It began to rain at one thirty on the afternoon of November 7, 1975. Mist, haze, and a dense fog blanketed Staunton Hill plantation with autumnal gloom and Meg had not ventured outdoors. Shortly after three on that afternoon, she was startled when Marios banged on her door demanding to know if she had seen Sasha. He was actually the second person who had come by to ask for her in the last half hour. The first had been John LeGrand, the handyman.

Marios wore his usual sweater and black pants. He looked small and dark and frightened and there was a wild cast to his usually mocking brown eyes.

"I haven't seen her." Meg told Marios. Then she advised him to check some of the tenant houses where Sasha often visited. How far could she have gone on such a gloomy day? "What'd she do? Leave you?" Meg couldn't resist joking mischievously.

But Marios had already turned and started walking away. When he came back again about an hour and a half later, it was to tell Meg that Sasha had had a terrible accident.

"She's killed herself!" he shouted. "She's dead! She's dying! Call the doctor!"

At first Meg thought Marios must be exaggerating; he always seemed so unpleasantly overemotional. No doubt Sasha had injured herself in the house. Was she actually bleeding?

"Hurry up! Get somebody!" Marios cried hysterically.

Meg reported an accident to the Brookneal Rescue Squad, since Marios seemed too upset to do it himself. Then she asked Marios to take her to Sasha. They walked out into the rain, past Staunton Hill mansion. As they passed the portico with its ten slim columns gracefully facing the Staunton River, Meg was surprised that they didn't go in. But Marios plunged on past the adjacent office building toward the circular stone wall running around the property.

Meg held her breath as they scaled the wall stopping at the ancient-Old World cedar where Sasha always went for target practice. Under the twisting branches of the massive, sheltering tree, in a sweater and blue jeans, Sasha was lying in a pool of blood.

She lay on her right side, her long wet black hair tangled and matted, clinging to her face. Her left arm was flung outward, her right hand resting by her head. Meg noticed that the blood and mucus that had run out of Sasha's nose and mouth had already congealed, as if she had been lying there for some time. There was no visible wound.

"Maybe she fell out of the tree," Marios remarked. He seemed to have forgotten suggesting to Meg that Sasha had shot herself.

"Please don't let her die," he murmured. Meg realized she would have to take over.

She forced herself to remember her college first aid. Injured people must be kept warm. She checked Sasha's pulse, noting with relief that she was still breathing. "Go get a blanket!" she ordered Marios.

Discreetly, she waited until he was gone to look at the exposed left side of Sasha's head for an exit wound. There wasn't any. Nor was there a gun lying among the wet pine needles. The ground was too thickly matted for her to spot any spent shells.

Lying near Sasha was the gray torso-shaped target board that was usually set up on the tree. Both the board and the tree were riddled with bullet holes. Whenever she heard shots, which was quite often, Meg would make her little boy come inside the house. Today she had heard no shots at all. But of course the windows had been shut against the coming rain. She started to pick the board up, then hastily stopped herself. She didn't want her fingerprints on it. Sasha's tall slender body lay huddled and unmoving, and Meg became increasingly nervous standing out there alone in the fine rain.

After what seemed a very long time, Marios came back from the Mansion House with a small, light blanket. He said he had been looking for the gun he kept hidden from Sasha under his bed, but hadn't found it.

It would only occur to Meg later that with Sasha lying on her right side, and apparently not having been moved, there was really no way anyone could have known whether she had in fact been shot. But at the moment she couldn't think of much else besides keeping Sasha warm. The blanket Marios had brought wouldn't do much good. Still, she took it from him and tucked it gently around Sasha, working from her feet to her hips, careful not to move her. She felt around Sasha's body but could find no gun.

It frightened Meg to see Sasha looking so cold and still with her usually dusky rose complexion so chalky. Marios was becoming more and more distraught and self-pitying. "My poor Sasha," he kept wailing. "You don't know how much I love her and now she's going to die." Meg ran all the way back to her own house to get a quilt.

Around five that same afternoon two visitors arrived at Staunton Hill, Sasha's godmother, Priscilla Jaretzki, and her friend Rainer Esslen. Sasha had invited them for the weekend and in fact had spent part of the morning in her father's wine cellar choosing champagne. She had also been baking a chocolate cake.

As the two visitors remembered it, Marios suddenly came running from the colonnade area of the Mansion House. He led them through the rain to the place where Sasha lay. Now three of the servants were clustered around her, having joined Meg Tibbs.

In her elegant clothes, Priscilla knelt down on the muddy ground beside her godchild. Putting her hand on Sasha's forehead, she noticed the black eye. She lifted Sasha slightly, thinking she might start her circulation, and saw a gaping black hole in the right side of her face, from which a thin stream of blood steadily trickled. Sasha had been shot. Looking around for Marios, Priscilla noticed he had disappeared.

"He was somewhere peepin'," John LeGrand said afterwards.

Fifteen minutes later the ambulance arrived. When William Gray Stimpson of the Brookneal Rescue Squad rolled Sasha over, he saw that both her eyes had gone black. There was blood all over his hands. He asked if anyone had seen a gun and then quickly ordered the area cleared. He and Wylie Marston, the paramedic, prepared to carry Sasha to the ambulance with Rainer Esslen's help. No one else seemed able to move.

Once Sasha's body was removed, John LeGrand lifted

Meg's quilt off the ground. "There's a gun back there!" he shouted just as the back door of the ambulance slammed shut.

Elizabeth Hamlett, the elderly arthritic housekeeper, for decades a retainer of the Bruce family, picked up the gun and rushed to the ambulance, followed by the handyman Buss Baker. Stimpson heard a banging on the metal door. When he opened it, Elizabeth in her confusion was pointing a gun between his eyes. He pushed her arm down and grabbed it, releasing the clip and clearing the chamber of a live round of ammunition.

The gun was a silver 22-caliber Manurhin-Walther PP Sport target pistol. Fired out of doors that foggy November afternoon, it would have made a high-pitched whining sound—a quick crack that would have been muffled by the rain.

When Meg saw that gun, a chill ran down her back. Had Marios squeezed it under Sasha's body while she was gone fetching the quilt? But she kept silent.

"I have been familiar with the Staunton Hill plantation for some fifty-five years of mature observation," Sasha's grandfather William Cabell Bruce wrote in 1936, "and, during that time, no grave crime has ever been committed on it, though it has had, at times, a population of between three and four hundred people on it; that is to say, no murder, no rape, no arson, no offense worse than petty Negro pilferings from the Mansion House storeroom, or pantry, or from orchards, cornfields, or hen houses."

His granddaughter, Sasha, would be the first person to be shot at Staunton Hill.

When William Stimpson turned the weapon over to the police, he reported that the hammer of the Walther had been forward when he took it from the trembling hands of old Elizabeth Hamlett. Since the gun had been fired once, someone would have had to put the safety down—or carefully pull back on the trigger while gently pushing the hammer forward with the thumb. This operation would normally require two hands; if it had not been done precisely, the gun would have gone off again.

With so severe a head wound, it would have been virtually impossible for Sasha to have pushed the hammer forward—or even to have moved the safety down. It was almost as unlikely that in her panic Elizabeth would have had the presence of mind to put the weapon on safety, calmly effecting this precautionary measure. John LeGrand had been too frightened to touch the gun at all.

But a murderer familiar with guns might inadvertently have put the pistol on safety without thinking.

In the ambulance Stimpson started Sasha on oxygen. At first she seemed to respond positively. Between Staunton Hill and Brookneal, a distance of about eight miles, she stirred slightly and mumbled something. After Brookneal there was no movement and no sound.

Hobbling back to the Mansion House, Elizabeth Hamlett found Sasha's sunglasses lying on the back porch outside the kitchen door, as if they had been knocked off her face. Buss told her he had heard Sasha and Marios arguing that morning in loud, angry voices.

The ambulance sped to the emergency room of Lynchburg General Hospital thirty-five miles away, arriving at 6:45 P.M. Stimpson put the pistol and the clip into an envelope and handed it over to Officer Carl Clemmons of the Brookneal Police Department, still convinced that the hammer had been forward.

Everyone had expected Marios to get into the ambulance with Sasha. Instead, he joined Priscilla and Rainer in their car as they followed to the hospital. During the ride he said little, except to murmur occasionally, as if perplexed, "Why did she do it? Why did she do it?"

At Lynchburg Hospital the nurses gasped as they removed Sasha's muddy clothes. A beautiful young woman, she was covered with bruises, some yellowed, others fresher; most had been received in the past four to seven days. There was Sasha's black eye, the fading bruise over the left eyelid. There were bruises on her left upper arm, on the front of both thighs, and on the lower part of her legs—as well as the fading one on her left eyelid. Dr Lewis J. Read, the medical examiner, later would wonder how they had been inflicted. Had Sasha been involved in a series of struggles, fighting off an attacker who finally had shot her?

* * *

Because Sasha was still alive, there was no way of determining the time she had been shot. She was examined first by Dr. Ramachandriah who found her in extremely critical condition. He asked Marios about the bruises all over Sasha's body. Sasha had thrown herself down the stairs, Marios said. The bruise on her left eye was caused by the recoil of the rifle with which she had been practicing.

At midnight Investigator B. F. Chumney of the Virginia State Police arrived at the intensive care unit and conducted neutron-activation tests on Sasha's hands and face. The test swabs he took were never examined.

At the Lynchburg Holiday Inn, Marios insisted that Rainer Esslen drive him right back to Staunton Hill. He was adamant about returning to Brookneal that night. Priscilla was astounded that Marios should be so anxious to leave Sasha. The doctors had warned them that a gunshot wound at point-blank range would probably be fatal. Sasha was likely to die at any moment.

Annoyed, Priscilla told Marios that Rainer was too tired to make that long drive. He had already driven down from Richmond that day. The road was dark, wet, and crooked. She began to feel wary of Marios and later she remembered feeling Rainer might even be in danger with this man. He might be a cold-blooded murderer who could do harm to her friend.

In the middle of the night Investigator Chumney collected Marios and drove him back to Staunton Hill. Special Agent J. W. Barbour of the State Police, the local sheriff, Burrel Brown, and Investigator R. P. Rainey, Jr., were waiting for them there.

November 8, 1975

AT 3:25 A.M., Marios was interviewed by Investigator Rainey. He told the police of Sasha's many past attempts to commit suicide. She had so many problems stemming from her unhappy childhood that she didn't want to live. Six months earlier, Sasha had attempted suicide by taking twenty sleeping pills. At that time she had left him a letter which they later destroyed. She had written that she feared she was affecting his life badly and that only her death would set him free.

She'd tried to commit suicide again only last weekend, Marios said. There had been a similar suicide note—this one too had been destroyed. But Sasha had only taken ten sleeping pills, so Marios had been able to bring her around by forcing her to drink a lot of water and to throw up. He gave the police the same story about Sasha's black eye that he had given Dr. Ramachandriah and that Sasha had told Meg Tibbs. But now he said he didn't believe that story himself. Sasha got the black eye by deliberately throwing herself down the staircase. She had been prone to falls since she was a child. A doctor had once told her that it was psychological; there was nothing physically wrong with her.

He admitted to the police that he had sometimes found it necessary to beat Sasha during the three months that they had been married. Three weeks before, in her parents' home in Washington, he "slung her" when again she tried to kill herself after receiving a "bad letter." Rainey asked nothing about the contents of this letter. He was interested only in knowing whether Marios hit Sasha with his fist, slapped her, or what. Marios demonstrated. He had slapped her with the palm of his hand open once on the cheek and then he had grabbed her and shook her again and again.

But he also hit her when they were alone together at Staunton Hill. "I slung her," Marios repeated to Rainey. He beat her when she was feeling depressed as a way of shaking her up. The first time he'd hit her was shortly after they met.

Sasha's problems, which led to her shooting herself, Marios said, were shared by her two brothers: "They had no family."

Until they went to the hospital, Marios said, he had not known the gun had been found next to Sasha. He said he had hidden the gun the past Sunday after the latest of her suicide attempts. He had placed it under a bed in his room. Rainey wanted to know if Marios thought Sasha was "crazy," if she'd ever been to a psychiatrist.

Unhappy people weren't crazy, Marios replied, although they behaved in unexpected ways.

He and his wife were equally wealthy, Marios told Rainey. Sasha's irrevocable trust was bringing in forty thousand dollars a year; he was worth a half million dollars himself when he married her. And he agreed, should it become necessary, to take a polygraph test.

Rainey told him to remain available for further questioning. Marios then asked if Sasha had died. Not yet, he was told, but she wasn't expected to survive.

The police asked to be shown around as they searched for a possible third suicide note. The one she had written the past Sunday had been scrawled on an envelope. They could find no last message from Sasha. But just as they were about to leave, Special Agent Barbour decided to look in the small office building near the tree where Sasha's body had been found. There in a wastepaper basket was an envelope torn into three pieces. Placing the fragments together, a small paragraph could be made out. Yes, Marios said, this was the note left by Sasha on Sunday, November second. It began "Mou husband mou."

The police were baffled.

What does *mou* mean, they wanted to know.

It means "my husband mine," Marios explained. Sasha was using *mou* as a term of endearment.

Fast-talking, hard-drinking, fortyish Marie Harper was Sasha's closest friend in Charlotte County. Marie liked her Jack Daniel's laced with ginger ale and her humor bawdy. After Sasha found out that Marie had been born on Staunton Hill plantation where her father was David Bruce's gamekeeper, they had become "buddies."

On Friday night she heard Sasha had been shot. And when she arrived at the bank where she worked as a teller on Saturday morning, the sheriff and the State Police were waiting for her.

Wary and shrewd, Marie was at first reluctant to say anything. Assured that the interview would be confidential, she opened up. Sasha was her closest friend, Marie said. Sasha had brought her a bracelet when she returned from her honeymoon in Greece in October. The police wanted to know whether Marie believed Sasha shot herself.

Marie said she found it difficult to believe Sasha would take her own life. Yet on Mother's Day, Sasha had attempted suicide by taking an overdose of Valium. Sasha had a very unhappy childhood and a past of which she was ashamed, Marie said. She did not believe Marios loved Sasha as much as Sasha loved him. Marios was very jealous.

Marie rambled on about financial details. Sasha and Marios were attempting to buy Staunton Hill from Sasha's brothers. Sasha had made an application for a loan at the Fidelity Bank. She had also cosigned a note for Elizabeth Hamlett's nephew which had become due. The bank sent a notice to Staunton Hill, but it had been returned to the bank on Thursday unclaimed. Sasha had been free to get together with Marie only when Marios wasn't around. She hadn't seen Sasha all this week.

Did Marie believe Marios shot Sasha?

Marie calculated quickly. If she were to say yes, where would that leave *her*? What if Marios didn't do it? She hedged. All she could think of anyway was Sasha lying in the hospital in a coma. She wasn't worried about Marios; he could take care of himself. But what would happen to Nicky, Sasha's youngest brother? Sasha was like a mother to him. How would Nicky survive this?

The police had a final question. What could have motivated Sasha to commit suicide? They were anxious to have done with this delicate case, for like everyone in Charlotte County they were scrupulously protective of the Bruce family. As one of the courthouse philosophers put it, "There are three types of people in this county: the whites, the blacks, and the Bruces.''

Marie told the police she didn't know what could have prompted Sasha yesterday to try to kill herself.

After the police left, Marie drove to Staunton Hill to see how Elizabeth Hamlett was faring.

The two women sat in the kitchen and answered the telephone.

"I think Marios was out for everything she had," Elizabeth whispered. "He's been trying to take over everything. Sometimes I had to hide Sasha's pills."

One of the telephone calls was answered upstairs. Marie had thought they were alone in the house. Elizabeth told her Marios was home. Why wasn't he at the hospital? Marie wondered. Maybe after the police questioned him he didn't have a car to get back to Lynchburg. Still, it seemed odd that he should be here with Sasha in a coma forty miles away.

When Marios came downstairs, Marie could tell he had been drinking. He seemed to be blaming Evangeline Bruce, Sasha's mother, for what had happened. "*She* killed her, *she* killed my wife!" he moaned. Marios invited Marie to come upstairs with him. "I want to show you something," he said.

In Sasha's bedroom he took out the white silk bridal gown Sasha was to have worn at her October wedding at the chapel in Washington where she had been confirmed. This religious ceremony had never taken place. "Sasha never got to wear it," Marios said sadly. "*She*" (meaning Mrs. Bruce) "ruined it. We sneaked out of the house in Washington and came back here and Sasha never got to wear her wedding gown." This killed Sasha, Marios repeated.

As if in a trance he moved toward Marie and put the veil on her head. "I want you to see how it looked on my Sasha. I just want to see how it would have looked on her," Marios said softly.

That evening when Marios went to Lynchburg Airport to pick up Sasha's brothers, Marie was with him. Nicky, a tall, skinny, gangling boy of twenty-four with dark hair and glasses, had left the Scientology movement with Sasha's help and was now working as a janitor at his apartment building in Portland, Oregon; David Surtees Bruce, twenty-seven, tall, blue-eyed, and fair, the image of his father, was studying Chinese in Seattle. The brothers had met up in Washington and caught the same Piedmont flight into Lynchburg.

At the Holiday Inn, Marie ordered cold cuts, cheese, and crackers; she and Nicky had drinks; David ate a turkey sandwich. The attempts at conversation were awkward. Marie observed that the brothers were not close and that David definitely did not like Marios.

Rainer Esslen came in and told the Bruce boys that their parents had returned to the Sheraton from the hospital. According to Marie, he begged them to be cordial when they met their parents at the hospital, but Nicky said he wasn't going to speak to his mother. "I'm not going to talk to her because she killed my Sasha," Marie says she heard Marios add. Marie remembers that when David phoned to make the arrangements Evangeline Bruce said she was too tired to see them. However, according to Mrs. Bruce, Rainer saw Marios and Marie hold on to David Jr. and urge him not to join his parents. The Bruces sat up and waited for their sons until very late.

Once Marie was gone, Marios began to talk nonstop, compulsively recounting what had happened. In the hours that followed he gave three versions of how Sasha had gotten that black eye. He said first she had fallen down the stairs. Later he said she deliberately ran into a wall; when she was upset, she would sometimes bang her head frantically against the wall. The third story was that during her suicide attempt last Sunday he smacked her hard in the face trying to bring her to after she had taken those sleeping pills. He hit her to bring her back to consciousness and that was how she got the black eye.

Marios told Sasha's brothers he had hidden the Walther under his bed because Sasha was so suicidal. He believed she might use the gun at any time—which proved that what happened was suicide and not murder. Not that anyone had yet accused him of that.

November 9, 1975

All Saturday night and into Sunday morning Sasha lay unconscious. At her bedside sat her seventy-seven-year-old father, David Bruce, the "Daddy" she adored. She died on Sunday morning at ten minutes past four. At six, Marios called the hospital and so was given the news.

In his report, Dr. Read described one gunshot wound to the right temple just above and in front of the ear with minimal external damage. The powder at the wound margins led him to conclude it was a contact or near-contact wound and he decided that Sasha must have held the weapon against her right temple with her *left* hand and in this contorted posture triggered it with her thumb; her right hand had stabilized her arm. Next to "occupation" on Sasha's death certificate he wrote "domestic." He ruled her death a suicide.

Ambassador Bruce decided there would be no autopsy, despite the violent character and circumstances of his daughter's death. When Bruce had talked with Dr. Read, he seemed more concerned with the bruises than with the gunshot wound. He told Read that Sasha had many emotional problems and could become extremely depressed. She had attempted suicide on several occasions in the past. Concluding that the ambassador was neither alarmed nor surprised that his daughter should have committed suicide, Read felt better about going along with the view that the wound was self-inflicted without doing an autopsy. Later he issued a hasty statement. "I talked to State Police investigators who told me the death appeared to be a suicide," Read said. There would be no coroner's inquest.

At nine thirty that morning, David Surtees Bruce called Kenneth Holt, manager of the Henderson Funeral Home in Brookneal. "We would like to make arrangements to have the burial today," Holt, who had been disturbed at home, was told. "Would that be possible?" Holt said it would, provided he could round up enough help to dig the grave.

Marios selected the coffin, a wooden one with no metal on it, like those used in Greece.

When Holt arrived at Staunton Hill, only young David, Nicholas, and Marios were there. The clothes had been laid out. Sasha was bathed by the undertaker, who dressed her in the floor-length white bridal gown that had never been worn. Then she was placed in the casket which was closed and locked. The body was taken directly to the cemetery. Marios told everyone Sasha would not have wished to be embalmed. She had once said she wanted to be buried simply, "like our grandfathers."

Only the immediate family and the household servants were present as Sasha was laid to rest in the family cemetery at Staunton Hill where from childhood she had talked of being buried. The grave was sheltered by the old stone wall covered with ivy. Millard Stimpson of the Presbyterian Church spoke. Buss Baker filled in the grave as Elizabeth Hamlett stood and wept. There was no vault and no container.

Marios says he heard Ambassador Bruce ask David how he was progressing with his Chinese studies.

"Very well," David replied.

"Can you believe that? Can you really believe that?" Nicky exclaimed, according to Marios.

"Even Al Capone would have cracked," Marios commented.

On this day of Sasha's funeral, Ambassador Bruce phoned Herman Ginther, editor of the Brookneal *Union Star,* and requested that Sasha's death not be reported. "Mr. Bruce was a gentleman," Ginther would say later to justify his compliance, "his father and my father fished together years ago." It was Mrs. Bruce who phoned *The Washington Post* and *The New York Times,* but it would take five days before the wire services carried the news of the death of Sasha Bruce.

At seven that morning Nick had called Marie Harper to tell her Sasha had died and that the funeral would be on Monday or Tuesday.

On Monday, having driven back from Lynchburg as fast as she could so as not to miss Sasha's funeral, Marie called Nick again.

"What time will it be?" she asked.

"I'll tell you when you get here," Nick answered.

"I won't even stop at my house. I'm coming straight on to Staunton Hill," Marie told him.

At Staunton Hill only Nick and Marios were home. David Surtees Bruce had flown back to Seattle. The Bruces were already in Washington, for the ambassador had an appointment with President Ford that day. Nick took Marie by the hand and they walked the eighty yards to the cemetery. There he told Marie that Sasha had been buried at four the previous afternoon.

"Marie, they didn't even give me time to shave," he said.

At the grave, an open area surrounded by towering trees, Marie broke down. There was only a pile of fresh red dirt to mark the spot, not even a daisy. Marie's sister had driven her to Staunton Hill and Marie sent her back to Brookneal to buy flowers for Sasha's grave.

"She was a rose and she deserved a rose," Marie said.

Later there would be a tombstone purchased by David Surtees Bruce, for which Marios insisted on providing the inscription: "Flower," his name for her in their good times. Sasha had often closed her notes to him with a delicately drawn four-petaled blossom.

Meg Tibbs too felt the desolation of Sasha's hasty funeral. On Tuesday she picked a bouquet of chrysanthemums and asked permission to lay them at Sasha's grave.

Storm clouds threatened as Meg and her husband made their way to the little cemetery. They passed the gnarled old cedar where Sasha had lain in her agony. The patchwork quilt Meg had put over her had been tossed on the ground. It was difficult to locate the grave, for it had rained again. A patch of black mud and a little stick now marked the spot. And a rose lay over Sasha's grave, Marie's rose.

As Meg put down her chrysanthemums, it began to rain. Leaves blew around wildly. The little graveyard seemed a lonely, unhallowed place. "I don't know if I believe in ghosts, but I think I do," Meg said as they hastily retreated. As Meg continued to live on at Staunton Hill there would be times when she imagined Sasha near. Fixing meals, she expected Sasha any minute to turn the handle of the kitchen door, as she was wont to do, and then rush in without knocking, crying, "Meg!"

*   *   *

From Washington that Monday, November tenth, Evangeline Bruce called Wendy Wisner, one of Sasha's oldest childhood friends.

Wendy remembers Mrs. Bruce saying in a hurried conversation that she was off to Brussels and that her daughter, Wendy's oldest friend, had just been buried. She asked her to spread the word, and she told Wendy that Sasha had married an awful man.

Dismayed, Wendy sent two telegrams to David Surtees Bruce. "Call me," she telegraphed frantically. "I need to talk to you. What's going on? Console me in my grief and I'll console you in yours."

There was no reply.

Is he protecting Marios? Wendy wondered.

And she thought: Sasha should never have been buried like that, even if she did commit suicide. There was something about it that didn't do honor to her life. But the Bruces had always concealed from the world what happened among them. If Sasha herself had orchestrated the aftermath of her death, she too would have wanted it this way. Silence concealing any unpleasantness from the outside world even if, as the scar healed over, it left an infection festering inside. Just so long as no one knew about it. Now a Band-Aid would be slapped over the scar so that no fresh air could penetrate the wound.

The Band-Aid remained in place for almost three years. Then, on September 8, 1978, Marios Michaelides was indicted for the murder of Sasha Bruce.

The Ambassador's Daughter

It is almost a commonplace that children of esteemed parents themselves lack self-esteem. Their burden is to do as well, to continue in the tradition of excellence which has flourished in the custody of their elders, to nurture and carry it forward.

Alexandra Bruce, upon birth given the Russian nickname "Sasha," was born in Washington, D. C., on May 1, 1946. From birth she was the beneficiary of a million-dollar trust. As a child she followed her parents from embassy to embassy. First there were the years in Paris, where David K. E. Bruce, having administered the Marshall Plan, served as ambassador to France from 1948 through 1952. The family returned to Europe in 1957 when he was appointed to West Germany. By 1961, when her father was awarded that diplomatic plum, the Court of St. James's, Sasha was ready for boarding school.

She grew up believing the world would be her arena. Life could be wrenched into any interesting shape; only imagination was required. And an "interesting" life was above all what Sasha, like other girls of her class, sought. For children like Sasha, however, such unlimited aspirations may be accompanied by guilt, an uneasy feeling that so much privilege has not been earned. In Germany her younger brother David was embarrassed to be driven to school in an embassy limousine while his classmates arrived in Volkswagens.

If her father had had his wish, Sasha once said, he would have chosen the life of a cardinal in Rome with the robes, the pageantry, and the splendor. The adjective she applied to her father's affection for her was "distant." As a little girl she cherished her walks with Daddy, waited like a puppy longing to be taken out.

Sasha never relinquished the compulsion to do well. But at an early age she seems also to have become convinced that she could never be good enough. Amid every opportunity, every advantage, she grew up feeling she was not valuable.

On Sasha's mother, Evangeline Bell Bruce, fell the conflicting demands of husband and children. Evangeline Bell was the granddaughter of Sir Conyers Surtees, an English MP. The daughter, stepdaughter, and niece of diplomats, she is said to have once remarked, "I vowed never to marry into the diplomatic service." She knew well the constant uprootings, the strain on the family such an existence made inevitable.

"It wasn't an easy life," she told David Schoenbrun, who covered the Bruces in Paris in the fifties, "never having a home, frequent heart-wrenching farewells to friends, struggling to learn new languages, always the foreigner, the outsider, wherever you landed." Evangeline's father, Edward Bell, an American, was in the foreign service for twenty years and had been deputy chief of mission at the old legation in Peking in the early twenties. Evangeline was three and a half when she left Peking the first time; she would return in 1973 as wife of Chief of Liaison David Bruce. Her stepfather, Sir James L. Dodds, was a British ambassador to Peru, and her sister was married to a British ambassador to Italy, Sir Ashley Clarke. Evangeline had lived with her parents in London, Tehran, Tokyo, and Peking, with her stepfather in The Hague, Stockholm, and Berne, and with her uncle in Budapest and Copenhagen. She'd been educated in London, Stockholm, Paris, and Tokyo.

She met David Bruce in 1941 when he interviewed her for a job with OSS (Office of Strategic Services), for which he was later to become chief of the European theater of operations based in London.

Evangeline had already pursued Chinese studies at Harvard with John Fairbank and spoke French, German, Italian, Swedish, and what she called "bad" Hungarian and Japanese. "I was very impressed with that handsome, seven-language girl," Bruce is said to have remarked. More than twenty years David Bruce's junior, Evangeline Bruce would go on to become an exceptional diplomatic hostess, calling herself her husband's "closest associate."

When the Bruces lived in Paris in the early fifties, Evangeline Bruce was named one of the best-dressed women by French arbiters of taste. Her style was always original and eclectic. In London in 1964 she was photographed wearing thick black lace stockings and square-toed shoes under a long white evening skirt. The year 1980 found her in her sixties on the cover of *Women's Wear Daily* wearing a spangled evening gown with fabric shoes to match, dancing with Hans Gleisner, Austrian Ambassador to London, at the wedding of Alexandra, daughter of Diana Phipps, to Austrian Count Frans Seilern und Aspang.

At a Washington costume ball that same year she was seen wearing a scarlet dress with a demure bow around her neck in the same scarlet fabric as the gown. The following summer she attended the couture showings in Paris at the House of Grès, praising the designer because "she seemed to do what she wanted without worrying about whether anybody liked it"; Evangeline herself wore a ten-year-old blue and gray printed chiffon, "my first and only Grès dress." On Sunday, December 7, 1980, in Washington she was general chairman for an honors gala at the John F. Kennedy Center for the Performing Arts. Later there was a White House reception hosted by the Carters and the Mondales. "It's a tremendous mix of people," Mrs. Bruce said. And in April 1981 a Sunday brunch at her Georgetown house was photographed for *Vogue* with such captions as "in front of the fireplace, a basket of fresh quail's eggs," "sprays of mimosa surround mushroom caps," and "puff pastry hearts brightened with tomato sauce"; her home was described as one of the most beautiful in the Washington area.

Indeed Evangeline Bruce decorated her homes and the embassy residences where she lived with a flair for the dramatic and the eye of the connoisseur. Sasha thought her mother added beauty to whatever she touched. At boarding school, Sasha longed for old-fashioned Christmases at Staunton Hill. But when in 1966, Mrs. Bruce had the Christmas tree at Winfield House, the ambassador's residence in London, decorated with oranges and lemons, tiny white candles and blue ribbon instead of tinsel, Sasha, then at Radcliffe, had to admit approvingly she found the effect "strangely traditional." In Europe her mother took her to museums and awakened her interest in art. The houses in which Sasha grew up were always filled with splendid objects, for David Bruce all his life had been a serious collector, delighting in old silver and rare porcelains.

But Mrs. Bruce's days were not her own and when David Bruce was chief of mission for the Marshall Plan based in Paris in the late forties, little Sasha and David (Nicky had not yet been born) were left temporarily in Washington with their English nanny until the Bruces could find a large enough apartment. Social functions were unceasing and her parents went out as many as six nights a week during Sasha's childhood.

In France, as the wife of the American ambassador, Evangeline Bruce was at her own desk by eight thirty in the morning, lamenting that she was not able to spend more time with Sasha, three and a half, and David, eighteen months old. A secretary would arrive and they would begin on the day's correspondence. Half an hour was then spent with the housekeeper, who presided over a staff of seventeen. Fifteen minutes were devoted to the chef. Then Mrs. Bruce returned to her mail, accepting no more than a twentieth of the invitations beckoning the attractive couple. There was always a luncheon party rarely attended by fewer than twenty. Then Mrs. Bruce would go shopping, visit the hairdresser, and attend official functions. According to newspaper accounts, Mrs. Bruce made sure she saw her children at least between five and seven every evening. After Sasha and little David were put to bed, there would be more receptions, exhibitions, a banquet, or a dinner party. In her spare time Mrs. Bruce worked on a book about the French Revolution.

One day a few years later, Mrs. Bruce, her two young sons, and Sasha were crossing the busy traffic circle behind the Arc de Triomphe in Paris when a taxi driver nearly ran them down. Mrs. Bruce began to scream in perfect colloquial French, berating him for nearly hitting her children. "My mother got so upset!" Sasha exclaimed, telling the story years later. She spoke of the incident almost with wonder, as if her mother's unequivocal demonstration of concern was of unique significance.

The routine in London was no less stringent. The Bruces became famous for their brilliant dinner parties at which political personalities joined the leading writers, artists, and intellectuals of the day. The Bruces, Arthur Schlesinger, Jr., remembers, "used social occasions with great effect, as a means of keeping in touch with the opposition."

Mrs. Bruce presided over a household of almost Victorian

formality. The Bruces had separate bedrooms. Mrs. Bruce would breakfast alone in hers. When David Bruce was appointed Ambassador to the Court of St. James's in 1961 by John F. Kennedy, Mrs. Bruce made what she called the "grave decision" of leaving Sasha and David back home in boarding schools. "There is a time in cultural expatriation when children should go home," she said. On Sasha's visits, she often wouldn't see her mother until midafternoon when they might take tea together. Mrs. Bruce busied herself with appointments and her children were not permitted to disturb her.

Shortly before Sasha's death, her mother told her she had obediently abided by her husband's wishes concerning the upbringing of the children. He was so worldly, Mrs. Bruce explained. As a young woman, she had assumed he had to be right about the children, too. She admitted she might have done things differently if it hadn't been for the demands of her husband's career.

The million-dollar trust Sasha received at birth had been made possible by David Bruce's first marriage in 1926 to Ailsa Mellon, daughter of Andrew, sister of Paul, and the richest woman in the world. David Bruce's father, William Cabell Bruce, was a United States senator from Maryland, but the family coffers had long been empty.

Sasha's great-great-grandfather, James Bruce, born in 1763, had been, after John Jacob Astor and Stephen Girard, the third-richest American of his day, worth two million dollars in 1837, when he died leaving an estate that included three thousand slaves. James Bruce was a merchant, moneylender, tobacco speculator, and founder of the chain store. "Nor did he *demand* his dues, but by gentleness and persuasive measures he obtained what was his," it was said of his moneylending practices.

In the aftermath of the Civil War, his son Charles lost plantations and slaves and southern securities. It was only the marriage of Charles's grandson, David K. E. Bruce, to Ailsa that made the Bruces solvent once more. Old Andrew Mellon took his future son-in-law aside, knowing he had nothing except his salary of twenty-five hundred dollars a year as vice-consul to Rome, where he had just been posted, and gave him a million dollars in his own name so that he might not be entirely dependent on his wife's fortune. Ailsa came accompanied by a ten-million-dollar dowry as well.

Their wedding drew three thousand guests, including the President of the United States, Calvin Coolidge. Ailsa was adorned with a hundred-thousand-dollar pearl necklace and a huge sapphire ("something blue"), both gifts from her father. Rich and titled rivals like Major General H. K. Bethell, a British diplomat and military attaché, and Prince Otto von Bismarck, grandson of the Iron Chancellor, had been by-passed in favor of the tall, blue-eyed, handsome Bruce, whose family pedigree was his only material asset. When he met Ailsa, he had been a mere lawyer and member of the Maryland House of Delegates, having defeated the local Democratic Party machine on an outrageously frivolous program, which included the protection of fox hunting, the repeal of prohibition, and the legalization of betting on horse racing.

But unlike upstarts like the Mellons, the Bruce family was indeed impressively rooted in the American colonial past. George Washington himself had once spent the night at the home of the guardian of James Bruce's first wife, Sally Coles; his second wife was the widowed daughter-in-law of Patrick Henry. The earliest known ancestor, "Charles Bruce of Soldier's Rest," had served with distinction in the French and Indian War and later as a captain in the American Revolution. In contrast, Andrew Mellon was the grandson of a poor potato farmer in the north of Ireland.

At the wedding of Ailsa Mellon to David K. E. Bruce, the bride omitted the promise "to obey," while the groom prudently chose not to include "with all my worldly goods I thee endow." David K. E. Bruce was never one to inspire ridicule! The reception at the Pan American Union boasted ten chefs and seventy-five servants tending a buffet of chickens stuffed with pâté de foie gras, Virginia hams, jellied meats, baked salmons festooned with decorations, and ice cream in elaborate paper containers.

While a Marine band in scarlet uniforms played on a balcony above the feasting guests, the divorced Secretary of the Treasury Andrew Mellon, Senator and Mrs. William Cabell Bruce, and the bride and groom labored four hours shaking hands with all their well-wishers. Tall, bony, and plain as she was, the bride looked handsome, if solemn, on her wedding day, dressed in an ivory point d'Angleterre lace gown over ivory satin, the drape of the lace overskirt caught by a buckle in the manner of the twenties. The veil was tulle, the cap banded with orange blossoms. And the train was nine feet long.

The patronage of old A. W. Mellon gave David Bruce a chance to make money in his own right. And so he did throughout the thirties, becoming director of twenty-five corporations, including Union Pacific, Alcoa, and Pan American Airways. His interests ranged from a Puerto Rico sugar plantation to the Rockingham, New Hampshire, racetrack (Sasha and her brothers loved to go to the races with their father and to place bets), Virginia newspapers, Texas oil, Fox films, parachutes, and even a project for denicotinizing cigarettes. Representing Averell Harriman and others, in 1933, he bid as a Washington unknown on the bankrupt *Washington Post,* losing to Eugene Meyer, father of Katharine and father-in-law-to-be of Phil Graham, who would become a close friend.

Bruce's first venture into the foreign service had not lasted long. In Rome, Ailsa soon fell ill with the lifelong ailment that some said was caused by bites from insects bred in the concrete of the building where they lived. She became chronically neurasthenic. Meanwhile Bruce wasted no tact on Benito Mussolini. "I've been here six months and my luggage is still being held by your customs," Bruce, age twenty-eight, indignantly told Il Duce. He received his bags within hours.

His marriage to Ailsa Mellon made it possible for David K. E. Bruce to redeem the home of his ancestors, which had been sold by his father out of the family in 1924. This he did on December 20, 1933, when he purchased Staunton Hill from the Staunton Hill River Corporation, a hunting club organized by his brother James. That he waited until the birth of his first child, Audrey, was typical of David Bruce, whose style would not have been to marry Ailsa and at once buy back Staunton Hill, as if he had married the richest woman in the world for this express purpose. His grandmother, Sarah Seddon Bruce, had almost lost Staunton Hill in the panic of 1896 after the death of her husband, Charles. Then, led by Endicott Peabody, a group of Charles's Harvard classmates and fellow members of the Porcellian Club rented a private railroad car and arrived at Staunton Hill, offering their assistance to the widow, who refused at once to accept charity. Later that afternoon they discovered the fabled Bruce wine cellar and so made a deal with one of Mrs. Bruce's sons, purchasing enough wine to pay off the mortgage on Staunton Hill. The rest of the day they devoted to getting drunk on Charles Bruce's fabulous wines. (His grandson David would be elected a grand master of the Chevaliers du Tastevin, a group of wine aficionados sworn never to let water pass their lips.)

When in the 1920s Staunton Hill was again about to be sold, twenty-year-old David K. E. Bruce told his mother he feared there would soon no longer be any great southern homes in the hands of the lineal descendants of their original owners. So strong was his pride in the blood ties uniting him with the Bruces of old, that he considered renouncing the world to assume the life of a Virginia country gentleman. "He'd better go into the diplomatic service for a few years and get polished up a bit before he begins to rusticate," was the opinion of his elder brother, James, at the time.

Staunton Hill, the old family place, was certain to influence for the better anyone who lived on it, young David Bruce believed.

With money no object, the improvements began. All the bathrooms were remodeled after those at the Ritz Hotel in Paris. The stone floors on which hunters had tramped were replaced with hardwood. A new colonnade, balancing the old, was built, thereby enclosing the courtyard. There would be four new bedrooms and a linen room. A new wine cellar would serve David Bruce's great passion. He set about furnishing Staunton Hill with handsome English furniture and bought hunting prints and paintings.

Staunton Hill always occupied a special place in the imagination of Sasha's romantic father. One day in 1942, flying back to Washington, a pilot told David Bruce that since he was the only passenger, he could choose any route he desired. And so he suggested that they fly over Staunton Hill which looked, he thought, tiny and odd, nestling there in the trees.

In later years Bruce chivalrously told Sasha he had loved Ailsa, dubbed "what ails her?" by a naughty Sasha and her brothers. But by the late 1930s the marriage was clearly in trouble. Bruce enjoyed the companionship of Ailsa's father and brother and took great pleasure in supervising the birth of the National Gallery of Art in Washington, becoming its first president, but he could no longer abide the social whirl of Long Island where he and Ailsa had settled. He was bored with business deals and his work as a tax lawyer and distressed that he was whispered about as a Mellon hanger-on. He felt he was wasting his life. He and Ailsa had long since discovered themselves to be temperamentally unsuited to each other. Often Ailsa sent Bruce to dinner parties alone, promising to appear later. Bruce would sit looking at his watch as the evening stretched on and still Ailsa couldn't summon the courage to grace the social gathering at which the witty, gregarious Bruce was in his element.

They were divorced in April 1945, Mrs. Mellon Bruce, as Ailsa now called herself, having once before crankily come and gone to Florida without accomplishing the agreed-upon task. The grounds were desertion and mental cruelty. A sum of money was settled upon David Bruce, who would remain a lifelong friend of Ailsa's brother Paul, and a devoted friend to Ailsa as well, arranging to have dinner with her whenever he found himself in New York.

Their child, Audrey, was a lonely, exceedingly shy little girl who was raised almost exclusively by her nanny, Virginia Parsons. Sasha barely knew her half-sister, Audrey, who was already thirteen when Sasha was born.

His connection to the Mellon family made possible David Bruce's later diplomatic career, in which Ailsa took no part. As an ambassador he entertained lavishly at functions for which the American government contributed barely enough to pay for the wine. Only his personal fortune, a direct result of his first marriage, allowed Bruce to serve with the appropriate flourishes which, he knew, eased and facilitated the business of diplomacy.

Evangeline Bell, handsome, self-confident, instinctively fashionable, unlike the dowdy Ailsa, would flourish in the environments of diplomacy, making a much more suitable companion for David K. E. Bruce.

David Bruce was forty-eight years old at Sasha's birth; from the beginning he seemed more like an adored grandfather than a father, the central figure of all family ceremonies. Sometimes he would enthrall his children with stories of his OSS exploits. His favorite one involved a D-day adventure with his boss Wild Bill Donovan. During the invasion of Normandy, Bruce had been Donovan's second in command. As the two men crept through the hedgerows together, Donovan remembered he had left his "death pill" on his bedside table at Claridges in London. "David," he said, "I must not fall into enemy hands. I order you to stay behind me. Shoot me if you see the enemy and make your way back to Claridges and see about that pill!" In another version, Donovan asked Bruce if he had brought along his death pill. When David Bruce confessed he hadn't, Donovan told him not to worry: "If we're about to be captured, I'll shoot you first. After all, I'm your commanding officer!"

Sasha often liked to talk about her ideal Christmas; she'd be sitting on the floor in front of the fireplace at Staunton Hill at her father's feet, the two of them reading with the dogs gathered around them. With her mother she would select and trim the tree. There were also ideal Thanksgivings at "the farm" when her father would go out in quest of one of the wild turkeys in which Charlotte County reputedly abounded but which always managed to elude him so that he invariably wound up resorting to the well-stocked freezer.

One snowy Christmas at Staunton Hill, Sasha and her father, in David Bruce's words, "whacked the bushes, pounded through fields and forests, in quest of quail and turkey without success." At night the whole family played poker. They reveled in the Virginia food cooked by Elizabeth Hamlett: corn pone, corn fritters, corn sticks, tomatoes broiled in molasses, yams with marshmallows, chicken livers, giblet sauces, spareribs (a big favorite), Brunswick stew, and turnip greens.

On Christmas of 1963 at Staunton Hill, recorded in David Bruce's diary, the three children put on a "broadcast" for their parents, their rehearsals shaking the flooring above and sounding, their father thought, like activities at a wrestler's training camp. When they came down for breakfast the following morning, he thought they looked "slightly seedy." The performance was put on at nine o'clock on New Year's Eve, Nicky presiding. The finale was a Spanish guitar feature with Sasha strumming her Christmas present, dressed in an Argentine poncho, a relic of her South American tour the previous summer. "Had the offspring been on public TV," David Bruce wrote, "they would have been considered irresistible."

The festivities continued on New Year's Day. Sasha and her father danced to Martinique records; the parents "did a few Bal Bullier numbers, to the delight of the youngsters." There was much clowning as they bustled through a hedge of liqueur bottles on the carpet and bellowed at each other in French.

"There never was so amiable a group; we laugh from morning to bedtime," wrote the ambassador.

David Bruce's normal schedule was of course even more formidable than his wife's. He told Sasha people thought when he came home from the embassy at night that there was nothing more for him to do. But every night there was a cable to be sent back to the State Department, and Sasha knew how he relished composing those cables. He'd also work on his voluminous diaries, which Sasha and her brothers were not permitted to read. The following telegram, classified as "confidential" and written in David Bruce's meticulous handwriting, triple-spaced on a legal pad, as was his custom, in 1964 just as Sasha was entering Radcliffe, offers a glimpse of her daddy's time was occupied and of the world with which Sasha felt she had to compete for his attention:

Between the distractions of internal administrative and personnel problems, receiving visits from peripatetic and fidgeting federal officers, giving cocktail parties for compatriots, addressing British audiences seemingly tolerant of endless flows of banal oratory, carrying out instructions to make representations to the British foreign office, all too often duplicatory of conversations already held with the efficient British Embassy in Washington, liverish representational lunching and dining, attending meetings of the Anglo-American goodwill organizations, running a barroom and restaurant for jetborne countrymen, turning night into day in an unceasing effort to cope with trivia, crippling my wrist with correspondence, attempting to preserve security with inquisitive journalists, maintaining courteous relations with 100-odd ambassadorial colleagues, it is quite impossible for me to concoct within the time allotted, namely a few days, a reasoned response to your 10-page memorandum of January 23, requesting comments on that hotchpotch of confusion suggested as a background paper for the President in connection with "the forthcoming Johnson-Douglas-Home talks"; I will close this somewhat lengthy midnight sentence by stating I will answer as quickly as I can, and without unwarranted bile, having already disposed, I hope satisfactorily, in a previous communication, of the weighty matter of how Mesdames Douglas-Home and Butler should occupy their leisure moments in Washington.

Bruce.

Her "dotty Daddy," as Sasha came to call him, was intensely preoccupied during her earliest years. When she was ten, he drafted a secret report for President Eisenhower in which he condemned CIA interventions in the governments of foreign countries. Such "king-making responsibility," Bruce argued, was in violation of international law and dangerously unilateral, since it was often done without the knowledge of presiding State Department officers. Despite his belief in the need for a strong intelligence operation, he found such "rogue elephant operations abhorrent." "Where will we be tomorrow?" he asked presciently. He was a brilliant negotiator, working always within the interstices of government, immune from what he considered misleading, vulgarizing, and damaging public debate. David Surtees Bruce later thought their father eschewed elected office in part to escape the unpleasantness of notoriety.

Whatever part of the world he was in, his appointment book on any given day listed ten names; his "take-home briefcase" was always crammed with reports. He was present, but not close to his children. Moments alone with him were rare.

One day at the London Zoo when she was twenty-two years old, Sasha watched as her father walked along tenderly holding the hands of two little boys, one his grandson, Michael Currier. Sasha trailed behind. Then, wistfully and utterly without anger, she turned to her companion and remarked, as if she were stating a simple matter of fact, "Never with us."

In 1952 when Sasha was six, David K. E. Bruce was appointed under secretary of state and the Bruces returned to Washington from France. Promptly she was introduced by her nanny to Terry Graham, whose father, John, was with the Treasury Department, and to Wendy Wisner, whose father, Frank Wisner, would become CIA head of clandestine operations; both had been judged suitable friends for Sasha by the Bruces.

In the backyard of the house of one of the girls, Sasha appeared wearing "funny" French clothes. Wendy and Terry decided her French mannerisms were absurd, her manners ridiculous. She was very correct and feared getting mussed up. At once Terry and Wendy teamed up to mock her, making fun of her Frenchified ways. But before long the differences dissolved and the three little musketeers were all tomboys in perpetual motion, sharing bicycles, horses, and blue jeans and climbing trees.

Their abiding rule was "no girlie things." Horses assumed great importance in their lives. When Sasha spent two weeks in Scotland with the Wisners, the girls rode two rented horses and camped out on the moors. At Staunton Hill they rode Fawzan, an old white horse who lived to be thirty-two and to whom Sasha became attached. Fawzan was one of the family; he had belonged to her father. In a favorite game one girl was the rider, the other the horse and they jumped hurdles on the Bruce lawn in Georgetown. In her third-floor attic room Sasha read the Black Stallion books and pretended she was in a fantasy land. She loved animals and taught her blue parakeet Turque to do tricks and follow her around the house.

The three tomboys considered themselves tough. Marking Windsor on the map of England in her atlas, Sasha wrote, "This is where the Queen lives. She's stinky and smelly. I hate her."

Secretly she hid a few dresses away in the back of her closet. They were there because she knew they had to be. She didn't enjoy them, but they were necessary. For such infractions Wendy and Terry had their revenge and one day they killed Sasha's turtle by putting Bab-O in its bowl. All prissy girl things were out. Dolls especially. Another day they set upon Sasha's French doll, which slept in a little French bed in the window of her room.

No one was allowed to touch this doll. But after throwing playing cards out the window and clogging the gutters, Wendy and Terry ripped up the French doll, tearing it limb from limb. Sasha stood by passively, making no attempt to stop them. Then they threw the doll out the window.

Later Wendy and Terry were ordered by their mothers to return separately to the Bruce house and apologize to both Sasha and her mother. Wendy shriveled before Mrs. Bruce's disapproval. Sasha stood silently beside her mother.

Twice a month on Saturday afternoon the three tomboys could be found wearing party dresses and party shoes at Mrs. Shippen's legendary dancing class held in a church hall in Georgetown. There boys and girls learned to waltz, fox-trot, rumba, and cha-cha. By sixth grade some girls became boy crazy and wore nylon stockings, high heels, and strapless bras to Mrs. Shippen's. Sasha continued to appear in her little-girl dresses. She was not interested in boys.

The values of the tomboy world prevailed. Now it was Sasha who scorned thirteen-year-old Wendy Wisner, fresh from two years in England and sporting an English accent. "Wendy is finished," Sasha told Terry. She was not to be their friend anymore, not unless she got rid of all those pretensions. And it was tomboy Sasha who got into endless fistfights with her brother David, once pushing him into a fireplace so that he got burned and she got spanked.

Sasha was a good student at Potomac School, many of whose pupils were children of government officials; rarely did she miss a day. She was too shy to be a class leader and felt she was not one of the "perfect people," those girls already so mature for their age. Sasha was childish, mischievous, playful, and seemingly untroubled. When the headmistress berated her for not wearing her school sweater on the hockey field on a chilly autumn day, "What's the matter with you? Don't you have any sense of hot and cold?" Sasha turned the line into a private joke to be enjoyed long after. "Can't you tell black from white? Don't you know hot from cold?" she would demand of friend and fellow-culprit Susie Colgate and the two would explode in gales of laughter.

Sasha's laugh was infectious, high-pitched, and joyous, if shaded by a note of hysteria. In his diary Ambassador Bruce wrote of Sasha's "usual high, but equable spirits." Sasha told her friend Steve Blodgett that once her mother told her that her laugh was altogether too much like a hoot and not at all genteel. In other words, Sasha had been made to feel it had been noticed in company.

Potomac School pleased her. She flourished under its unusual program, which included art, bird watching, band, drama (Sasha played a nobleman in *Saint Joan*), folk dancing on May Day (her birthday), and chorus in which everyone sang. She did well in its structured academic program, excelling, not surprisingly, in languages; Latin was a favorite. Excellence, of course, was expected of her. School was a secure base and she became so attached to her Potomac jacket that she wore it right through the summer. She was a girl scout and during the summer of 1954 at Camp Macjanet in France won a prize for camping, for which her name was inscribed on a plaque. She became fascinated by the Loch Ness monster, by her ancient Bruce ancestry which went back to the town of Bruis in France and to the Norman Conquest, as well as to King Robert the Bruce, and by everything Scottish. She learned the names of all the different tartans.

After-school activities were often organized by Mrs. John Graham, Terry's mother. It was Mrs. Graham who took Sasha, Terry, and Wendy Wisner to the movies or ice-skating or horse-back riding, driving them back and forth. Sometimes Sasha felt as if she were an extra person, invited along thanks to the courtesy of others.

Winter afternoons Terry and Sasha would get off the Potomac School bus together and have tea and cinnamon toast at the Grahams'. Mrs. Graham was always there, and Sasha was treated as one of the family. In the Bruce household self-restraint and decorum were expected. Sasha was not allowed sweets; fruit was permissible, but not cakes or pies. There was no food between meals, no sneaking into the kitchen for snacks. A style of perfection was to be cultivated and years later people would watch incredulously as Sasha, drying the dishes, would polish a single glass for fifteen minutes before moving on to the next.

*   *   *

Of the three Bruce children, Sasha was acknowledged as the leader and the strongest—the most responsible. She called herself the "manchild." She was also the loneliest, although David also remembers having some lonely times. David K. E. Bruce had had one "Mammy" who did most of the bringing up and whose picture he carried with him to Europe when he was twenty-two. But his children had a succession. One girl named Yolanda, nicknamed "Yo-Yo," was a favorite. When an orphaned French girl dubbed "G" took care of Wendy, Sasha was drawn to her as if she were an older sister. But there was also one nanny whom Sasha hated and called a witch behind her back. She was in charge of seeing that Sasha, aged six or seven, performed in the bathroom every morning after breakfast. And there she had to sit and wait, regardless of whether the urge was present. With that nanny there was corporal punishment.

There was also a succession of Evangeline Bruce's barking, yapping, biting dogs. Dogs were a passion for Mrs. Bruce, who once told a *Vogue* writer, in response to a remark about the inevitability of dogs becoming as interesting as people, that the difficulty "begins when they become more so." In Georgetown it was Sasha's job every day to feed them—a chore she so hated that, uncharacteristically, she complained bitterly about it to Wendy. Ordinarily Sasha never openly questioned anything her parents did and she was always taken aback by Wendy's battles with her own mother. Sasha was especially jealous of her mother's favorite dog, Brucie. When Brucie died, his ashes were buried in the garden.

In Washington, Sasha was in charge of preparing the daily meal for four springer spaniels, a chore that had to be completed by a certain hour. If she had started a game with a friend and was delayed, making it impossible to have the meal done on time, she became terrified that her mother would be angry at her. If one of the dogs made a mess in the house, it was Sasha's task to clean it up. Terry Graham remembers—although Mrs. Bruce denies this—that one dog named Mosey became a neurotic; if Mrs. Bruce whispered certain lines in French, Mosey would become frightened, crouch down on the floor, and urinate.

One of the spaniels, whose name was Minty, belonged to Sasha. But when the dogs began to fight among themselves, Mrs. Bruce decided to give Minty away and keep the others.

Sasha found out where he was sent and for a while was determined to visit him. A decade later, however, at Winfield House, Sasha and Mrs. Bruce could be found together bathing "the boys," the springers just rescued from the British quarantine. Sasha told her friends that on her arrival she was certain to be greeted by the springers clamoring for her affection. "Dreamers!" she called them playfully.

Of all the mothers, Sasha's was unique, more fun to be with than any other adult that Sasha's friends knew. Mrs. Bruce alone had the imagination to lend herself to the children's way of thinking. She talked to them as if they were grown-up; she confided in them. Once she told Sasha her own mother had been a stiff, formal lady and she wanted to be close to her daughter, closer than her own mother had been to her. Sasha reported to her friends that her maternal grandmother was the worst mother she had ever heard of, and that Mrs. Bruce had had frequent adolescent depressions.

Mrs. Bruce felt she and Sasha always had a close and loving relationship. Even when her daughter was a little girl, she treated her and her friends as equals. "Do you *really* think that?" she might ask. She was their charming friend, as if no age difference separated them at all. One morning at Staunton Hill when Sasha and Wendy made a great display of eating burnt toast with no butter for breakfast because they said they preferred it that way, Mrs. Bruce enjoyed burnt toast with them. She laughed at their jokes, declaring that Wendy should be nicknamed "Wen-wen" and not, "Wen," since that meant "mole." She signed her letters "Mrs. Groose." This splendid older friend could also be a coconspirator and when ten-year-old David was caught smoking in the guard house at the ambassador's residence in Germany, she allowed him to smoke in her sitting room instead.

For Sasha and Terry, nine, and Wendy, eight, Mrs. Bruce created what she called The Thursday Club. Mrs. Bruce personally did the cooking, living up to her reputation as a great spaghetti maker. And she seemed to delight in these evenings as much as the little girls did. She permitted Sasha and her friends to visit her boudoir. Among her possessions was a diamond stomacher, a gift from her Uncle Harold that was said to stretch clear across her belly even when she was pregnant. And there were ball gowns unlike anything belonging to the other mothers. The three tomboys were given the run of the elegant Georgetown mansion, well aware that they would never have been given such freedom at the Grahams' or the Wisners'. Always they gravitated to that exquisite boudoir until finally Mrs. Bruce would stop them and say they were making too much of a mess.

Mrs. Bruce was also famous as a storyteller, regaling Sasha and her friends at the table at Staunton Hill with hair-raising tales of the Germans and the Japanese. She created the tradition of each family member reading aloud from a chapter of a book after dinner, and suffered endless games of Old Maid. At Staunton Hill she told ghost stories with such vividness that one night Sasha and Wendy raced through the colonnade after they had been put to bed to find comfort with Mrs. Bruce in her bedroom.

There was a magic about Mrs. Bruce. If she entered into the spirit of an occasion, it seemed there was nothing she wouldn't do. It felt glorious to bask in her approval. One Easter she dyed eggs with the children. Later she joined in the Easter egg hunts. When Terry didn't win a single game, Mrs. Bruce, always observant, took Terry under her wing and saw that she won something. At Staunton Hill, Mrs. Bruce put together photograph albums of the children's growing up.

Mrs. Bruce and Sasha composed what Mrs. Bruce calls "a Nabokovian satire" and a minihistory of Staunton Hill. There was an air of excitement in the Bruce household. Mrs. Bruce taught Sasha to feel at home anywhere in the world, to thirst for knowledge and experience. She must not miss out on anything strange, beautiful, or inspiring. Idleness was frowned upon, no lazy Sundays reading the newspapers and dropping off to bed. In the south of France one summer Sasha was given a choice: she might visit the Meaght Foundation museum in St.-Paul-de-Vence, or explore the countryside; in Paris it might be Versailles, the Museum of Modern Art—or a fashion show.

But Mrs. Bruce also had very definite ideas of how a young lady should comport herself. An offhand remark of her mother's could hurt Sasha for days. Sasha penned notes to her mother even when they were living together in the same house, requesting permission to do the most ordinary things. The time her mother spent with her was precious and never enough.

If you ever meet my mother, Sasha told her friends, you might be taken aback at first, but then you would like her.

At eleven Sasha had to leave Potomac School because her father was returning to Europe as the new ambassador to Germany. Marios Michaelides says Sasha told him she was so upset that she went down to the silo at the lowlands near the Staunton River and there strangled her pet cat, leaving its body behind, and telling no one. Later at St. Timothy's School when she had to read aloud in German class a story about two children tearing out the eyes of birds, she began to cry uncontrollably and had to stop.

In Germany the children remained in their "exclusive preserve," the top floor, where they had to remain when their parents entertained. They amused themselves playing with the dumbwaiter, learning, David Surtees Bruce says, that as long as they remained out of sight, they could do pretty much whatever they wanted.

Sasha was thrown into a German-speaking school and for three or four months couldn't understand what was being said. She found it hard to make friends and the Bruces sent for Terry Graham to keep her company. The girls played on the huge estate in Bad Godesberg with its dogs, deer, and swimming pool. A seemingly endless stream of servants attended to their needs. They rode horses at a nearby riding academy, which Sasha had begun to frequent by herself out of her loneliness.

Halloween of 1959 found Sasha at thirteen back in Washington, scraping out a pumpkin for a jack-o'-lantern. That night her parents took her to her first "mixed dinner" at the John Grahams'. Her father told her she looked "lovely."

Sasha wasn't sure she was pretty at all. She had frizzy black hair. And she was physically less developed than other girls her age so that she was nicknamed Runty. Her mother was handsome, witty, elegant, and sophisticated, everything Sasha was certain she was not. As she entered adolescence, she grew ashamed of how she looked and uncomfortable in social situations.

Sasha's was a childhood of high energy and of loneliness. There were moments so dark she could share them with no one, pain so acute it may have led her either to do injury to a pet cat—or to tell Marios that she had as a way of defining her earliest years. It was a childhood for which Sasha would later feel she deserved particular understanding, compassion, and even pity.

At St. Timothy's School, where she went as a sophomore in the fall of 1961, her depressions began in earnest.

Christian Gentlewomen

The school Sasha and her parents chose was an Episcopal academy for daughters of the elite located on an isolated road in the hilly countryside outside Baltimore. Of the thirty-six girls in Sasha's class, every one came from a wealthy family. Several, like Jane ("Trickster") Frick, were socially prominent as well. There were descendants of genteel New England bloodlines, like Julie Clark, whose ancestor was Alexander Hamilton, and Rosalie Hornblower, whose family went back to John Aldrich. The southern girls were the richest and produced superb clothes whenever the St. Tim's uniform—gray skirt, white blouse, blue blazer—was not mandatory. The Chicago girls took private planes in and out of places like Vail and on Father's Day their fathers would sit in the back row and place bets on the Kentucky Derby.

At St. Tim's, under the genteel eye of Miss Watkins, the highly cultivated daughter of an Episcopal priest, Sasha and her schoolmates would be guided along the pathway to becoming "gracious leaders." As "Christian gentlewomen" each would make her contribution to family, community, and country, serving others out of a sense of chivalry and noblesse oblige. During Lent, Miss Watkins read *Jane Eyre* to her assembled charges as they sewed baby clothes for the poor. At Christmas, each girl curtsied as she was given a sprig of holly by Miss Watkins. Then they departed for their holidays in dresses and suits, never blue jeans.

"Oh dear, that makes me cross," Miss Watkins would demur in response to a slightly off-color remark. Politically conservative, she'd defuse too progressive an idea with "Oh, but don't you think that's a terribly broad statement?" A less threatening notion might elicit, "Oh, isn't that interesting!"

St. Timothy's offered little free time for morbid adolescent introspection. Inwardness and self-doubt were considered enemies. Two bells sounded each morning summoning the girls to breakfast. They would march back to clean their rooms, then proceed to study hall. Every morning there were compulsory prayers and on Tuesday, Thursday, and Sunday nights, longer services. Sports—tennis, hockey, horseback riding—were vigorously pursued every afternoon; some girls, but not Sasha, kept their own horses in St. Tim's stables.

The Bruces were serving in London in 1961. Sasha and Wendy were to enter St. Tim's together that fall. Wendy resisted, rebelling against the idea of an Episcopal, southern girls' school that offered training in the profession of ambassador's wife. Wendy's mother, Mrs. Wisner, an active alumna, enlisted Sasha's help. "Make her see it's a good idea to go to St. Tim's," Mrs. Wisner implored. Sasha prevailed.

Sasha entered energetically into the spirit of St. Tim's, thriving on the rigorous discipline. The structured atmosphere allowed her a freedom she found exhilarating. "[Miss Watkins] liked to have us create within limits because she said it molded character," Sasha's class wrote of their formidable headmistress in their yearbook and Sasha thoroughly approved of this approach. Although she was not religious, she was even moved by the required Sunday evening chapel services at which, she wrote, leaning "if vaguely" toward God, she looked through the windows at the "mottled blue and black sky in its immensity and felt a certain peace."

One Christmas she sang carols in German before the assembled student body. On another occasion she put on a skit in perfect French dramatizing a driving lesson; she scratched a pie tin to imitate the screeching of brakes. She was a bell ringer, playing at concerts in St. Tim's revival of church bell ringing in old England; she played Don Pedro in *Much Ado About Nothing* and was a member of the Self-Government Board, Current Events Board, and the French, Spanish, and Camera clubs, as well as "Dramat" and Choral.

Bright seniors were encouraged to design their own courses and Sasha organized a seminar in the history of art. She took another seminar in Russian history and enjoyed studio art. Greek mythology and Greek plays fascinated her. Her probing questions in history class revealed her background in the world of diplomacy and it was apparent that the Bruces had educated her well. When Arthur Schlesinger, who had known David Bruce since OSS days and Evangeline even earlier, visited as a guest speaker, he sought Sasha out. Natural and simple, Sasha was not as sophisticated as many of the others, but she was among the brightest in her class at a school where academic excellence was expected of its privileged pupils. "If your parents have *Reader's Digest* on the table, throw it away!" a teacher named Mrs. Stockley advised.

Sasha's was called "a collegiate wonder class" with everyone bound for college but the troubled Jane Frick. "Roses with a few thorns," as Miss Watkins put it. "Trickster" Frick got "x's" or "tidy crosses" for unseemly behavior and often lost her weekend privileges. Sasha did not get "tidy crosses" but befriended many who did.

If Sasha performed with distinction from the start, Wendy Wisner hated St. Tim's her first two years, finding its values antiquated. She rebelled by doing poorly in her courses. When she finally excelled during one marking period, Sasha was ecstatic, throwing her arms around her old friend as if she had achieved something monumental.

Sasha took the honor rules of St. Timothy's very seriously: no smoking, no drugs, no gum chewing, no leaving the campus without permission, no washing of hair or studying on Sundays—no activity unbecoming to a St. Tim's girl. But when an administrator named Miss Bement opened a letter to Sasha from Mrs. Bruce, Sasha reacted with violent indignation. Miss Bement was a hated figure and once, unkindly, she had told Jane Frick she would "never get ahead." Now furious at this breach of ethics and invasion of her privacy, Sasha told her she was never to open her mail again; to emphasize the point she threatened to call her mother. Embarrassed, Miss Bement backed down and apologized.

From the time she began at St. Tim's, Sasha was overly sensitive to any mention of her distinguished family. "For God's sake, don't say anything about Sasha's father. She doesn't like it!" Mary Wisner warned the others. Mrs. Bruce rarely came to St. Tim's and the girls began to believe Sasha was troubled that her mother didn't care enough. When Mrs. Bruce did visit, Sasha seemed embarrassed about how special, how handsome, and perfect she was. Yet when her mother sent her fancy dresses in the latest style from London, even when they were the wrong size, Sasha was elated, crying, "Mummy sent some dresses for me!"

*   *   *

As her best friend at St. Tim's, Sasha chose Sally Clark, a girl from a small town in Maine—the one member of the class who was not going to have a coming-out party. On her first day, Sally read Sasha's nametag which said "Alexandra Bruce, England" and thought "She must be English." She had never heard of David K. E. Bruce.

"You shouldn't feel like a hick," Miss Watkins told Sally somewhat later that first autumn. "You're bright enough and nobody here is better than anybody else." Spirited and rebellious, Sally would become both class president and "Head of School" (president of the student body) when she and Sasha were "sixes" (seniors), though she would repeatedly be bounced from "group one" for such infractions as lighting a cigarette in Boston Airport (to which she confessed). Sasha hoped she and Sally could be roommates when they went off to Radcliffe together.

With her sweet nature and willingness always to make time for others, even for girls who were not considered "cool," Sasha was popular at St. Tim's and several girls considered her their closest friend.

Through frenetic activity Sasha was able to keep her demons at bay her first two years at St. Tim's. But in her junior year she often described herself as "depressed to emptiness." She spoke of her "crazy moods" and said once "thank God for the little things in life—it's about all I do thank Him for sometimes." A sense of hopelessness overtook her and under "self-image" in the St. Tim's yearbook she would be described as "schizophrenic."

Sometimes between four and five in the morning she would take long walks in the cornfields adjacent to St. Tim's. It was considered odd for girls to want to be alone and solitary walks at any hour were not encouraged. Yet often Sasha could be spotted running by herself in these cornfields which, the following year, as a "six," she willed to Wendy Wisner as other graduating seniors willed pictures of boys to underclassmen. Or she would wander there with Jane Frick who would be chosen "Brownie" mascot to Sasha's "Spider," both boosters at the annual Thanksgiving basketball game. Sasha and Jane shared an excessive ebullience and after graduation went off with Nick and Mrs. Bruce for a week or two to the Scottish highlands. There they searched for the

Loch Ness monster. "We know he and others are there!" Sasha impishly joked, revealing what her friends called her "romantic propensities." (A year and a half after Sasha's death, Jane Frick committed suicide; she'd been firmly convinced that her friend had been murdered.)

Moods of dark despair would be followed by moments of high animation. Sasha would dance about, flinging her arms over her head, skipping here and there as she made her way between classes. As Spider mascot, representing the class spirit, she shook her wand with tinkling bells attached to it, and danced about, raising everyone's spirits in a wonderful concentration of her essence. At such times Sasha seemed an aerial spirit, whimsical, ethereal, a bit fuzzy around the edges so that you couldn't quite pin her down.

"I can imagine her dancing around in front of Marios with that free spirit of hers," one of her best friends at St. Tim's later mused, "crying, 'Go ahead! Go ahead! Shoot me! Shoot me! Hee. Hee. I don't want to live anyway!'"

Lonely, childlike, and increasingly high-strung, Sasha reacted intensely to two deaths which occurred during her years at St. Tim's. In August 1963, Phil Graham, long a favorite of Sasha's (no relation to Terry), killed himself. Once Phil Graham had written to John Kennedy that only painfully had he "learned the value of wisdom, slowness, and the kind of calm sense owned by a handful of men such as David Bruce," and he had been a family friend for years. Sasha, Terry, and Wendy were in Terry's basement when they heard the news. Sasha's reaction was one of deep despair.

Then when John Kennedy was assassinated three months later, Sasha became hysterical, locking herself into one of the St. Tim's bathrooms, unable to stop crying. "If I could give my life to bring him back . . ." she wept. "The two most exciting, dynamic, brilliant, wonderful people in my life are dead." For days after Kennedy's death Sasha would speak to no one; her reaction was more extreme than anyone else's. The southern girls at St. Tim's shared little of Sasha's sorrow; to them Kennedy represented civil rights and was well gone. Yet even the Kennedy assassination brought Sasha unwelcome notoriety. When she received a letter from her mother on embassy notepaper, it created quite a stir. Once more she was a celebrity, special, different from the others.

* * *

During the summer between her junior and senior years, Sasha joined St. Timothy's Latin American Seminar, an intensive three-and-one-half week swing through six Latin American countries. Her responses revealed an inquiring mind dissatisfied with received truths. Reality belied the Washington briefings at which the girls were informed that the Alliance for Progress and American aid were transforming Latin America. Sasha found the trip more a grand tour than an educational experience.

In the official photograph, picturing the seven St. Tim's girls with the six public school girls who had been invited along to mingle with their privileged counterparts, but never did, Sasha looks as conservative as the rest of the group, tall and thin and smiling, wearing high heels and a print dress with a Peter Pan collar. But once abroad she pursued areas of inquiry of her own, siding with those who confronted the American ambassador to Argentina, demanding a reaction to the Birmingham crisis of 1961: Bull Connor had sicced his dogs and let the Ku Klux Klan loose on thirteen black and white Freedom Riders so that Kennedy had to instruct federal marshals to move in.

"Well, we're trying very hard to reassure everyone . . ." the man replied lamely. Sasha looked at her friends and they nodded in agreement. "He's not telling the truth. He's trying a diplomatic dodge," Sasha said.

In São Paulo, Sasha and a few others sneaked off by themselves and picked up some Communist students in a café just outside their hotel. Sasha took the lead and asked the questions in good Spanish, which served in lieu of Portuguese. Unwilling to accept that self-help, American aid, and the Alliance for Progress would put an end to endemic poverty, she wanted to know what the Communist movement had to offer.

One day, half in jest, she remarked that some of the dictators had done a "rather nice job" of turning chaos into order. They were doing some good things for the people. She asked many questions about the *padrone* tradition because she thought it bore some similarity to her own family history.

When they returned to St. Timothy's, the girls were questioned by their language teacher, Stanley N. Frye. What have

you seen? he wanted to know. Sasha told him she wanted to
help the Brazilian people.

"How are you going to help them?"

One of the girls talked about American aid.

"Do you think that under a feudal system with a few
land-owning families in control American aid will help?"

Oh, yes, most of them said.

Frye despaired. The idea that a system could be changed
was as foreign to these "St. Tim's" as it was to their fathers.

Sasha adored Stanley Frye and her attachment to him grew
in her senior year. So strong was her obsession with Frye that
for years to come she would measure all future suitors against
him. Invariably they would be found wanting.

At St. Tim's, Sasha and the other girls almost never saw
boys their own age. At times they didn't bother to wash their
hair for a week. They ate gluttonously and most gained
weight. When Toby Wolff (brother of Geoffrey, who would
write *The Duke of Deception* about their childhood) declared
himself "in love" with her, Sasha replied, "Pshaw, I don't
feel that way at all." At Maryland Hunt Cup weekend the
girls were permitted to invite male guests and over the years
there was a dance or two at a neighboring school but there
was little contact with those boys again. It was all very chaste
and Sasha was a virgin at graduation.

Mr. Frye was different, different from her cool, remote
father and from the pale Washington boys Sasha knew from
Mrs. Shippen's dancing class with their pasty faces and sweaty
palms, except for Laudie Greenway, who put cherry bombs
in the toilet to enliven those painfully awkward afternoons
and who had put Toby Wolff up to that declaration of love.

Frye was handsome, mysterious (was he from Georgia in
the Soviet Union or from Wisconsin?), odd, and ethnic-
looking, but certainly exciting to girls fed on a pallid emotional diet. He had a thick black mustache and sparkling hazel
eyes, a large nose, shaved-off hair, and a flat head and he
was only in his late thirties. His posture was stiff and military
straight and he walked around the campus like a Cossack,
proud and self-confident. He was like no one Sasha had ever
known.

At St. Tim's, Frye taught Russian, German, and Spanish,
but there seemed no language he did not know, from Serbo-

Croatian, Czech, and Turkish to Greek and Mongol. The only language of which Frye said he was ignorant was French. "French is a dying language," he would assert, daring disagreement. He was a marvelous teacher, whose tactic was to get a rise out of these well-bred girls so unaccustomed to thinking for themselves. He pitied them for their narrowness, but he was not unkind. Gruff, playful, ironic, Stanley Frye sought to infuse the insulated world of St. Tim's with real life.

Iconoclastic, he broke countless St. Tim's rules, keeping a dog called Nokhor, who was a constant threat to Miss Watkins's Saint and Timothy. When a teacher entered a room where girls were gathered, they were expected to rise and say, "How do you do, Mr. . . . ?" remaining standing until invited to sit down again. Frye would bow and in a voice laden with irony say, "Ladies, *please*!"

He detested snobbery and ordered the southern girls to stop trying to get rid of their accents, as they were inclined to do. "You're southern! Talk southern!" his voice would boom out. When his Spanish class followed required religion, the girls asked him questions and he was not beyond crying out "Garbage!" for he was more interested in nature and the harmony of the universe than in God or Christianity. Other teachers spoke their minds, but the girls felt that Frye really meant what he was saying.

They discovered he had studied in a monastery with Tibetan monks and this added intrigue to his persona. Once a Tibetan monk in red robes with a shaved head, speaking no English, visited him. In the afternoons the monk could be found sitting by Miss Watkins's pool, smiling and saying "How do you do?" when the girls passed. One girl wrote a poem: "I never thought I would see a Lama at St. Timothy's."

Sasha took German and Spanish with Frye, but not Russian, in which she said she was not interested. In German class she was self-deprecating, pretending she needed brushing up, minimizing her abilities; she did not reveal that she had lived in Germany. She seemed inhibited, as if there were many things about which she could not be open.

Frye saw she needed discipline and was determined not to treat her as if she were special. "Sasha, blow your nose!" he would command her in class. For so much understanding, she adored him and he became one of the most important people in her life.

Unlike the other teachers, Frye opened his home to the girls in the evenings and weekends. Sally Clark argued with him about everything from child rearing to racism, but Sasha became his most frequent visitor. She had grown up believing there didn't have to be distance between herself and grown-ups and so threw herself into the friendship without the decorum observed by the other girls.

Frye became Sasha's hero, a romantic ideal. He painted icons, which hung in his living room, and he sang in Greek, Turkish, and Russian, accompanying himself on the guitar. He was sensual and passionate and he was interested in her as an individual, rather than in what her family did and who they were. Eyeing her dark hair and dusky coloring, Frye would tease her. "You're not a Bruce!" he would declare, knowing how this would delight her. "You're a Gypsy! You haven't got a drop of Scottish blood!" Then Sasha would pretend to be angry. She craved family life, Frye saw, behaving like an abandoned orphan waiting patiently to be adopted. Many nights, violating one more St. Timothy's rule, Sasha would knock at Frye's door and they would listen to Rumania and Hungary on his shortwave radio.

With Frye, Sasha could be herself. During fierce arguments she would stamp her foot and demand, "How can you think such a thing?" Frye was known to bait Sasha even on the issue of civil rights. "The niggers should never have been freed. . . ." "Oh, Stan!" Sasha would cry. He saw her as an intelligent, genteel, natural, gracious young woman who needed direction and purpose. She saw him as father, teacher, friend—and fantasy lover.

Sasha became the ethical conscience of her class and as a "six," or senior, came into direct confrontation with Miss Watkins, whom she otherwise admired. Miss Watkins was advisor to all the senior girls and during one of their required conferences, Sasha demanded to know why there weren't any black or many Jewish students or teachers at St. Tim's. The year was 1964; the civil rights movement was at its height. It disturbed Sasha that the only blacks at St. Tim's were the cooks and other help who once a year put on a singing performance out of antebellum days.

Miss Watkins reserved her reply for one of the mandatory prayer meetings at which the entire student body was assembled. "Someone asked me why there are no blacks and Jews at St. Tim's," Miss Watkins began, omitting the name of the questioner, "and rather rudely implied that was because we didn't want to have black and Jewish students and teachers. I want you to know that none have applied who are qualified. If you can find students who might be qualified, go ahead." She suggested Jewish students wouldn't want to come to St. Tim's because, unlike the Catholics, they could not attend Episcopal services. (In fact, one member of Sasha's class, Bettina Looram, was related to the Rothschilds, but she had been brought up as a Christian.)

Some of the girls thought Miss Watkins feared the parents of the southern girls might pull them out of school if they had to room with a black. Blacks are different from what we are and they wouldn't be comfortable in this environment, she seemed to be saying. We would not like to make anybody uncomfortable.

Many admired Sasha for taking her stand. Miss Watkins's response only pointed up the disparity between what was happening in the country and in the South in particular and the values of St. Tim's, which so failed to address themselves to the moral issues of the time. This would be the last of Miss Watkins's twenty-eight years as headmistress; many thought she preferred the less rebellious class preceding Sasha's (memorialized at St. Tim's by the chapel built by the family of Kassie Wilson, a student who had died of encephalitis). Miss Watkins should have retired with the girls she loved best, Sasha and her friends came to think—not with those "roses with a few thorns" who were already exhibiting signs of becoming the college class symbolized by the massacre at Kent State.

During a brotherhood assembly held in the blue assembly room with its giant cross, Sasha again expressed her strong moral sense. The theme was tolerance, love—and prejudice. Miss Watkins presided. A priest had also been invited.

Sasha stood up and asked, "What do you do when you are prejudiced?" Everyone was shocked. Was this an admission of intolerance? Then she added in her chidlike way, "I'm prejudiced against people who are prejudiced." It was Sasha, the others thought, who had nailed it by raising the issue they were in danger of evading: What do you do when you really are prejudiced?

That same year, her last at St. Timothy's, Sasha was made one of the six members of the Honors Council, the student government which, in practice, usually confined itself to endorsing Miss Watkins's views.

When Wendy Wisner lied to Miss Watkins about having attended a "starred" or mandated piano recital, the headmistress enlisted Sasha to convince Wendy to be honest. Both as a friend and in her official capacity as a member of the Honors Council, Sasha was to let Wendy know that the worst thing she had done was to lie.

Almost in tears, Sasha confronted her childhood friend.

"Wendy, I really want you to tell the truth," Sasha urged. "I think this is important. You've got to tell the truth!"

"I'm not going to. I'm just not going to do it," Wendy said, determined not to fall into the "two-minus" group, which meant sacrificing weekends off campus.

Sasha became desperate.

"Please. Do it for me. As a friend. I think it's really important. Think about what you're doing."

"Look what I would sacrifice. All my weekends. Come on."

Then Sasha played her last card.

"It's honorable!"

But Wendy never did admit to Miss Watkins that she had lied about attending the piano recital. A chasm opened between her and Sasha. Sasha was trying to please her mother, Wendy thought.

Sasha's time at St. Timothy's was inextricably bound up with her infatuation with Stanley Frye and years after graduation she would turn up at his door, testing his indulgence anew, as if his was the home where they had to take her in. One day in 1965 she hitchhiked back to St. Tim's in a snowstorm; she was dressed inappropriately in summer clothes, a mismatched purple blouse and brown skirt. She told Frye she was broke and he had to give her bus money back to Radcliffe. At eleven thirty one night in 1969 she turned up in Indiana where Frye was studying for his doctorate. When he became angry at her for coming without notice, she sat down on the floor and refused to move. Rejected as a woman, she might win his attention as a little girl, the forlorn waif bedeviling her father-teacher.

Repeatedly Sasha tried to find ways to join the Frye family. One day walking in the woods she turned to Frye's son Roderick and asked, "Aren't I your godmother?" "Aren't I Roderick's godmother?" Sasha asked Frye. "Yes, Sasha," Mary Frye, his wife, intervened. Roderick's godmother had died; there didn't seem any harm in it. The Easter after she left St. Tim's, Sasha returned all dressed up, sat down, rolled up her sleeves, and painted Easter eggs in gold leaf with the Frye children. When her incessant talking proved irritating, Frye turned her over to his wife.

Rarely did Sasha speak to Frye of her mother, although she often mentioned David Bruce. It was terrible that the British failed to appreciate Bruce, horrible that the family spaniels had to be quarantined. Once she laughingly created for Frye the image of her eccentric father ("dotty Daddy") sitting on the roof of the mission in Peking. Although she never complained of her father's neglect, it was plain he had no authority with her. Frye thought she was torn between identifying with the family and an obvious if unacknowledged need to break away from them by coming to terms with what had been lacking in their family life.

But there was more to Sasha's fantasy. Frye became the impossible man, the lover whom against all odds she must win away from others. With Frye she set up an emotional struggle ordained to fail as if, believing she could never gain her real father's attention, she had to recapitulate this defeat with another admirable adult male.

Frye tried to wean Sasha from this infatuation, even joking about the new headmistress, Miss Miller. "If I hadn't been married, I would have married Miss Miller," he told her. She rose to the bait. "Oh, no you wouldn't. What are you saying that for?" On one of Sasha's visits he danced with Lydia Greeves, sister of one of the teachers, a dark-haired young woman Sasha's age. On another he danced with Rona Earle, Sasha's friend. Both times Sasha was enraged. Mary Frye was one thing; new competition was intolerable.

No one ever remembered seeing Ambassador Bruce at St. Timothy's. For Sasha's graduation Mrs. Bruce arrived without him, accompanied by another family. The Fryes watched

from their porch as she rode up the hill in a large black car.
All they glimpsed were her fine long hands arranging a scarf.
Later she did not mingle but, elegantly aloof, remained apart
from the teachers and other parents. Evangeline Bruce never
made the acquaintance of Stanley Frye, her daughter's surrogate parent and imaginary lover.

Sasha's destiny, her classmates decided in the St. Tim's
senior yearbook, was "to be a Sappho singing the song of the
Orient and the West."

Foreign lands, foreign adventures, inevitably awaited her.

The Bitch-Witch

Sasha had already decided on her first adventure, a dig with the University of New Mexico field school in archaeology.

Two St. Tim's classmates, Julie Clark and Rosalie ("Rosie") Hornblower, would join her. But first there was her formal entrance into society at the Washington, D. C., debutante ball. A private party was given for Sasha and Terry by the widowed Kay Graham, who was now publisher of *The Washington Post*. A certain amount of ill-feeling emerged with Mrs. Bruce injured at the suggestion that she couldn't bother to make arrangements for her own daughter.

There was also a dance organized by Terry's mother at the City Tavern; again Mrs. Bruce remained aloof from the preparations. For this occasion Bunny Mellon, wife of Paul, designed fake orange trees with scented eucalyptus boughs and real oranges. Sasha and Terry agreed the effect was fantastic. Sasha's favorite escort on the "deb circuit" was Laudie Greenway, whose uncle, Lauder Greenway, became Ailsa Mellon Bruce's companion after her divorce. Once Laudie appeared at Staunton Hill armed with a Luger pistol. He owned four Harley-Davidson motorcycles and was outrageous enough to appeal to Sasha despite his impeccable family background.

Bound for the dig in Albuquerque, Sasha told the army corporal sitting next to her on the plane that she was part Zuñi Indian. When the plane began to descend from the mountains, she uttered a high-pitched shriek of joy that sent a chill through her friends. She had failed to bring enough money for the six-week course and had also forgotten her sleeping bag. "But the "three high-society girls," as they called themselves, had come to the Southwest "to live," and nothing could dampen their spirits.

Wherever there was mischief, Sasha was to be found.

Riding to town on Saturdays with her dirty laundry, she played "figurehead" by putting her head through the sun roof of the speeding Volkswagen. It was Sasha's idea to build a campfire with cow dung and to make a torch out of a lighted Tampax. She was eager to sleep out at the rattlesnake-infested site and to explore nearby caves in the middle of a rainy night to provide a suitable atmosphere for ghost stories. Her witty remarks were much relished by the group. "If the Seventh Day Adventists feel that the world will end and Christ is coming, he's it," she said of a charismatic lecturer named Devereau.

Sometimes her play got rough and Sasha went out of control. One day during watermelon break on the hot, dusty site she sprinkled a boy with water, and he threw her under the water-filled tarpaulin called a Lister bag. Emerging filthy and wet, Sasha demanded Rosalie Hornblower's knife. "Knife throwing," Julie recorded in her diary. "Sasha nuts and dangerous."

When Sasha was upset, Julie usually tried to help. Often unable to think of anything to say, she wound up scratching Sasha's back. One night in a "non-Sasha mood," she told Sasha she couldn't take much more and left her alone with her peculiar intensity. At St. Tim's Sasha had been Julie's idol, but her dark moods and hysteria were becoming very wearing.

Fortunately, the high-spirited moments would return. One night Sasha concocted a birthday cake with ice cream and butterscotch sauce and then danced in with her creation. Still a "vestal virgin," as all three "St. Tim's" were called by the others in the group, she settled her affections on a boy named Lee and spent a night alone with him in the woods. The next morning she made her way back exuberantly, jumping over cactus and sage.

When she first arrived at Radcliffe that fall, Sasha spoke obsessively of Lee, describing herself as being "in her own private hell," hardly able to bear "the agony and longing and beauty and tenderness." With adolescent self-dramatization she vowed to meet Lee in a hundred years and go on a roller coaster ride with him; not even a century would make a difference in her feelings for "her littlest angel," as she called him. Love meant suffering, "*ein Gottverdamdest leben*,"

Sasha wrote to Terry Graham. "Everything but our feelings are ruled by time; they're impervious to it."

She told Laudie Greenway there was no hope for them; he was "too real" for her.

She came to Radcliffe as high on despair as she was on hope.

Cliffies of Sasha's day divided themselves into three "flavors": peach, chocolate, and lime. Peaches were clubby and social; they wore coats with fur collars, went with boys who smoked pipes, and majored in fine arts or English. Chocolates came from public high schools, wore large plaids, eyeglasses, and thick boots. The grinds of Radcliffe, they majored in science or math. Some joined Phillips Brooks House, the social service organization; others were simply obsessed with high grades, going on to graduate school and careers. The limes were the intellectuals, the arty ones who had already lived in foreign countries, hung Greek shoulder bags over their arms, and had pierced ears. They were loners who seldom made many friends.

Sasha came from an upper-class family and majored in fine arts, but she abhorred the thought of being called a peach. She got high marks and worked at Phillips Brooks House, but she was no chocolate ambitious for a career. And if, like the limes, she knew Europe and wore a poncho, she scorned their self-conscious ivory-tower elitism.

It seemed important to Sasha to try to live down to something. She refused to pluck her thick, dark eyebrows and wouldn't use makeup, although with her high dusky color it didn't matter. She wore thong sandals and a man's shirt borrowed from a current boyfriend, undoing the buttons of the button-down collar and opening it to make it seem more feminine. A Peruvian poncho became her trademark.

Some remember Sasha walking through Harvard Yard, a tall, slender figure, her long dark hair unruly, her clothes dark, her entire appearance somber. She still thought herself ugly and so let herself go, putting herself out of the competition either by being slovenly or by dressing like a little girl.

One day, Mrs. Bruce, visiting Cambridge, invited her to lunch at the Ritz Carlton Hotel. Sasha appeared in jeans and they weren't permitted in the main dining room, but had to

descend to the café, and there was even some question about
that. Later Mrs. Bruce tried to make a joke of it. She and her
daughter almost didn't get anything to eat in Boston because
Sasha wore pants.

Mrs. Bruce's visits to Cambridge, however, were important times to Sasha, who all her life longed for her mother's
companionship. Together they made certain "pilgrimages"
(Mrs. Bruce's term) to places of significance to the Bruces.
Sasha's friend Maeve Kinkead decided Sasha was an eighteenth-
century person cherishing family traditions out of a sense of
continuity and respect for the past.

In 1964, Radcliffe College was still a world out of Mary
McCarthy's *The Group*. Pants were not to be worn to class,
boys were banned from the women's dorms, and the only
place women could congregate was in the basement of the
Memorial Church in Harvard Yard. There were scarcely five
women on the entire Harvard faculty and no closeness or
intimacy with women teachers or deans was possible, because
the few in evidence were intensely insecure about their own
positions.

But in choosing Radcliffe, Sasha was following in the
footsteps of her mother—and her great-grandfather Charles
Bruce who came to Harvard in 1845 determined to study
French until he could speak it fluently and read Madame de
Staël in the original. He paid for a private tutor in Italian and
intended to make himself a good Latin and Greek scholar
despite what he saw as Harvard's inadequacies in those subjects.
Soon Sasha's brother David would join her in Cambridge.

David Bruce advised his daughter to select courses for the
sheer joy of learning, subjects she wouldn't have taken
otherwise, with no rationale. Sasha picked Chinese. There
was no need to prepare herself for a career. The Radcliffe
woman was encouraged to believe she was one of a favored
few, as if that were an end in itself. Her appropriate demean-
or was noblesse oblige, an idea Sasha had already begun to
detest at St. Timothy's.

Sasha was determined not to be defined as "a Bruce" at
Radcliffe. She hated people who sought her out because of
her family and never called them back. Her women friends
had to take life seriously and do things well. If they were silly

or social, she wouldn't see them. She did not apply the same discrimination to her choice of men.

As a freshman, she shared a shoebox-sized room with Maeve Kinkead, whose parents wrote for *The New Yorker*. Maeve was sensitive, literary, and scornful of pretense; the two girls were kindred spirits, dark-haired, beautiful, ethereal. Maeve was the more sophisticated, Sasha madcap and childlike. Both enjoyed being rude to people they thought were frivolous. Absurdities titillated them; they thought it hilarious that the Harvard computer produced the fact that Sasha's mother was deceased.

Blue-eyed, mannered, and witty, Maeve was a counterpart of Sasha, whose dark eyes were still full of light as she began at Radcliffe. "Oh, Maeve, you're so beautiful," Sasha would cry, and then Maeve would answer, "Oh, Sasha, *you're* so beautiful." Such self-mocking exchanges produced gales of laughter. Sasha's birthday fell on the first of May, Maeve's on the last. They sent each other obscene limericks for their birthdays.

Soon after her emergence at Radcliffe from the organized world of St. Timothy's, Sasha volunteered to work at a correctional facility called Lyman School for Boys, a social welfare project of Harvard's Phillips Brooks House. Already Sasha scorned prep school products like herself, who she thought were intellectually developed, but emotionally cut off, lacking "patience with people and tolerance." At Lyman she could learn, as she once put it, "what the other 98 percent of the population was like."

Several days a week Sasha tutored a group of juvenile delinquents in reading, literature, and history. Her high-pitched, infectious laugh would ring out and she'd get them to tell jokes and laugh at nonsensical things. If she needed to be forgiven for her privilege, they forgave her. Sasha recruited Julie Clark, but Julie felt out of place at Lyman. The chasm between the Lyman outcasts and the Harvard volunteers seemed too unbreachable, and she quit the program.

Sasha, however, saw no real difference between herself and these boys except money, and hers was unearned. She sympathized with their rebellious spirit, their defiance of respectability, and their contempt for anything that was sham and spoke of her own "JD life." The boys were lucky in having a freedom she lacked—the freedom to be poor and anonymous, to take chances, to act out devilish pranks forbidden to her. As David Bruce's daughter, she always had to fear getting her name in the papers, doing anything that would embarrass her family.

Lyman was a backward, Dickensian institution. Boys would have their heads shaved for various infractions and be sentenced to scrubbing wooden floors, isolated in a "discipline cottage" for two to three weeks. There were rumors of forced homosexuality. One hot night a black Harvard volunteer named Wes Profit, having taken a bunch of boys to the gym for basketball, decided they could have a swim. The pool area was dark. Wes approached in search of a light switch. Turning a corner, he came face to face with one of the cottage masters, a man in his forties, standing over two boys, forcing one to have sex with the other while he watched.

During Sasha's freshman year, one boy told her that he planned to run away to Florida. She had long conversations about infinity with her Florida-bound delinquent. A moonbird would fly to earth, picking up pieces of dust and carrying them back to the moon; when all the earth was deposited there, this would be just the beginning of infinity. She asked other Harvard volunteers whether she should tell the administration of his plan to run away, but of course she knew she wouldn't.

She developed a friendship with a boy named Paul Kennedy who at the age of twelve had shot and killed his stepfather. It was an honor for Sasha to have been chosen as Paul's tutor; she was selected by the school as someone who would not be judgmental. When she saw him for the first time, he wore a little blue jacket, like a pea coat, and a small hat. Although he was fourteen, he looked like a child. He seemed so sweet and so forlorn that Sasha almost cried.

Sasha tutored Paul and was instrumental in bringing his brightness to the attention of the school. She arranged for him to get financial aid so that he could leave Lyman and attend Phillips Academy at Andover. She pushed him and she succeeded. With Paul, Sasha played the same big sister role she did with her brother, Nicky.

For four years, no matter how heavy her classwork, how pressing her exams, Sasha honored her commitment to the Lyman program, although she believed the best thing that could happen was for this barbarous place with its open toilets and public humiliations to be closed down by the state. She was the most dedicated of all the volunteers, seeing her role as that of friend to the boys, someone they could tell what was troubling them. They respected her and if she said "Don't do that," they obeyed. They knew she cared and so she could be tough with them if necessary.

By the end of her freshman year, she seemed the most likely choice out of the thirty volunteers to become leader of the Lyman program. Everyone thought she combined the emotional and intellectual qualities to run it. But she declined, turning the office of coordinator over to two Harvard men. She was afraid her wealth and class would make her a target for criticism and that this would hurt the program.

Referring bitterly to her Bruce heritage, Sasha told a friend in her freshman year that she came "from a long line of Scottish pissants, narrow-minded, penny-pinching, small-minded Calvinists who bred guilt in people and never gave them a chance to be themselves." It was unfair she was a female, unfair she had been firstborn because so much was expected of her, unfair that she always had to behave "properly." If she had been Sasha McGillicutty, then she would have had a chance. Once she said she chafed under the strain of being locked in "a genealogical prison."

At Lyman she refused to be in a group picture, turning on her heels and walking quickly away. Unexpectedly she would invoke prerogatives of privacy, a hauteur which surprised her friends.

She held a heavy curtain in front of whatever happened within her family; only rarely would she articulate that anything was wrong. Her friends knew only that Sasha wavered between the exhilaration of endless expectation and the burden of too few limits. "Life's a trifle *too* interesting for anyone's peace of mind," Bettina Looram, her old St. Tim's classmate, told Sasha during these years. It seemed essential to Sasha that she learn where her inherited privilege stopped.

"It's so much easier for other people," she complained to Wes Profit, who so shared her commitment to the Lyman program that she dubbed him her "official biographer." For others, Sasha felt, "life included surprises, like brightly colored packages set out under the Christmas tree.'' Someone like Wes might open them and experience delight, but there would be no more surprises for her. For Sasha, life would have to be a matter of renunciation because she'd always had everything she wanted materially. Still she could never quite give up her advantages.

All the time she was at college, the income on her trust accumulated steadily. She lived on a generous fixed allowance. Yet in March of her freshman year she told Terry Graham she didn't have enough money to get from Cambridge to Washington and again the following November she had to tell Wendy she couldn't come to a party at which Laudie would be present because she was ''dead broke.''

Depression stalked her. Proud of being ''anti-Freud,'' she would not search in her childhood for the causes of her despair. Things were not going well; probably they never would. To examine the roots of her misery was to be disloyal to her heritage.

Peering in the mirror, she dubbed herself the ''bitch-witch.'' She swung between being self-deprecating and imperious. Cruelly, she manipulated people into baring their souls, then took verbal swipes at them so that they felt they had been held under a microscope without compassion. Held accountable for her arrogance, she would become vulnerable, too weak to bear the consequences of her actions. The rage within her, the violence, would erupt sporadically. She hated babies, she said. If you dropped them out of the window, they'd sound like tomatoes, squishing as they hit the pavement. Cruelty provided a further occasion for her to hate herself.

It was fashionable at Radcliffe to be depressed over exams, unrequited infatuations, and the general pointlessness of life. But with Sasha depression was more than a fad.

Letters from her mother—or Stanley Frye—that she found emotionally insufficient would send her into hiding. She'd lock herself into her room and no one could gain entry. ''No talking really ever gets through to me,'' Sasha explained once, ''except in tones of voice.'' Like a school of dolphins, her friends, the Lyman crowd—Sally Clark, Wes Profit, Peter McCaffery, Julie Clark—or Maeve Kinkead, tried to nudge her to shore.

But seeking help was an admission of defeat. It was her

duty to take charge of her own life, removing this burden from her busy parents whose obligations made the self-sufficiency of their children necessary. It was as if talking about her pain would have caused her parents to be lost to her.

Rock music became an obsession. The Beatles were always on her phonograph—or "Red Rubber Ball" or "Turn, Turn, Turn." The line, "For you I'm just an ornament, something for your pride," struck a note in Sasha. "Stolen minutes of your time are all you had to give," the singer of "Red Rubber Ball" complains, countering at the end with "I don't need you at all." As if it were a litany, she sang this song over and over.

One day in her dormitory room Sasha made her mother sit down and listen to "Lady Madonna." In an offhand way she told Evangeline she liked the rhythm—and waited for some greater communion. Mrs. Bruce's response was understated, not hurtful, but a bit dry and sardonic, as if to say, "but this isn't serious," as Sasha must have known it would be.

Perpetual motion became one of Sasha's methods of chasing away the demons. She would go for two or three days at a time without sleeping, and not only during exams. She stayed up all night talking with people. It was as if she needed both days and nights to keep all her separate lives going: her commitment to Lyman, her lovers, classes, friendships, her concern about the family, especially for Nicky who was languishing unhappily at St. Paul's School. Her own animation made life interesting to her; her imagination and sensitivity allowed her to survive pain much longer than might have been expected.

Already she had begun to wonder whether her own view of things was sane. "My sister undervalued herself a lot," her brother David would say of Sasha during those years. Friends took to calling her "the black Bruce."

She began to take drugs: pot, acid, speed. Terrified one midnight, she phoned Frye and told him she had been running down an alley chasing cats. Shortly before her death she told him she feared she was losing her mind because of all the drugs she took while she was at college. (At Winfield House in London during this period David and Nicky gave LSD to one of Mrs. Bruce's dogs.)

Suicide became an obsession. She said she didn't care whether she lived or died, and she spoke these words often. One day she came back to the dorm and confessed, "I rode my bike down the hill and didn't put the brakes on. I was going really fast and it was exciting. I thought, 'If I get killed, big deal. If I'm going to be okay, then I'm going to.' " Death seemed gratifying in a world emptied of pleasure, those brightly colored packages under the Christmas tree long since opened and discarded. The moment of self-obliteration promised a new sensation.

She painted her bicycle in psychedelic colors: pink, green, and silver. Then someone stole it. Two months later, driving through Harvard Square, Sasha spotted her bike, complete with its metallic configurations. "Stop the car!" she cried, "There's my bicycle. I'll see you back at the dorm." She leapt out of the car and stole it back, telling no one how she did it. She just turned up at the dorm with it later.

Sasha went on a roller coaster at an amusement park that spring of her freshman year. At the top of the stepest pitch she uttered an eerie, strange scream, as she had on the airplane to Albuquerque; it issued from deep within her, a shrill cry of completion accompanying a dangerous moment. It both frightened and thrilled her companion, Steve Blodgett, so sexual was it in its call, so obviously was it set off by gratification at being carried off by a force beyond her control. She liked being passively overtaken by danger without having had to engineer it herself.

She told Sally Clark she had promised her godmother, Priscilla, that if she ever seriously thought of killing herself, she'd call her up first.

"My godmother said she was afraid I wouldn't live past thirty," Sasha admitted. She always took to heart what her godmother said, but continued to speak of suicide as a logical, rational alternative.

One night she composed a ditty: "One thousand tears or clowns in a day keep suicide away." Then she boasted of possessing an animal's instinct for self-preservation. "That's one of the most conceited things I ever heard," Wes Profit said. "It's strange to think I'm alive by the grace of a conceit," Sasha punned back. She said she could always see herself as if from a distance, understanding a lot in the midst of everything. But that never helped.

In January 1965 a friend of Laudie Greenway's, a girl Sasha's age, jumped out of a window in New York City. She was typical of their generation, Sasha thought. For Sasha and her friends there would be civil rights work, antiwar marches, the cornucopia of intellectual resources Harvard offered, but Sasha increasingly felt she had nothing to live for. The more fervent her activity, the more pervasive became her sense of futility.

With music and drugs, sex became another avenue of escape. Often Sasha attributed her depressions and suicidal feelings to failures with men. It was impossible to find the right person, always a struggle to commit herself to anyone. Telling Mrs. Bruce of a young man who might have been appropriate for Sasha, Evangeline Bruce says, Nicky commented, "He's too nice. Sasha wouldn't like him."

Promiscuity was a predictable reaction to virginal St. Timothy's, where birth control was considered a cheap thing to do. On Christmas vacation of that freshman year the subject of sex came up between Wendy Wisner and Sasha when they met in Washington.

Wendy was now a senior at St. Tim's. "You just can't. It's not right. It would spoil everything if you did," she insisted.

Sasha looked at her condescendingly, as if to say, "Little do you know, child, but you'll learn."

Wendy was shocked. Was it possible that Sasha—? But she had not been to New Mexico with Sasha the previous summer. Sasha confided no more.

Later Sasha had a similar conversation with Sally Clark.

"I don't think I'd do it. I'd be afraid of getting pregnant," Sally, still the St. Tim's vestal virgin, admitted.

"You don't think of it at the time," Sasha answered dryly.

At first Sasha alternated between men who were threatening and those who were safe. She met David Irons in her natural science class. He had gone to summer camp with her brother David and had been instructed to look her up. He was a St. Paul's graduate and a member of the *Harvard Lampoon*; his father was headmaster at Groton. They went to movies and plays, strolled up Garden Street arm-in-arm, and kissed good night. Together they visited Nicky at St. Paul's and David at Groton. They talked of art and politics (he found her views relatively moderate). But they did not become lovers.

Sasha treated David Irons as a brother, enlisting him as one of the few friends with whom she would discuss her family. She spoke about the Bruces as if she were forgiving *them*. She had been forced to understand them since she was the strongest. The tension with their mother was treated more as her brother David's problem than as her own.

Sasha urged David Irons to read Konrad Lorenz's *On Aggression*. He thought she treated psychology as a tool toward understanding her Lyman ward, Paul Kennedy, never herself.

With Steve Blodgett, she went a little further. They met at Lyman. She admired Steve for his ease with the boys and his ironic attitude toward Harvard.

Sasha frequented working-class dives with Steve Blodgett. They'd act like children together, shooting water pistols out of car windows and then pretending innocence with straight faces. It troubled Steve that he was not of Sasha's class, but she never made him feel clumsy or inadequate. She was accepting, tolerant of other people's excesses and personality quirks. She received you, Steve thought. The dark side of this was she felt she *had to* be interested in others. And yet she made it clear you couldn't need anything from her.

He brought her home to Vermont with him. "The sun hitting scarlet crimson trees," Sasha exclaimed, "is enough to make me scream in disbelief. Such a color should be contained more strictly than Communism!"

They seemed to be drawing close, but one day Sasha announced to Steve: "I can like you so much and I won't be liking you any more than that!"

Steve laughed. At first he didn't believe her. But she said she meant it. Their relationship would be limited. There was a man with whom she was in love.

She did not speak the name: Stanley Frye.

In her early years at Harvard there was always more than one man at a time; they were all held at a distance which could never be bridged. Her lovers were all told of this "someone else." And if a relationship ended, Sasha seemed more relieved than sorry. It was better that she be absolutely free, she said. Then, should things work out with her "longtime love," there would be no impediment on her side. And if she had to be alone, she could still be happy, knowing she was close to "him" and didn't have to worry about hurting anyone else. She was always sad inside because she could not live with "the beloved one." But just that he existed made her happy. She was intensely happy just to know the beloved.

"Does it bother you?" she asked Steve.

He said no, but from then on he knew he couldn't permit himself to grow too fond of her. It was difficult to reach her anyway because there were so many things she didn't like about herself. He had to assure her repeatedly that he liked her, and he could never convince her he thought she was beautiful. Once she said she'd really like to live with many different men and go from one to the other.

At a dinner one of the Lyman volunteers angrily accused her in front of the assembled group of not having any feelings. Then he got up and walked out. Sasha smiled.

When others criticized her, she accused *them* of being unkind. Once she said something devastating to Steve, then tried to spin away her cruelty with verbal gymnastics: "I'll go bury the word in the snow, and it won't come out again until it thaws. By then it won't matter since words don't sound so harsh when it's warm. I'll just say you're not nice. You'll take that as a compliment—perhaps."

One night she and Steve went to see *Breathless*. The nihilism of the movie exacerbated Blodgett's own depression. He said he felt like hurling himself off a bridge.

"Was your mother unkind?" Sasha asked. Steve thought the question insensitive and primitive. He overdosed on acid and wound up in the infirmary.

Sasha came to visit, full of advice. You'll have to learn to compromise with life, she said. It was something she'd been forced to do early. He needed to be tossed around a bit in order to grow up. But he had to do it by himself. Her abruptness chilled him and he thought, she wasn't someone you approached in weakness. Sasha did admit to guilt for having encouraged him in his feelings for her since she could give so little. The song "Master Jack" explained how she felt about him: "It's a strange, strange world, and I thank you, Master Jack. You taught me all I know and I'll never look back."

A young man named Tom Dolembo fell in love with Sasha's sense of fun. They visited Mount Auburn Cemetery where he recited "Ozymandias," which he knew by heart. In homage she pelted him with snowballs. She was sensitive to his poverty and insisted on going dutch. Yet she soon became a night creature, disappearing until the early hours of the morning, telling no one where she had been. Sometimes she complained that the men at Harvard were soft and weak. They lacked distinct personalities. She was looking for a hero.

Shortly before her death, Tom Dolembo tried to convince her one last time that there would be no heroes. Your hero is married and selling beer and pizza in Denver, he wrote her.

One of her boyfriends said Sasha behaved like a man who never had a father.

Sally Clark, who was so close to her, would be shocked by the extent of Sasha's sexual activity when she learned about it later.

Marios Michaelides would say that even at Radcliffe Sasha had begun to degrade herself sexually. Once she confessed to him that she lured a black Lyman volunteer to a room where they could be alone together. There she proceeded to tease and excite him, arousing him to a point of frenzy only at the last minute to spurn his sexual advance. Exasperated, he raped her. A pattern of courting sexual abuse had begun early and secretly.

About some things, Sasha seemed strangely innocent. One night she received an obscene phone call. For a long time she couldn't figure out what the man meant. It was something about eating. But Sasha assumed it was a dinner invitation and went on talking until the caller finally said, "Okay, okay, lady," and hung up. "You know, I think we just got an obscene phone call," she told Sally.

"What did he say, Sash?"

"I don't know. He was talking about eating. I was dreaming about sugarplums and he woke me up. I started talking to him. Then he got flustered and hung up."

From her friends Sasha hid her seriousness about her studies, mourning that she wasn't "talented" and couldn't "do anything" really well. Yet she did superbly even in subjects that didn't interest her, like required science, receiving a better grade in that course than David Irons.

Gracefully intellectual, Sasha had tastes as a freshman that she would carry into the future. Already she had an interest in the medieval art of Europe. Perhaps because of Stanley Frye, the Near East beckoned her even back then, and she delighted in *The Alexandria Quartet*. She shared her father's admiration for scholarship. One day at Staunton Hill she proudly showed a friend a first edition of Dr. Johnson's *Dictionary*. At Radcliffe she carted her personal set of the *Encyclopaedia Britannica* from dorm to dorm.

Hating to be thought "special," however, she attended the traditional Bogart festival during the final exam period after freshman year and let it be known that she was having "frequent hysterics" over Chinese, in which, she lamented, bluffing was out of the question. Exam eve she threw all her possessions out the door of her room. Then, abandoning their books, amid more hysterics, she and several girls called the Audubon Society for the wild bird report. Frantic giggles greeted the announcement that two white owls had been sighted in Rockport and five evening grosbeaks in Cambridge.

That summer of 1965 she went on the second of her archaeological expeditions, this one sponsored by the University of Pennsylvania. Her father had known the professor in charge. "Would you like some company?" Julie Clark asked. "You'd better find out if there's space," Sasha said distantly. Secretly Julie used Sasha's name and was signed on at once.

On their way to Turkey, Sasha and Julie spent five days in London buying gear. At Winfield House Julie found wheatmeal digestive biscuits and a carafe of water by her bed. Mrs. Bruce was cordial, if remote. Being high-minded at the dinner table was debilitating.

At one lunch Julie alluded to an unpleasant stand she thought the United States was taking. But David Bruce would not be drawn into a debate. "Yes," he agreed, as if it didn't matter what he felt personally, "but I am a representative of the United States."

Once Sasha heard her father joke about *his* father's advice as he left for Europe in 1918, having dropped out of Princeton in the hope of joining World War I. "David," William

Cabell Bruce told his son, "I'd rather see you come home dead on your shield than know you were responsible for destroying the virtue of one of those fine Frenchwomen."

The night before they were to leave for Turkey, one of the maids told Sasha her father wanted to see her. Sasha and Julie entered Mr. Bruce's bedchamber where they found him in a dressing gown reclining on his four-poster bed.

He wanted to warn them of possible sexual harassment in Turkey.

"I hope you girls have a good time," David Bruce said. "They have different customs there, so in case anyone asks, just cross your legs and say no!"

At the site in Gordion there were two jobs open, working in the field or cataloging and cleaning objects in the lab. Julie and Sasha flipped a coin; Sasha was the winner and chose the inside job. She wanted to spend her time with the beautiful golden objects Professor Young had found in three Hittite burial mounds. Archaeology made her amazingly happy, Sasha said, and more certain of what she was doing "hanging around this mass of earth" than anything else.

The two girls lived with a Turkish family; soon Sasha was speaking the language, which she found straightforward and easy. The beauty and mystery of Turkey, the primitive peasant life, drew her. She said she scented danger even as she landed in Ankara and found herself faced with dark, swarthy, if not exactly hostile people. She responded to the restlessness in the streets that lasted far into the night, augmented by the continual honking of horns as automobile drivers engaged in endless confrontations. The people's faces betrayed an outward fierceness, almost a cruelty which, she thought, contrasted with the sickly weak sweetness of the air, like incense. She liked the music with each note not quite the tone it was meant to be and observed that everything she was accustomed to was in a major key, while everything in Turkey was in a minor one. Discord—threats of danger—aroused her interest.

The tough, barren strength of the countryside also appealed to her. One of the villages so touched her that she envisioned settling there. Then she mocked herself for such romanticism. "Peasant life, that's for me. Yup, fresh bed, fresh eggs, fleas in the bed, goat fights, herds of stupid, bleating sheep, sunsets bright red at both ends and pale, feverish white in the middle because at 106 degrees it's too hot to see colors, a low unpainted mud brick house to share with the animals in winter, great white long-haired wolf-sheep dogs that smile and bite alternately, communal water trough, visiting Gypsy bands, women fishing in the rivers, lamb and yogurt, up at five with the sun, dark at eight, no plumbing or electricity.''

One day in July her mood plummeted. She went to town for mail and supplies and learned that Adlai Stevenson had just died. Again she behaved as if this death were too much to bear, as she had done when Paul Graham and John Kennedy died. She disappeared into her room and didn't emerge for three days. When she spoke of Stevenson afterwards, it was in the tones she usually reserved for her father, as if there were something godlike about him. Each time it was as if her father had died.

Tom Dolembo had been right when he told her she craved heroes. Speaking of those who failed to measure up to the standard set by David Bruce, she was biting and sarcastic. She called Henry Kissinger a "screw-up," quoting her father on two projects to which Kissinger had been assigned and which David Bruce had said he mismanaged.

The melancholia touched off by the death of Stevenson colored Sasha's sojourn in Turkey. She titled one of her letters "DEATH: or How All Roads & Letters Lead To Death by S. Bruce." She had told Steve Blodgett that one of them was likely to die this summer. She composed his epitaph, a cryptic "Vacuums and the Nightingale." Sasha decided that she wouldn't die *this* summer, but maybe she would the next. She taunted her friends with the threat of suicide. Then she rationalized her morbidity. It was more likely that she would die the following summer when she planned to join an excavation in Greece which involved underwater archaeology.

One day she entered the burial tomb of King Midas from which, however, the king himself, "with all his goodies," had been removed. Clutching a lantern, she walked along the dark passageway to the high-ceilinged wooden room where she lay down in Midas's empty grave. "It fits me well! A king! A king!"

On hashish, she wrote, "Sleep screams. How do you think

sleep sounded the night Macbeth murdered sleep?'' At dark moments she would invoke Macbeth and Duncan's blood. Later, on an airplane trip, she "awoke to see the rosy fingers of dawn well-tainted with Duncan's blood spread across the horizon."

Through the haze of drugs she pictured herself a pheasant in a land of turkeys, always the odd person out. That's the one joke someone forgot to play on me, Sasha now said, as if in earnest, the joke of making me a turkey!

"Well, I'm better off this way," she decided, "but what does 'better' mean, and then, again, what does 'I' mean?"

She wrapped herself in ironic labyrinths of language, designed to deflect her pain: "Turkeys leave strong-smelling trails and pheasants have long trailing tails. It all comes to the same thing when you're shot. Death equalizes everything. But what about life?"

She seemed to know her destiny was to be shot.

She helped a family with threshing and wore herself out turning around in circles on a sled with spikes in the bottom pulled by two horses. The children laughed at her. "They all love to see me suffer," Sasha said. "It's good and good for you. What if 'Onward Christian Soldiers' marched to the top of the hits until someone remembered that history moves in cycles and it was time to crucify Christ again?"

She signed one of her letters from Turkey "Sally's dog."

But it was only the summer of 1965. She still was able to pull herself up short. "I kind of covet life the sunny-side up," Sasha said. The cracked egg was one of her favorite metaphors.

After the dig, Sasha and Julie explored the Near East, boarding a train from Ankara to Istanbul. At the Topkapi Palace they admired Chinese porcelains as Sasha joked, "If my father were here, he would try to steal those!" (Years later David Bruce, visiting Kinloch, the estate left by Audrey and Stephen Currier, would bypass the elaborate greenhouses. "Take me to the china!" he demanded. And so he was led to the Kinloch pantry where in special display cases stood more than fifteen important sets of china. Bruce could identify them all!)

*   *   *

In Paris before her return to Cambridge, Sasha bought a postcard picturing the Place de la Concorde, site of the execution of Marie Antoinette. She said she preferred "the French way of death to the American way of life" and signed the card "Marie-face." Was Marie Antoinette already her double?

The Black Bruce

Wendy Wisner visited Sasha at Radcliffe in the fall of 1965. Giddy with excitement, she spent her time dashing around Cambridge. One day she returned to the dorm to find Sasha waiting for her.

"Wendy, I have something to tell you," Sasha said.

Her tone brought Wendy down at once from what she would later call her "high butterfly horse."

Sasha sat holding a wet washrag.

"I want you to know your father* has just shot himself."

That was all Sasha had to say.

She didn't elaborate, didn't throw her arms around Wendy for consolation; she was just there. She attended to the necessary details, arranging for Sally Clark to drive them to the airport. She wouldn't permit Wendy to make the trip back to Washington alone.

On the plane, Wendy felt awkward about their silence and tried to make conversation. She ventured a remark about politics.

Sasha looked at her as if to say, "What *are* you thinking about?" Conversation on Wendy's part was not required.

Wendy got up and went into the bathroom where she collapsed in tears. Through the door she heard Sasha admonish the stewardess who was about to intervene.

"Don't bother her," Sasha said. "Just leave her alone."

Although it was the middle of the semester, Sasha remained in Washington for a week, through the funeral, standing by in case she was needed. One day she took Wendy to lunch. They didn't see each other the rest of the time. But it was essential to Sasha that she be there for her friend. Then she went back to school.

---

* Frank G. Wisner, director of clandestine operations for the CIA and an intimate of Dave Bruce's, had resigned from the agency in 1962 after a nervous breakdown.

*   *   *

During sophomore year Sasha gained a lot of weight, grew slower and more lethargic. To push back negative impulses, she took more courses—one semester she enrolled in six. She spent more time at Lyman, too. If there had always been hills and valleys, now the valleys were growing deeper. When she talked to her friends, she couldn't attribute her despair to any cause. She thought of it as metaphysical.

One night in heavy snow, returning from a party with Tom Dolembo, Sasha, drunk, took off at a run and gave Tom quite a chase before he caught up with her.

"You haven't the right to feel this way about yourself," Tom said angrily. "I'm not going to let you do this to yourself."

"I'm feeling worthless, overtired, and confused," Sasha told him.

That spring she and Tom went wading in the reservoir. Suddenly he turned to her and held her head in both his hands. He felt a terrible loneliness overtake him and he burst out crying.

Once he had worked in the steel mills, he told her, and had to hold a man's head after the man had fallen; he could feel the man's life slipping away, his dying, even as he held him. Now he felt the same way about Sasha, the same terrible loneliness, the same sense of life slipping away. Sasha tried to understand. Then, as usual, she gave up.

When anyone did break through to her, address her pain, even as she fought tooth and nail to hold them off, she was intensely grateful. They had passed a test. If someone set limits for her, she equated it with caring.

Most of the time, though, people took her at her word. Friends protected her fragility. Sasha Bruce was gay, gentle, tentative, cryptic, poetic, elliptic—and interesting—but always more unhappy than happy. And she could think up a rationale for any behavior, however irrational.

"Knowing you are doing the wrong thing for months corrodes a not-too-solid bank of self-respect," she once admitted obliquely. She thought of herself as a "bad person," someone tainted. If anyone really knew her, they would discover her evil. Few were allowed to come close enough to make that discovery.

At Cambridge, she acquired the reputation of being "intensely private."

Sometimes Sasha called herself a "masochist," but always ironically and in a situation where she was not punishing herself, where the term was obviously inapplicable. Irony, nuance, anecdote, laughter were her modes; she didn't slop around in psychological jargon.

She'd longed for the day when she would get her driver's license. When she bought her first car, she drove it to Washington, accumulating speeding tickets all along the way. Someone said she drove like a bat out of hell. She adored marathon drives; sometimes she would drive twelve hours without stopping to a cabin she had purchased in Maine as a sanctuary. Speeding through New Jersey on one of her trips south, she was stopped; a judge ruled she was never to drive through New Jersey again.

Changing gears gave her a strange sense of power. She wrote Sally Clark that she thought she had a racer's mentality. As soon as she was in third gear she longed for a wide open stretch of road and the thrill of controlling her speed without having to worry about other cars—or people.

During the summer of 1966 the Lyman volunteers created an intensive program. In the spring they had written proposals for summer funding. After Peter McCaffery wrote his, Sasha told him she didn't have time to write one because exams were coming up and asked him to do hers as well. His roommate happened to be on the committee which approved the proposals and one day he told Peter, "You wrote a great proposal and it was accepted. But Sasha's was poorly written. It wasn't nearly as good as yours and didn't have any good ideas in it. She really submitted a sloppy piece of work."

Horrified, Peter confessed at once. "I wrote that one for Sasha. That was my work and if you're going to blame somebody for a sloppy proposal, blame me."

"It serves me right for not having written it myself," Sasha said when Peter told her what had happened.

He told her not to worry. He'd admitted the work was his.

But suddenly Sasha became furious. "Oh, Peter, shut your mouth! How could you say something like that!"

Then she walked out and didn't speak to him for a week. "Keep your mouth shut!" she'd cry if he ran into her on campus. It was a matter of keeping up appearances. Something she'd arranged in one corner of her life had become public in another. And it was unseemly that excuses be made on her behalf.

All of Sasha's reactions were similarly intense that summer. The Lyman group had become a surrogate family; everything that happened generated incommensurate emotion. She treated each person with a baffling mixture of intimacy and formality, demanding that they be intensely involved with each other as well.

Once she announced her plan for a commune at Staunton Hill. They would make their own clothes and live off the land. She would have twelve children and they would all run wild and free on "the farm." Geoff Beane, Wes Profit, Peter McCaffery, Sally Clark: they would live there together.

During that "frantic Lyman" summer she lived with Sally Clark and Marcia Nye in a building on Hampshire Street that was so like a slum that Sally's mother nearly drove off the road when she saw it. Down the street was the S & S Restaurant which they dubbed the "SS" restaurant. To go there for dinner, they decided, they would have to be accompanied by ten men who would encircle them so they wouldn't be attacked.

Each day Sasha went out to Lyman, tutoring three or four hours with the responsibility for ten boys. She taught one boy by associating historical names with food: William of Orange, Napoleon. One Sunday night a seventeen-year-old in the summer program turned up at the apartment on Hampshire just as Sasha was giving a party at which there was no small quantity of booze.

"What are you doing here?" Sally demanded.

He said he'd been released for the weekend.

"Oh, he's here already," Sasha interrupted. "We can't just let him go. Come on in! Join the party!"

The next morning she drove him back to Lyman, incurring the wrath of the administration because it turned out that although he said he was due back at eight on Monday morning, he wasn't supposed to have left the grounds at all.

When one of the boys, who was eighteen, asked Sally if he could date her when he was released, she thought, Oh, no, what am I going to do? But such things didn't bother Sasha, whose attitude was "They're my friends!"

The seventeen-year-old who crashed Sasha's party rented a hall and decided to give a dance to make money. He hired a band and spent one hundred sixty-five dollars, but hadn't arranged for any publicity so the hall was empty the night of the affair.

Sasha insisted that all her friends hop into their cars, drive down to Harvard Square, and accost people in the street. "There's this great dance going on. Do you want a ride? We'll take you. It only costs so much!"

Mark Nye believed he was in love with Sasha that summer. Being with Sasha was like climbing a mountain you could never conquer. But he refused to go to Staunton Hill because he didn't want to confront the class difference between them.

His dream was to take her to the Grand Teton Mountains in Wyoming, get her away from all the social ice-skating.

Sasha said she'd like to go. But she never did. Nye grew jealous, jealous even of the time she spent with her Lyman charge, Paul Kennedy. But his real rival, he felt, was Stanley Frye.

Frye was her "special person," Sasha told Mark. "Yes, he's married," she conceded, "but he may be getting divorced."

Nye tried to argue her out of it. This is ridiculous, he'd tell her. How often do you see him? What do you do when you do see him?

Sasha would become evasive, saying only that she had a commitment and that was the way it was. There'd be days when the shadow of Frye wouldn't come between them. But later she'd again invoke this old attachment. It was her safety valve, Nye thought, a way of remaining uncommitted to anyone. Sometimes Sasha tortured him by saying Frye was not the only other man she was close to.

Observing Sasha's relationship with Mark, Peter McCaffery concluded Sasha liked *the idea* of loving people, but didn't actually feel much for them. He took her to Connecticut one weekend to meet his family. His father, a former television newsman named Kevin McCaffery, tried to make eye contact with her all weekend and failed. Later he warned his son: "Watch out for this woman. She's a two-edged sword." A man might want to make Sasha happy and satisfy her, Peter decided, but it was impossible to locate her center, to discover what touched her. Anyway they both agreed a sexual relationship wouldn't be the best way for them to express their affection for each other. Peter stayed a good friend and was there for her one time when she took sleeping pills and had to be taken to the hospital to have her stomach pumped.

Throughout that intense Lyman summer Mark engaged in combat with Sasha, struggling for her loyalty. One night he gave himself a birthday party. Considering Sasha his girl friend, he expected her to attend. At the last minute she said she wasn't coming. She was tired from the long day at Lyman and wanted to rest. She instructed Sally to convey the message.

Refusing to accept her decision, Nye called the apartment. He let the telephone ring for twenty minutes without stopping. Sally grew nervous. She knew Sasha had been there when she left. She drove back to Hampshire where she found Sasha stretched out on a bed, somewhere between sleeping and waking, out on drugs. She hadn't wanted to be at Nye's party. He'd put pressure on her and she'd retreated.

Over the telephone shortly afterwards Sasha told Mark she didn't feel the way he did. Mark lacked depth, she told her friends. She wouldn't sever the connection entirely, however. They'd had good times together; it just didn't mean more than that. What could she do if Mark didn't believe her?

When one of her friends who was interested in Nye herself at the time upbraided Sasha for not letting him go, Sasha gave one of her usual oblique defenses. If something was still good, even though you knew it would spoil before long, you didn't throw it in the trash can in anticipation.

Taking the fall semester off, she fled from Mark to London.

The following June, just as he was about to graduate, Mark had a nervous breakdown. His roommate cornered Sasha then and accused her of causing it, condemned her for wielding her emotional power over Nye for manipulative ends.

But Sasha's own friends forgave her. Nye had always been successful with women and had viewed it as a challenge that Sasha wasn't attainable. That wasn't her fault. Nye had been wrong. He'd thought she felt more than she did. He should have acknowledged the distance Sasha had demanded. And yet—there was no denying that she had something to do with his breakdown.

Sasha's mood was black as she flew over the Atlantic that fall, downhearted at being away from her friends. Her plan was to live at Winfield House with her parents. But this reunion was accompanied by great emotional trepidation. "I'm beginning something far tougher than twenty Lyman summers and the thought of it appalls me," she admitted. She busied herself in London taking piano lessons and expressed relief with typical Sasha self-mockery that the book she was using preferred "simple Purcell to difficult 'Mary Had A Little Lamb.' " Capturing Mrs. Bruce for an hour one day, she gave her a piano concert, warming to her mother's pleasure at her progress, although she knew Evangeline was tone-deaf and probably only appreciated seeing the "spastic" attempts of her fingers on the keyboard.

In her room at Winfield House she tried writing, shut off from all distractions, but the words wouldn't come. She remembered Mr. Lisle, her English teacher at St. Tim's, telling her it was useless to write if you cannot, and so she went back to her reading. She bought secondhand books in Chinese, archaeology books by early explorers, books on magic from the 1880s and immersed herself in learning. At the Victoria and Albert Museum she examined the unicorn tapestries, Indian prints, the massive casts of doors from German and Italian cathedrals. Through London University she took an extension course from the Warburg Institute of Art in French Impressionist and Postimpressionist painting. It was more informative than inspiring, but she delighted in the gossip about the painters. She went on English country weekends and on one of them met a publisher who guaranteed her a job when she graduated. She had no intention of taking it, but liked the philosophy the man espoused; he approved of having many interests and never following one to the exclusion of the others.

Her father had bought a set of teach-yourself books and records for Italian and so she gave up her Spanish and Turkish for still another language. And she entered a Radio London contest for thinking of the most words ending in the letter "x"; she knew she'd never win the five-hundred-pound prize because she was using only a "concise" dictionary.

Catching herself using a cliché in a letter to Sally, she added, "And now I have used the last of our happy banalities, and may jump off the tower in peace."

In London, all this frenetic activity rescued her from despair—just as it had in Cambridge. In what she called her "ivory tower existence," she now immersed herself in the ancients, declaring her favorite writer was now Herodotus. She decided Mesopotamia was at the root of all Western civilization, the origin of both Bible stories and Greek myths, and found in the epic of *Gilgamesh* an analogue for the Book of Job. "The sun of the ancient world offsets the lack of sun there has been in my world these past few months," she wrote Sally.

Friends let her know that Paul Kennedy missed her. Although she felt guilty about deserting him, she didn't write but sent him a message through Sally Clark saying she was thinking of him and would write later. She felt uneasy about the Lyman counselors reading her letters, she told Sally. It wasn't that she planned to say anything subversive; she simply couldn't stomach the thought of the preslit envelope.

Not all of Sasha's letters to her friends in Cambridge were gloomy. She thoroughly enjoyed the fact that the top half of her Potomac School class, supposedly a "best-ever" class, had dropped out of college—herself included—this semester. Finding this dropout rate "delightful," she impishly contemplated mailing a survey to the headmistress, Miss Preston.

In November, like her mother and Ailsa Mellon Bruce before her, she was presented to the Queen and what she called "countless other members of the Royal family." "My curtsy nearly dragged Her Majesty down to floor level," Sasha joked, "since I could not keep my balance." She did what she called her "kowtow" to all the appropriate people, all the while casting her cool, appraising eye on what she saw as just another "usual" diplomatic reception filled with court hangers-on, trumpets, and champagne. But although as a little girl she had written of the Queen, "She's stinky and smelly. I hate her," and although she saw the occasion through her habitual lens of irony, attend she did. "The Court of St James's, that strange euphemism for England adopted for diplomatic purposes," Sasha remarked, "was in full swing. It was more Miss Miller than Ella R.," she concluded, referring to the two headmistresses, the Miss Watkins she respected, the Miss Miller she despised. "It was Ella R. without the warmth of tradition."

She enjoyed her talk with Lord Snowdon, comparing docks in London and Boston. Before marrying Princess Margaret, he had frequented the London dockland, she remembered, and had a beautiful Chinese mistress. But being her father's daughter, she refrained from mentioning *that*. Lord Snowdon advised her to go down to the docks on a foggy night, being sure to take a responsible person with her. She thought she might enlist her brother David.

At Thanksgiving lunch she enjoyed explaining this favorite holiday to the assembled "Brits," as Dvorak's New World Symphony played in the background. She felt like the first settlers in a foreign country inviting the native Indians ("Brits in this case") to share in the mood of thanks. She noticed the "Brits" did not take the comparison with native Americans as a compliment.

The high point of her semester abroad was a trip to Paris with her parents. At Notre Dame Cathedral she lit a candle to Our Lady and remained kneeling for a long time. Sunday night at the chapel at St. Timothy's flashed through her mind. She felt soothed by a past where moral norms were not ambiguous. Humbled, she made herself direct these feelings toward God. Then, feeling "very medieval," she ascended one of the towers.

Up there she saw herself as Victor Hugo's hunchback, at one with those equally deformed creatures, the gargoyles around and below. She felt as ugly and hated as Quasimodo. But when the bells of Notre Dame rang, she felt inexplicably happy. It was sunny; the sky was very high and clear.

Tragedy struck the Bruce family in January 1967. David Bruce had never been a close, accessible parent to Sasha's half-sister, Audrey. "Did my duty on Father's Day at Nicky's school, Beanvoir," he wrote in his diary for 1959. "Doubled it by sending Audrey a telegram of birthday congratulations." By then Audrey was married to Stephen Currier, no favorite with his father-in-law, perhaps because he lied when he said he had graduated from Harvard, or because they eloped and the ambassador felt Stephen had taken advantage of his shy, diffident, and very rich daughter.

Currier in turn entertained no kindness toward David Bruce.

At one point Audrey contemplated divorce, requesting the name of a good lawyer from her father. After Bruce made a suggestion with great alacrity, Audrey changed her mind, foolishly telling Stephen of her father's enthusiasm for the dissolution of their marriage. Having barely known his own father, Richard Currier, Stephen could be abrasive on the subject of fathers in general and once he called his father-in-law "a glorified messenger boy."

One night that January, Audrey and Stephen chartered a small plane to carry them from Puerto Rico to the Virgin Islands where they planned to hook up with a yacht on which their young son Michael awaited them. Stephen was in a hurry to reach his son to say good night. The Curriers made an exception to their rule this once and decided to fly together.

Stephen had his secretary call around to different charter companies. Only Airplane Charterers, Inc., with one plane in its fleet, was available. A recent theft had left it without its inflatable raft.

On this January night it was already dark by 6:45. The air was full of turbulence. At 7:15 their last radio message came. At 7:30 a Navy P2V plane at the same location as the Currier two-engine Piper Apache radioed that to escape moderate turbulence the pilot wanted to climb to ten thousand feet. Below, at eight hundred feet, the Curriers were being buffeted about. The plane evidently hit water, filled up at once, and went under. No wreckage was ever found.

The oldest child of the Curriers, Andrea, was eleven, the same age Audrey had been when her father divorced Ailsa to marry Evangeline Bell.

With Evangeline, David Bruce flew to New York; he remained there with Ailsa as the search went on.

Departing from London, Sasha felt as if the family had once again disappeared into a mist and she was left to her own resources. "By definition an impossible situation," she said, "since I have no resources." Before Audrey's death, Sasha had begun to think of her half-sister "an awful lot," even going so far as approaching one of Stephen Currier's cousins to arrange a meeting. She thought of Audrey as her "only sister" and had decided to ask her father if it "would make trouble" if she went to see her. Their distance was "a real gap which often bothers me." But now Audrey was dead.

As she prepared to return to Cambridge, her mind seemed a chaotic jumble. She talked of wishing "to recover a logic I never had." Her brother David told someone he had given up on his sister and when this came back to her, it stung.

That spring of 1967 Sasha met Bear Barnes, a young man who her friends were all-but-unanimous in agreeing would have been perfect for her. Barnes was a great-grandson of J. P. Morgan and president of the Porcellian Club, of which her own great-grandfather Charles Bruce had been a member. He was also president of Phillips Brooks House, although his social consciousness did not extend to his participating in so scruffy a project as Lyman. "Sasha, you've gone over to the enemy camp," Wes Profit said.

They met in a course on Northern European Renaissance painting. Bear was tall and blond with clear blue eyes; he was handsome and worldly and, according to friends who had shared summer homes with his family on Mount Desert Island, sexually precocious—when Bear was sixteen, he was already dating women of nineteen and twenty. He was intelligent, calm and gentle, and as guilty about his privileged background as Sasha was about hers. To Bear it was always a source of embarrassment when people found out about his connection with J. P. Morgan. Sasha took him to the working-class bars she had discovered.

Bear admired Sasha for her emotional energy, her strong feelings, and the individualism that meant she didn't care what the rest of the group was doing. He sympathized with her painful sense that her parents cared more about their careers than about her. But they didn't communicate well. Neither was open or emotionally frank. As usual Sasha treated many feelings as too dark to express, although it was obvious that she didn't value herself.

They were lovers from the spring of 1967 to the summer of 1968, yet they never discussed the deaths of Stephen and Audrey, Sasha's own childhood, or David K. E. Bruce. If Bear knew about Bruce's flamboyant days in OSS, it was because he was majoring in British history. He knew that Sasha adored Nicky and felt she didn't get along well with David, with whom she constantly sought rapprochement. They argued about commitment—whether they had an "exclusive" or a "primary" relationship. Sasha complained that Bear didn't love her enough.

When they spent the night together, Sasha parked her car in front of her own dorm so that it wouldn't be spotted near Bear's apartment. In the morning when he went to class, she felt uneasy being left alone on someone else's home ground. They always fought without yelling. It seemed they barely scratched the surface of the turmoil which grew between them.

Once Sasha visited Bear's home on Mount Desert Island. The weather was terrible. Although Bear knew Sasha hated sailing, he insisted they go sailing all day, returning to the house only at night. At the end of the third day, Sasha got into her car and drove off without a word.

She called him "Sweet Bear," but rarely would she say "I love you" or "I really care for you." Bear sensed that if he made a commitment, Sasha would run away. Yet his mother, observing the two together, accused him of treating her badly, of transmitting the message, "I care for you, but don't come so close."

Frye was held up to him as a rival, but Bear didn't take this seriously. He felt she didn't have a parental relationship with her father and so, he thought, father and lover were confused in her mind. Invoking Frye was not an act of malice against him; Sasha was simply expressing her very strong need. In his run-down fourth floor tenement apartment, she created a splendid birthday dinner for him. He had painted the floors bright yellow enamel and the bathroom blue with a white floor. Sasha brought him a blue vase matching the walls and a yellow enamel pot matching the yellow of the floor.

They alternated between joy and distance. They took their spring 1968 vacation in the Virgin Islands and spent most of the two weeks together submerged in the sea. "Lovely world," Sasha wrote to Tom Dolembo, "but as I went deeper into scuba diving, I realized I was not ever going to give up the sun." Yet she loved gazing down at the fish. "Even the barracudas seem friendly behind their vicious-looking masks. Perhaps," she pondered, "that's the way I look to them, too. Anyway there was no bloodshed."

As time passed, Sasha and Bear drifted apart. He was a conservative, he decided, while she was increasingly involved in romantic notions of the outlaw. He thought in her own person she was acting out the death throes of their social class.

Sasha attended antiwar demonstrations, but never became a radical. The summer Lyndon Johnson ordered the bombing of North Vietnam, she and David Irons spent an idyllic afternoon at the Henley Royal Regatta watching Harvard classmates row and race. Returning to London, they learned that both the embassy and Winfield House were ringed by English demonstrators. "Right on!" Sasha cried. She went to the big demonstration against the war in New York in 1967.

On the way to the 1969 Washington demonstration she and Geoff Beane stopped to walk along a canal. They heard shotgun blasts and laughed about hunting going on so close to the city. When they got back to Sasha's car, they saw that one entire side of it had been blasted with holes. The Jeep had Massachusetts plates and a string of reddish purple beads hanging on the rearview mirror. Sasha had just seen *Easy Rider* and laughed about the plot of that movie coming to life. In Dupont Circle she fell victim to tear gas and retreated to her parents' vacant Georgetown house where she sat crying until the chemicals wore off.

She was pressured by some of her Lyman cohorts to make a stronger political commitment, but she was afraid of getting publicity that might undermine her father, whose views on Vietnam, she knew, were moderate. Bruce felt our military had utterly failed to profit by the sad lessons of the French war in Indochina. As ambassador to England he attempted with Harold Wilson to make a deal with Kosygin offering the cessation of American bombing of North Vietnam in exchange for assurance that the DRV would stop moving troops into South Vietnam—only to be thwarted by Rostow and Johnson, who made only the small concession that they would not resume the bombing until Kosygin left London—this so as not to embarrass Bruce.

Like David Bruce, Sasha felt that it was absurd not to take the viability of the American political system as a given—she worked briefly for Eugene McCarthy in 1968. She believed her father represented the best the Western democracies had to offer. He stood in her mind as noble, the keeper of a worthwhile tradition. To break with this through political radicalism would have meant breaking with the best part of herself. At a cocktail party in London in 1968 she punched Andy Niven, son of the actor, in the nose for making a deprecating remark about David Bruce. Her father's moderate views on Vietnam had been misrepresented, Sasha said. He had integrity and sustained it in an environment that enjoyed little.

When the SDS took over the administration building at Harvard, Wes Profit, now president of Phillips Brooks House, was all for expressing solidarity. But Sasha, in the Bruce tradition, came up with a compromise that was both moderate and supportive of the rebellion.

Phillips Brooks House was independent, not owned by Harvard. Sasha decided that even if the university was closed to demonstrators, Phillips Brooks House, which owned its corner of the yard, could remain open.

A genteel benefactress had left money to Phillips Brooks House so the volunteers could have tea and cookies every day. Since this was hardly the fare they appreciated, the cookie fund had grown enormously. Sasha came up with the idea of Phillips Brooks House supplying cookies to all the demonstrators who had taken over the administration building. Hundreds of boxes of expensive cookies were dispatched to the SDS; there was even a picture in *The New York Times* of munching demonstrators. Sasha arranged that the seats in the Phillips Brooks House van go to voters who would vote no in the Vietnam referendum that summer.

In the spring of 1967 Sasha told her mother she planned to drive cross-country in her Jeep that summer. Her mother replied that it sounded like fun. Friends thought Sasha really wanted Evangeline to object, to say we want you home! The trip was to be an adventure, total freedom, being as rebellious as the Lyman boys. Sasha and Rona Earle began it together; Terry Graham joined them later.

Sasha's behavior was erratic, unpredictable, and distressing, particularly to Terry. She insisted she was so afraid of bears that at night the three girls had to lug everything out of the Jeep and put it in a washhouse. Sasha would lie awake all night frightened that the bears would come. She was suddenly excessively miserly and many a night refused to pay six dollars a night for a motel, infuriating Terry who longed for a

bath—at least once every three days. At a Harvard field site
in Arizona, Sasha insisted that the three of them stand out in
the hot sun in a temperature of 110 degrees picking up
potsherds.

The worst of her impulsive ventures into danger came in
Colorado, when it was her idea that they pick up two
hitchhikers, Marines gone AWOL. Terry said it was foolhardy,
even perilous. But Sasha insisted and treated it as a lark.
When the Marines said they knew a great swimming hole,
Sasha agreed to drive off the main road for miles. Then she
went skinny-dipping in the mountains. She got involved with
one of the Marines and drove to the house of one of his
friends in Los Angeles. There was no way Terry could reason
with her.

On this trip Sasha took a considerable quantity of ''speed.''

When she returned to Cambridge in the fall, Sasha was
overdrawn in her checking account by a considerable sum.
The bank sent her an unpleasant letter and Sasha in turn
became indignant that they should have done so. Suddenly
she was a Bruce, invoking the prerogatives of her class.

Wes Profit chided her. ''Sasha,'' he said, ''if I overdraw
my bank account by two dollars, they send me a nasty letter
and I have to go down immediately and deposit funds. Here
you're overdrawn by several thousand dollars and you're
upset with *them*. You've been traveling around the country
for three months writing checks on a nonexistent bank balance;
you have to expect them to be upset. This is the first time
I've known you to use your name and your family in that
way. Now you've got this poor guy thinking someone's going
to come along and withdraw all the funds out of the bank
unless he sends you a letter of apology. It isn't like you!''

''Well, he wrote me a nasty letter, and I thought I ought to
make him feel it,'' Sasha said.

She hated to use birth control. She had a diaphragm, but
most of the time left it in its case. One day right after she and
Bear had a fight and he told her he was ending the relationship,
she found out she was pregnant. ''Rather than have the baby,
I'll throw myself down the stairs,'' she screamed at Bear.

It was December 1967. Sasha fled to England, but it never
occurred to her that she could have gotten an abortion there.

She feared trying New York because the news might leak out and the publicity injure the family.

The Radcliffe scuttlebutt was that abortions were legal and routine in Jamaica. In January she and Bear flew down for a weekend, each paying their own way. Sasha's hysteria was exacerbated when she discovered they had been wrong; abortions were illegal and she was doomed to a back room somewhere on the island. Alone briefly in their hotel room she tried to kill herself. But finally they found a half-acceptable doctor's office where Sasha was given a D.&C. The cleanliness left something to be desired and afterward she had an infection. They were gone only for that weekend; by Monday morning Bear was taking an exam at Harvard. When she confided to Maeve that she had tried to kill herself, Maeve thought the entire choice of Jamaica had been inexplicably self-destructive. If an intelligent woman becomes pregnant, there are other options than a back room in Jamaica! But she held her tongue.

With some misgivings, Sasha had chosen to major in fine arts as opposed to a field of more immediate social purpose. To Linda Seidel, her instructor in tutorial, Sasha confided that it was her mother's influence which brought her to art. She spoke as if Mrs. Bruce were a special friend whose abilities Sasha appreciated.

At first Sasha considered writing her senior thesis about the social consciousness of the Postimpressionists. But medieval art touched her more profoundly. She had become fascinated by the work of a relatively little-known manuscript artist, referred to only as "the Rohan Master." What appealed to Sasha in his work was the brutal frankness of his imagery. He hadn't been swayed by the courtly frankness of his imagery. He hadn't been swayed by the courtly conventions of the fifteenth century. Instead the bodies of the Rohan Master's figures are hunched forward, leaning earthward, as if weighed down by alien and mysterious forces. His corpses are elongated and emaciated, their flesh as pale as wax. Melancholy and anguished, he traced the suffering that suffused early Christianity. Sasha, as Steve Blodgett had noted, was "receptive to pain." Perhaps she saw her own in the minutely depicted agony of the wracked and tortured souls that filled the pages of the Rohan Book of Hours.

The skies in the Rohan plates are dark and somber. A

Madonna has unnaturally short, spindly arms and a swollen head; Saint John turns toward God, as if with a violent motion of his head, reproaching the Father for his hardness of heart. The overriding theme is death.

Included as well in the Rohan Hours is a fine Saint George slaying a dragon, with the horse stepping on the dragon, the kind of innovation typical of this artist. Saint George would become Sasha's talisman as she began her work with icon painting; the Christian moralizations she wrote about in her thesis would resemble the icons she later studied and sold in London.

Allowing her to reach down to the darkest of her own obsessions, the thesis on the Master of the Rohan Hours became Sasha's major preoccupation for a time. At moments she grew impatient, complaining she was tired of looking at things as small as illuminated manuscripts. Playfully she said she wished she could write about the architecture of water towers instead.

But the final result of her work was inspired and she was proud of her accomplishment. She was awarded a *magna* with the highest honors. Three years after graduation she sent her thesis advisor Seymour Slive a deluxe edition of the Rohan Hours, published in France. It was Sasha's way of telling Slive the subject was still close to her heart. The Rohan Master's conviction that pain stalks our most innocent moments was one Sasha shared. His was a mood from which she only fleetingly escaped as she entered the final six years of her life.

Even while she was working long and hard on her thesis, Sasha continued in her commitment to Lyman, always with what she and Wes Profit called "radical designs." Periodically the governor of Massachusetts visited, but his inspections were announced well ahead so that by the time the official party arrived, the boys were in clean clothes and the school was immaculate.

It was Sasha who finally saw to it that Lyman School was permanently shut down. At first she and Wes enlisted some of the staff people to discuss how to bring this about. Then they began to have conversations with state agency officials in Boston. But her stroke of luck came when she discovered that a Senate committee had come to investigate all correc-

tional facilities in Massachusetts as a result of a riot at
Walpole Prison. It turned out she had met one of the senators.
"I know him, Daddy knows him!" she cried.

Sasha called the senator and urged him to investigate Lyman School, making a surprise visit. Many of the prisoners at
Walpole had been at Lyman earlier in their criminal careers
and Sasha told the senator, "If you want to see how they get
to Walpole, you ought to come out here!"

The committee visited Lyman unannounced and were appropriately shocked. The state followed with a lengthy report
and the school was closed down. Boldly effective in fighting
for what she believed, Sasha accomplished the end for which
the Lyman group had been struggling since the autumn of
1964.

One night at Cronin's, one of the working-class bars where
she hung out, Sasha announced that she planned to go to
Chicago to attend the National Democratic Convention. It
was the summer of 1968.

"We have plans for them!" Sasha announced. "We've got
snipers!"

"Who told you that?" Tom Dolembo asked her.

"I've got sources."

"You're up against the United States Army," Tom said.

"If the government opens a corridor, the blacks will get
them!"

"Daley knows what you're up to."

"We have it all planned. There are these black militants . . ."

"You'll never get out of Grant Park. The police will see to
that," Tom said. The demonstrators represented anarchy and
wouldn't get anywhere with the electorate. This was the
unfortunate legacy of the assassinations of Martin Luther
King and Robert Kennedy.

Sasha listened and changed her mind. It would not be
through radical politics that she finally broke with respectability.

Instead of going to Chicago, Sasha went to Israel in July
1968 on the last of her archaeological digs. The site was a
Phoenician city. There she lived on a kibbutz, excavating five
days a week from four in the morning to noon, and keeping
to herself. She found the boys in the group gutless and dull,
like her socially appropriate Harvard schoolmates.

In Israel, Sasha became passionately pro-Arab. She wrote that she saw the Arabs in old Jerusalem as oppressed and forgotten, the Jews as their jailers. The streets of the old city seemed reminiscent of the Casbah in Pontecorvo's movie *The Battle of Algiers*, which she had seen three times in one week in February 1967. She thought she had a "natural predilection for the Arabs" and got into heated arguments with young Jews whose attitude, she thought, was that Jerusalem was "just a filthy, smelly Arab town." Her hackles rose, she said later, when she heard "Zionist talk" about the glories of the Six Days War. Then, characteristically, she became appalled by her own "anti-Semitism," even as she watched it resurface amid new tales of Israeli heroics.

What excited her in particular was the land. She said she wanted to return to Jerusalem to live. She traveled to Jericho, to the Dead Sea, to Bethlehem, to Hebron. She was as moved by the Galilee region as she had been by old Jerusalem. The kibbutz was called Neve Yar, which meant "dwelling by the sea," and it reminded her of how Lee, the boy who had been her first lover in New Mexico, liked to recite Edgar Allan Poe's "Annabel Lee." Thoughts of Lee and the New Mexico dig made her feel her archaeological career had now "come full circle."

She never went on another dig. Even as she threw herself into projects, there was always a sense of impermanence, of finality, of things rapidly approaching a dramatic, inevitable end.

"Do something with your life!" Stanley Frye demanded on one of her visits.

"I am," she insisted, and mentioned the archaeology.

Frye was not convinced. There was something dilettantish about it. In Sasha's compartmentalized life, archaeology had held one precarious place. No single interest was compelling enough to justify a commitment. A goal might have meant slowing down, and, inevitably, what she feared most: introspection, self-examination. She danced away from any confrontation with herself, as if she couldn't risk what such a quest might bring, as if it were altogether too dark.

In August after she returned from Israel, Bear came to London to spend time with her, but she broke off the relationship. He stayed for five days and then went home.

The entire Bruce family went off on a vacation together the day he left. That fall of 1968 as he was about to leave for Philadelphia, Bear met Sasha in Harvard Yard. She was now dating a graduate student who had been an instructor in one of her courses and Bear felt she was deliberately taunting him by wearing this man's sweater. It was over between them for good.

Sasha's friends were distressed when she walked away from Bear Barnes. They believed he loved her and that this was the only healthy relationship she'd ever had. Others saw her withdrawal from Bear as inevitable. Sasha was a citizen of the world; she could never have ended up as a schoolteacher's wife. Bear was too goody-goody, too dull. Sasha's knowledge and temperament were so varied, she was so mercurial, that a good, solid, dependable man would have bored her.

From September 1969 through June 1970 she lived in another shabby tenement, this one at 900 Massachusetts Avenue, on the wrong side of town, halfway between Harvard and Central squares. In the middle of a shower, the water would go off and stay off, but Sasha didn't mind. Once there was a domestic dispute in the apartment next door. Sasha and Sally heard a loud, piercing scream and rushed to the rescue, banging on the door. Opening up, an annoyed woman turned on them: "Oh, go away and stop bothering me!" she yelled at her saviors. The roof leaked and when the landlord finally fixed it, he sealed up Sasha's cat into the roof. Sasha came home and heard Catastrophe mewing. To release her pet, she opened up the roof all by herself and Sally came home to find a gaping hole in the ceiling with tar dripping from it.

For respite she drove to her A-frame cabin in Maine. She became friendly with her neighbors and told her Cambridge friends she liked "the flavor of places" and was most relaxed, most herself, in the presence of solid, simple people.

Later an acquaintance moved into her cabin and lived there without paying her rent. "Kick him out," Frye advised. "I don't know how," Sasha said. She was constantly being taken advantage of, as if allowing herself to be exploited were a means of atoning for her privilege.

Once Bear was gone, a new pattern of obsession emerged. There was a string of older, married men who were all black.

Sasha would struggle in vain to woo them away from their wives. Increasingly she was drawn to those who might punish her, whose love she couldn't hope to win, who would demonstrate that Sasha wasn't worthy of anyone's full attention. If only she could find someone who would return her love, she lamented, she could cure her depressions. Once she asked Terry Graham's parents if she could use their New Hampshire house for one of her weekend liaisons with a married black lover. The heights of the respectable had been scaled. Her hunger for adventure grew. At workingmen's bars she picked up what she called "earthy" types. The men who were both black and married she pursued unrelentingly.

Sasha made a case for going out with married men. Your freedom remained intact, she said. They were older and might teach you something sexually. But when the pain of rejection assaulted her, she complained: "Isn't it awful that every time I find someone to love, he turns out to be married? If only I had met him years ago. . . ." Often the men promised to leave their wives for her, but they never did. With little encouragement she treated each one as a serious relationship, worthy of a life commitment. She demanded absolute devotion. When it was not forthcoming, she became hysterical.

One of these relationships with a black married man Sasha termed "sad." She couldn't see the man often. Her attitude was, "I know I'm not worth more than the little you're giving me." She was proving she was worthless, not as valuable as the man's wife.

She even developed a romantic interest in Peter McCaffery when he became involved with someone else. When Peter's girl friend, Diane, came to Harvard for a visit, Sasha locked herself in her room for an entire weekend. Sally stood by the door and tried to coax her to come out. "Okay, if that's what you want to do to yourself, I'll see you when you come out," Sally told her.

When Peter married Diane, Sasha visited them in Brooklyn and insisted on sleeping on the kitchen floor.

Once when Sasha started up with the husband of a friend, Sally said she disapproved.

"You're right. It's not a good thing to do to a friend," Sasha agreed. Then she defended herself. "He's not happy with his wife; I want to make him happy. He's happy with me. It brings a little joy into his life.''

One night in 1969, Wendy, Terry, and Sasha met in New Hampshire for a reunion. They sat around the fire late at night and discussed the psychology of suicide, the difference between the person who commits suicide and the one who commits murder. Sasha thought there was only a very fine line between the two: both were overwhelmed by the same feeling of despair. Suicide was the desire to murder someone else but not being able to do it. In both cases there was anger, which could be turned either against society or against yourself.

"Generalities of right and wrong betray a frightening obtuseness,'' Sasha said. There were no moral 'absolutes.

Now she often told friends she was frightened of killing herself. She wasn't worthwhile; continuing on in what she was doing was too painful. With Wes Profit and Geoff Beane she made a pact that a telephone call would be made to one of the others should one of them decide on suicide. As a sophomore Wes had told Sasha he was going to do himself in—she had talked him out of it.

One day in 1969, after she had graduated, returning from a weekend in New England with Maeve Kinkead, she deliberately drove her car into a snow-removal vehicle. Maeve was badly frightened. Luckily neither of them was hurt. Crossing the boundary of Sasha's privacy, Maeve urged her to see a psychiatrist. Sasha agreed something dire would happen if she didn't go into therapy.

Sally Clark tried another approach. "It's screwy to be going out with so many married men,'' she said. "You're very unhappy and maybe you should try to find out why.''

She went to a psychiatrist who had a group practice in Brattle Square. Her plan was to move to Maine, do independent interdisciplinary study in the history of thought—the connection between iconography and mythology—and commute to Cambridge for therapy. For a brief time, she seemed to be settling down.

The psychiatry was carefully mapped out. It would be a long-range program. She needed years of psychoanalysis, she was told. Therapy would just be reconnoitering and treating symptoms.

Sasha recoiled. Part of being responsible for herself meant

that she had to be in control; she had to be ready when her father made one of his characteristic, passively benevolent approaches: "What are you up to now?"

"I don't want to live like that," she said, refusing the prospect of years of analysis in Cambridge.

"I never met anyone like her," the psychiatrist later commented. "I have no idea what will happen to her."

After graduation in the spring of 1969 she returned to London to help the Bruces pack for their move to Washington. On her return to Cambridge, she did social welfare work, leading training seminars for community organizing and research on land reform and rural improvements in the South. But when one of the love affairs with a married man turned sour, she quit her job.

The summer of 1970 she toured Sikkim, Nepal, India, and Tibet. In India she found a child lying on the road, struck down by a car. She approached a group of boys on their way to a Siva temple, but they refused to intervene. So Sasha hired a taxi and took the child to a hospital where she paid for his treatment. Then the boy's mother and the local villagers were furious that she had interfered with the child's karma.

Wandering through Tibet, she acquired what she thought was a wall hanging and sent it to Stanley Frye. But what arrived was a foul-smelling horse blanket, and he knew she'd been cheated again. All that summer she was heavily on drugs.

In London before she went off to India, Sasha had met a Greek in the British Museum who introduced himself as Anton von Kassel. Like so many of the men she pursued in her last years in Cambridge, he was both married and a pickup.

When she returned to Cambridge, she terminated her therapy for good. She was going back to England, she confided to Sally Clark, to start a new life with this man she had met. "Maybe I need that analysis, but maybe my relationship with Anton will work everything out, so I'll try that first," she said.

That fall of 1970 Sasha approached her friends with an unusual request. She was collecting passports to get prisoners out of Greek jails; the man she was in love with, Anton von

Kassel, required American passports to enable oppressed Greeks to flee.

Wes Profit laughed. "I can see no earthly way my passport can be useful. I can't imagine there would be any blacks!"

"Oh, we'll take care of that," Sasha told him.

She seemed to believe the passports would in fact be used to help Greek dissidents. Her friends could easily get new passports by telling the government they had been stolen. She became angry when anyone refused her.

"Are you sure it's not for heroin? Be careful," Tom Dolembo warned.

They're revolutionaries, Sasha assured him. It was for a greater good.

"I don't like Greeks," Tom said.

To convince Bear Barnes to help her, she invoked their old love, and throughout the conversation created the image of Anton von Kassel as a wonderful, principled Greek who had been expelled from his country and whose friends were now in danger.

Terry Graham was unmoved by Sasha's passport story. The poor starving Armenians, the poor helpless Greeks. She wasn't going to help Sasha rip off passports. Sasha had always been an honest person. Now she seemed gullible. She wasn't doing this out of any convictions of her own; she was just obsessed with another man. And there was a disquieting note to the way she asked, as if it were a mischievous game.

But Sasha could be persuasive and some of her friends did surrender their passports, convinced that Anton von Kassel was what Sasha claimed him to be.

In December 1970, David Irons drove Sasha to Logan Airport. She had chosen a night flight to London and it was dark as they made their way along the shortcut which Sasha promised would shave five to seven minutes from their driving time. That she viewed her move as permanent was apparent from the amount of luggage she was taking: several bags and two large stacks of records tied with string. It was clear she was moving house. She seemed very nervous.

Sitting beside David, Sasha became more open with him than she had ever been. She had driven her car off the road more than once, she confessed; one time it had been totaled. Now, in retrospect, she admitted these were conscious acts.

She spoke of "attempts," never actually using the word "suicide," always elliptic, as she had been trained to be. She was, after all, David Bruce's daughter, the David Bruce who years afterward spoke still of the Kennedy assassination only as "that distressing event."

"I do things that scare me," Sasha said. "And I always know what I'm doing. Now I'm going to London. It's thoroughly frightening."

"Why are you doing this?" David asked her.

"There's a man there who makes me scream with laughter."

She told David Irons how to contact her. She would be living at Anton's house, under the pseudonym A. Bell, her mother's maiden name.

At the check-in counter, suddenly pointing to her luggage, she asked the man weighing the excess baggage, "What would you do if I told you there was a bomb in there?"

The London Episode

Anton von Kassel's New Grecian Gallery was located on Brook Street in Mayfair, just down the road from Regent Street and Liberty's. One entered from the street, but the icons themselves were displayed at the basement level in a room shrouded in darkness. Elegant, startling, dramatic, von Kassel's new gallery was like nothing the fledgling icon trade had seen. Every inch of the walls was covered with black velvet and the floors too were dark. Spotlights threw their beams directly on the icons. At once the spectator was transported into the realm of the supernatural. Somber and austere, the basement area simulated the atmosphere of a Byzantine church where it was so dark one could make out only the candles.

Upstairs in the small entrance room beautiful, long-legged secretaries with no discernible function idled about polishing four-inch-long purple fingernails and there was the atmosphere of a nightclub. For these jobs Anton von Kassel interviewed girls in the darkened room below with the spotlights trained on them, as if they too were icons.

It was said of Anton that his charm was so great that in his presence before you knew what was happening, you found yourself writing him a check. He had memorized books on manners and etiquette and his letters were sprinkled, judiciously, with phrases in French and Latin. He was a man who pressed his advantage to the point where his entire credibility was called into question. Yet the icon demimonde was respectful of his boldness. Anton had talked the Dean of Westminster Abbey himself into renting him the Chapter House for his first icon exhibition in the late sixties. He had invited the Sotheby's expert to estimate the icons there and when the man assigned them a quarter of the value von Kassel considered them worth, he angrily sent off a solicitor's letter to Sotheby's.

People had expected the manager of the fancy new gallery to be Anton's wife, Maria Andipa, who had been involved with him in the Grecian Gallery on Walton Street. But when the New Grecian Gallery opened in 1971, it was Sasha Bruce, daughter of the former ambassador, who was the manager, seated in a little office off the basement exhibition hall. When Maria Andipa's old friends called, they were told only that she "was out." The newspapers were informed that the *New* Grecian Gallery had moved and so Maria had to change the name of her own shop to Maria Andipa Gallery. Anton had split the original Brook Street storefront into two galleries; in the other he opened a surrealist section called the Acoris Gallery named for his and Maria's son. There Anton hung fake Dalis and held a grand exhibition of Magrittes, Di Chiricos, and "Dalis" with Mme. Magritte herself in attendance, and prospective clients unaware that most of the paintings were either there on consignment or were owned by banks.

Maria Andipa had known about Sasha Bruce for nearly a year. In late 1970 her marriage to Anton, punctuated by screaming matches and fistfights, had become so debilitating that Maria had taken a trip to Greece to recuperate. On her return she found a telegram on Anton's desk in their five-bedroom penthouse apartment on Eaton Place. A woman named Sasha announced she was returning to England and wanted to know where she and Anton might meet. In a fit of rage Maria turned over the place from top to bottom until she ferreted out more letters. One Anton had casually left lying around. A bunch had been tossed into a bureau drawer.

Maria had met Anton when she was singing in a London nightclub to support herself and her son Amadis by her first marriage. A well-dressed Greek introduced himself to her as a theatrical agent and film producer. Maria laughed and called him "one of those." But he returned the next day having arranged for her to meet with an Italian woman who ran a big theatrical agency in Mayfair. For Maria, as for Anton, there were the goals of Mayfair, associating with the titled rich and the high life.

The Italian woman spoke of von Kassel as if he were an important man and Maria was impressed. He promised to put her on television. She learned that his real name was Antonis Hatzinestoros, but he said his grandfather was an Austrian nobleman descended from King Othan and so he had a right to call himself von Kassel even if he was only the son and grandson of Thessaloniki hairdressers. Short, soft-looking, chubby, and baby-faced, he was several years the tall, sensual Maria's junior. He even had dimples. He wore glasses and this made him look like a combination of Peter Sellers and a Marxist revolutionary. He said he had gone to Cambridge; his conversation was clever and he had plans.

Von Kassel promised to adopt Amadis, whose own father had refused to see him and who, Maria said, had left her as soon as he found out she was pregnant. Anton said Amadis should call him Daddy. He sent Maria roses and presents— from a hat to a gold pencil—all in exquisite taste. She had originally come to London as a Miss Venus of Greece with plans to study at the Royal Academy of Dramatic Arts. Now she was destitute. Anton was sympathetic.

For a year they lived together enjoying themselves on money sent from Salonika by Anton's father. One day Anton came home driving a Jaguar he had mysteriously acquired. Maria says she told him to get rid of it. "But it's so nice and shiny," Anton said in his quiet way. When his father finally cut him off, disgusted by what he thought was the playboy life-style of his son, they became poor. Nonetheless, Maria married him in 1967. Immediately she applied for a Harrods credit card in the name "Baroness von Kassel" and made plans to enroll Amadis at Eton.

Maria had been born in Jerusalem and it was she who introduced Anton to the icon business. But by the time he opened the Grecian Gallery, he let her know she was to remain at home. Soon she became pregnant. When his partner Charles Churchill, who had made his money in a greeting card business, grew tired of paying Anton's bills, the Grecian Gallery collapsed. Anton decided to quit the icon trade, but Maria objected. "You're mad," she screamed. "It was me who started it and you're not going to give it to anybody. I'm going to take over the icons!"

Anton seemed to relent. Maria calmed down. They rented another shop on Walton Street. But Anton said he wanted his own gallery and it was then that he found the place on Brook Street. Anton was to sell his surrealist paintings on one side

and Maria the icons on the other. Then, just before the
opening, he told Maria she would not be needed; he had
found someone else to look after the icon gallery. He took all
the remaining icons from Walton Street before Maria figured
out what he was up to. But she did know the other woman
had to be "Sasha."

"I don't know what to do without you," Sasha had written.
She spoke of Anton's beautiful dark eyes and how she was
unable to forget him. She offered him airline tickets, anything
so long as they might meet. Having come of age, she had
access to her fortune. The income on her irrevocable trust had
steadily accumulated and she had a revocable trust as well.
Sasha was ready to begin spending.

David Bruce served as ambassador to Great Britain from
1961 to 1969, the longest anyone had ever held that post.
Afterwards the Bruces were frequently in London where they
kept an apartment at the Albany. In July 1970, Bruce was
appointed chief negotiator at the Paris peace talks to end the
Vietnam war, a thankless task that lasted a year. Coming out
of what Mrs. Bruce called his "fourth or fifth" retirement, in
May 1973 he became the first American envoy to Peking,
where he served as head of the United States People's Republic of China Liaison Office until October 1974. By late
November the Bruces were on their way to Brussels for what
would be Bruce's last post: permanent American ambassador
to NATO.

In March of 1970 David Bruce informed his three children
in a letter written jointly to them all, with a copy for each,
that although he had not intended to make any more substantial gifts to them in his lifetime, circumstances had altered
that decision. Ailsa Mellon Bruce had died in 1969, reputedly
the wealthiest woman in the United States with assets in
excess of five hundred million dollars. She had left her
former husband what he called a "handsome legacy." David
Bruce was of course not mentioned in Mrs. Mellon Bruce's
will; the trusts that passed to him were written so that they
would not become public.

Sasha and her brothers were made a gift of the contents of
Staunton Hill in an undivided interest. Bruce told his children
there was nothing particularly valuable in the house, no excep-

tional furniture, fine art, or silver; the china he called "ordinary." Using an appraisal made in November 1960, which estimated the contents at $51,039, Bruce said $100,000 was more than what they would bring at auction; even in Charlotte County the amount would be "risible." The furniture was in bad condition and had never been restored, although Bruce had to admit there was plenty of it.

The children were to pay the insurance, state and local taxes. The deed of gift of personal property, an "irrevocable gift," was drawn up on April 1, 1970. Someday, their father told them, if they wished, they could purchase the plantation itself from their mother, to whom he planned at that moment to leave Staunton Hill in his will.

Later that year Sasha went off to London with little thought of Staunton Hill, or, for the present, of her father's gift.

"Where shall we meet, inside London or out?" she had written to von Kassel. She said she was so preoccupied with thoughts of him that she couldn't even play with her cat, Catastrophe. She had tried to write many times, but her hand trembled and it took a long time before she could summon the courage to begin.

Anton agreed to meet Sasha in Norwich, far from the shrewd eyes of Maria. But somehow Maria discovered the name of their hotel, and that they were registered as Baron and Baroness von Kassel.

She rang the number.

"I wish to speak to Baroness von Kassel!" Maria demanded. If there was a Baroness von Kassel, wasn't it she?

Anton came to the phone.

"Who is it?" he asked cautiously in his soft, barely accented English. When he realized who it was, all he could manage was a weak "How did you find out?"

"You bastard!" Maria screamed. "So that's where you go with this girl and you call her Baroness von Kassel!"

"Sasha or me!" Maria yelled in fury when he came home.

"I can have you both," Anton answered slyly. "What's wrong with that? You're my wife and I love you. She can be helpful because she's got money. I'll give you presents; you'll live like a queen. Who cares?" He bragged about Sasha's influence in London; she could call a theater or restaurant at a moment's notice and be given the royal treatment.

''Either we're married or get out,'' Maria says she declared then. ''I don't want the money.''

''I'm going to live with her,'' Anton said, and promptly moved out of the Eaton Place penthouse to a town house at 27A Charles Street.

In their first heady days together, Anton seemed interested in everything Sasha said or did. He wore Edwardian-style clothes, black pin-striped suits, the most expensive silks, leathers, and suedes, and he expected Sasha to match him in elegance. He made her exchange her poncho and thongs for elegant costumes; when she returned to Cambridge for a visit, she asked Maeve Kinkead to teach her how to apply makeup. It was Anton's idea that she pluck her thick, dark eyebrows. He remodeled her, telling his friends, with a knowing air, ''She's handsome, but not beautiful.'' She knew nothing about cookery, but he ruled that at Charles Street only Greek food be served and so she rushed out and bought a cookbook. He taught her to bring the Cuban cigars he favored or his pipe on demand. He said a gentleman never carries money and so she carried cash for him in a cigar box. This is what a Greek woman does for her man, he told her.

They had talked of art and Oriental civilizations that day in May 1970 when they met in the British Museum. Sasha thought him erudite and the prospect of working with him in an icon gallery was tantalizing. Icons were not a new art form for Sasha. Stanley Frye had painted them and she had admired icons in the churches during her summer of 1965 in Turkey.

Anton von Kassel seemed to care genuinely about icons, explaining to Sasha how they had been neglected and how no one cared about their preservation. He created in her an enthusiasm for this untrammeled branch of art, virgin territory for the scholar. He liked to see her studying, he said. Intelligent clients were the ones he preferred; if he admitted that he sold fakes on occasion, it was to people who deserved to be sold fakes. Sasha seconded him in this. It didn't trouble her when he said he could get any number of Greek icons at a time when it was illegal to export antique icons from Greece. And before long she knew that he got his Jerusalem icons by paying off a certain Bishop Arcadios.

So elated was Sasha about working at the New Grecian

Gallery that she paid Terry Graham's way to London for the opening. Art and her linguistic skills were merging with her lust for adventure and illegitimate excitement.

A wealthy architect named Beresford Willcox walked into the gallery from the street, never having taken any notice of icons before. So successfully did Sasha convey her enthusiasm that Willcox became a major collector, charmed by this intellectual girl in her twenties. Sasha was generous and fair and once when she didn't have what Willcox wanted, she told him, "There are some very nice icons on exhibition at the Temple Gallery right now."

The Temple Gallery was the best icon gallery in London; for von Kassel, Sasha created the second best.

"Shut up," she said playfully when Helen Mark offered to pay her a commission for sending Beresford Willcox to her gallery. When Helen confided she was traveling to Corfu, Sasha sent her a book about Corfu the next day with a note attached: "This may prove useful to you if you read it."

She never gave the impression of pushing an icon on a customer; the person himself would have to raise the question of price. Only later would Sasha add, "You know, it's a good price. You haven't paid too much." Or she might say, encouragingly, "That was a very fine icon you bought."

The atmosphere she engendered at the New Grecian Gallery was intellectual, never commercial. Once she even invited Willcox to the house on Charles Street to show him one of her personal icons, a fifteenth-century processional work from Novgorod which had been paraded through the streets to inspire the troops. "Would you like this book?" she asked shyly, offering Willcox a volume on early Russian icon painting.

Her favorite icon subject was Saint George slaying the dragon; he was ideal man thrust into the cosmos, his existence threatened by forces from below. She bought her parents a seventeenth-century Greek Saint George, commissioning Claudio Astrologo to restore it for her with particular care. Pleased by his work, Sasha wrote a thank-you note and when Claudio's son was born, she presented him with a small icon of Saint Celianos, patron saint of maternity.

She attended the icon auctions at Sotheby's and Christie's, spending thousands of pounds. It seemed she would pay anything for one of the icons Anton had preselected; he himself never came with her. Often she wore a fur-lined embroidered Indian coat and sat in the back so as to have a good view of the proceedings. She wasn't always elegant, however. Sometimes she arrived with her hair unkempt and once wore black patent leather moccasins with one of the soles flapping loose. "She's David Bruce's daughter," someone remarked. "Why doesn't she buy herself a decent pair of shoes?" "Is *that* David Bruce's daughter?" someone else interjected. During the emotionally trying moments at auctions Sasha remained self-controlled, keeping her feelings well in hand. But for all her poise there was general agreement that Sasha nearly always overpaid.

At the New Grecian Gallery Sasha handled the icons, wrote the catalogues, and arranged the exhibitions. She became a virtual expert in *rigatino*, the only proper method of restoration. With *rigatino* tiny lines match one color to another so that you can distinguish what is original from what has been retouched.

At Claudio Astrologo's studio, where many New Grecian Gallery restorations were done, she sat for hours watching him work. Von Kassel began to boast that he'd taught her everything she knew, but it soon became apparent that she knew more than he. In his presence she was subservient, never venturing an opinion about an icon. Still, people marveled at her taste and the high quality of her writing and thought she would have become an expert given another five years.

Meanwhile they lived the high life. When they began together, Anton was already in debt for one hundred twenty thousand pounds, about a quarter of a million dollars, and had taken to borrowing at high interest just to sustain his old loans. Unaware of this debt, Sasha gave him twenty thousand pounds to start the gallery.

After Sasha arrived, von Kassel increased his fleet of automobiles to include, in addition to the Jaguar, a Rolls-Royce, a Ferrari, an antique Bentley, and a Range Rover, the vehicle Sasha preferred. He took clients to the best restaurants, always paying cash; the next morning his guest would receive a box of Havana cigars valued at sixty pounds. He frequented the Clermont Club, London's fanciest gaming establishment, where gamblers played for high stakes in a town house designed in 1742 by William Kent; even David K. E. Bruce had to admit when he was first taken there that the house was the loveliest on Berkeley Square, its staircase "of unusual perfection," the Gothic chairs in one of the gaming rooms "wonderful." An "intent-to-game" form had to be filed at least forty-eight hours before one was permitted to gamble and "you could come without a jacket if you owned a country." Parking his Rolls with the valet, Anton played backgammon and rubbed elbows with Lord Lucan and the other luminaries who frequented the Clermont.

He wanted to impress Sasha's parents that he really was a baron so they could not help but respect him, although once he confessed to Claudio Astrologo that he had bought the title. (Skeptics concluded he had picked the name out of a book, or simply made it up; he knew in England you could call yourself by any name and it was unlikely, given his character, that he would have paid to be called von Kassel.)

With the capital provided by Sasha, he bet heavily on racehorses and rented a country house in Hampshire and a cottage on the Isle of Wight, as well as a flat in Jerusalem where Sasha had been longing to live since her Israeli dig. He spent three thousand pounds to divide the kitchen at Charles Street so they could have a separate dining room. Then there was a yacht purchased for fifty thousand pounds in Brazzaville, Congo—which sank en route to Europe. It had not been insured. Maria Andipa gloated and said God was beginning to punish Anton for his evil ways.

For a time the New Grecian Gallery flourished. Between 1972 and 1973 the business was said to be worth eight hundred thousand pounds. Openings were lavish affairs attended by bank managers and financiers; compulsive over-reacher that he was, von Kassel even invited the personal banker of his chief rival in the icon trade, Dick Temple, to a private showing.

At these openings, Sasha presided as hostess, a bit nervous but poised. Catalogues that cost one hundred fifty pounds a copy were given away free. The parties cost nearly six thousand pounds each and there was food, champagne and strawberries, and free posters. Once von Kassel chartered an airplane and he and Sasha transported clients from London to

Germany for one night so they could see an exhibition. Having borrowed close to a million pounds, Anton paid his secretaries more than a hundred pounds a week, an unheard-of salary for London in those days. At the beginning Sasha poured money into the New Grecian Gallery without putting anything on paper and not even keeping receipts.

Occasionally old friends from home would visit. Annie Borland, a St. Timothy's classmate, was invited to dinner with Sasha, Anton, and a Lebanese friend of Anton's who told them he was in the market for Redeye missiles. "It's a weapon which you lift onto your shoulder and it shoots off a rocket," he explained. This man talked nostalgically of what an oasis Beirut once had been.

At another dinner Anton taunted Sasha. "In twenty years there will be a plaque on the house on Charles Street reading 'Sasha Bruce, American patriot,' like those blue plaques on historical buildings," he sneered. Sasha energetically defended American policy while Anton took special delight in calling American political attitudes naive. The English were inefficient, von Kassel pronounced, while the Americans were just stupid.

At times he'd sit in the presence of Sasha's friends sulking, not bothering to talk at all. On other occasions, he'd try to stir things up. Her friends neither liked nor trusted him. He never took the point of view of a woman seriously and he became unpleasant if you disagreed with him about anything. Despite his baby face and dimples, there was something menacing in his air.

In June 1970, a month after meeting von Kassel, Sasha had flown back to the United States to attend Wendy Wisner's wedding. On the morning of the ceremony, Wendy, Sasha, and Terry Graham rose early and ran out into the fields around Wendy's country house in their bare feet. The fog was just lifting and they laughed remembering all the good times they'd had together. Wendy and Sasha longed to find a horse and just ride off.

Sasha brought an elegiac mood to that day. She seemed sad and confessed to having had a fight with Anton already. At this most romantic of weddings, she seemed wistful, as if she'd missed her own chance to be happy. Wendy felt as if Sasha were saying that she once had dreams of a day like this, but they were gone for her. She wished the best for Wendy, her little sister. But she had permanently lost something simple and precious from her own life; such a day was not in her future.

Barbie Hanson Pierce, Sasha's roommate during her junior year at Radcliffe, spent a year in London with her husband. Soon after their arrival, the Pierces invited Sasha and Anton to dinner. They were due at seven thirty. At eight Sasha telephoned, and again at eight thirty, and still again at nine. Each time she said they were still planning to come. A bit after nine, they finally arrived, Sasha magnificently attired in a black velvet suit and a white blouse spilling over with ruffles, more elegant than Barbie had ever seen her. Furious, Barbie slapped the dinner onto the table. At ten, the doorbell rang. It was the minicab Anton had ordered in advance to pick them up.

On another occasion the Pierces bought theater tickets for all four of them only for Anton to fail to appear as Sasha endlessly apologized for him. Finally they entered the theater without him. Emerging, they found Anton waiting outside in the Range Rover and they went on to dinner. In the middle of the evening they switched over to the Rolls-Royce and went gambling at a Greek club in Bayswater where the lady croupiers wore evening gowns and a valet at the door parked Anton's car.

Anton seemed mortified that Barbie's husband wasn't wearing a tie. But he insisted on giving the Pierces fifty pounds each. "It's yours," Sasha said. "Everything you win, you get to keep. Anything you lose, you don't have to pay. It's an old Greek custom."

By now Sasha seemed to consider herself Greek. "A Greek would say, you naive Americans, you girls from St. Timothy's, you don't know how the world works. You don't understand the way Greeks do business," she said on another occasion to Annie Borland.

In the early days the one obstacle to Sasha's happiness seemed Maria Andipa's refusal to give Anton a divorce. Once Maria's sister telephoned Sasha. "Don't be stupid," the woman pleaded. "This man is married. He was married before to a woman in Greece with whom he had a daughter and whom he deserted. He has two children. Why do you want to be involved with him?"

But Sasha only replied haughtily, "This has nothing to do with you. It's between me and Maria."

Finally Maria herself called Sasha, determined to get her husband back. "He's married," Maria told her. "I've got a child. Why do you want to get involved with a man like that when with your position and money you could have anyone in the world?"

"Well, it's up to him," Sasha answered.

Disapproval was now what Sasha craved. She may have felt her parents' preoccupation with respectability only concealed an absence of love. Later Sasha would admit that if her parents had made more dramatic efforts to separate her from Anton, it would have made her want him only the more. By the time she moved to London, she was determined not to allow anyone to fulfill her need to be rescued, a need that conflicted with her stronger desire to be annihilated.

Maria was not one to take the loss of a husband lightly. At first she thought she could outlast this neurotic, hysterical girl who was probably more interested in spiting her parents than in Anton himself. Maria kept hoping the Bruces would intervene, cutting short Sasha's tenure. One day Sasha phoned Maria's house while Anton was there visiting Acoris. Sasha's voice was agitated as she demanded to speak with Anton.

"How dare she have the audacity to ring up here!" Maria railed. That young woman was buying Anton's love. Now she thought she had a right to be angry if he visited his son. But Anton enjoyed the charade. What better way of controlling Sasha than continuing to see Maria, who was, after all, still his wife?

In June 1971 the London press, led by William Hickey, gossip columnist of the *Daily Express*, discovered that the daughter of former Ambassador David K. E. Bruce and a Greek were living together on Charles Street. There was a knock at the door. Innocently Sasha came down only to have flashbulbs pop in her face. She did not deny that she was living with Anton von Kassel.

The publicity was intolerable to the Bruces. It continued to rankle that her mother was upset that, as Sasha put it in a letter to one of her Cambridge friends, she was "living in sin.'' Her mother was embarrassed even to give one of her friends her address, Sasha said, because Mrs. Bruce thought "even a number and street might give away her daughter's shameful life of sin.'' Even as she persisted in living in a way that distressed her parents, however, she remained concerned with winning her mother's good opinion.

Mrs. Bruce now insisted that Sasha at least maintain a separate residence. She found her daughter an apartment at the Albany, a residence for the rich, elderly, titled, and privileged, located, very discreetly, just off Piccadilly. In and out of London, the Bruces maintained their own apartment there. No place could have been less in keeping with Sasha's tastes, yet she allowed herself to be installed at this symbol of vestigial aristocratic entitlement.

Her apartment was furnished formally and resembled a hotel suite. Sasha's name was put prominently on the door. Secretly Sasha vowed she would never actually live at the Albany, but she did use it as a place to meet her American friends. Anton always put great pressure on her not to invite people he didn't know to Charles Street.

Sasha worried that the publicity had set her mother against her. She had broken a family taboo by causing them public embarrassment. She found some comfort in attributing her parents' distress to their old-fashioned sexual mores. She convinced herself they objected to her living with a man who was not her husband rather than to her association with a dangerous demimonde. She called their criticisms hypocritical and out of date. Didn't they care that she was happy? And there was no one to disabuse her of the notion that as the ambassador's daughter, nothing bad could really happen to her. "When you're rich and powerful, whatever happens to you, you survive it,'' her brother Nicky would later comment.

According to Terry Graham, Sasha believed Mrs. Bruce attempted to use the moral authority of her favorite aunt, Mrs. Ashley Clarke, as a means of dealing with the von Kassel situation. Sasha reported her mother said, "Your aunt is so thoroughly ashamed of how you're conducting your life that she does not wish to see you.'' But when Sasha ran into her aunt on the street and repeated what her mother had said, her aunt was cordial. No, she was not passing judgment on her niece; no, her niece was not damaging the family name and reputation. Sasha's relations with her mother worsened.

Terribly worried about her daughter, Mrs. Bruce persisted in trying to bring Sasha to her senses. She tried to convince her to spend holidays with the family. She quietly refused to acknowledge Sasha's work at the gallery as a real job, knowing how much her good opinion meant to her daughter.

Hating to be on bad terms with her mother, Sasha called it a war of nerves in which both sides lost. As usual David Bruce left the disciplining of Sasha to his wife. An old auction hand himself, he allowed Sasha to believe he derived pleasure from imagining her bidding at auctions. He teased her and in her presence told people she had become quite an "expert." One day he invented a whole series of stories about her work at the gallery. Glancing over at Mrs. Bruce, Sasha couldn't help but register her mother's disapproval. "Mummy," she said, recounting the moment later, was "dying of shame." When Anton spoke nastily of the Bruces, Sasha became angry but she was equally resentful of the notion that she was misusing her advantages and besmirching the family name.

According to Maria Andipa, a man pretending to be in the market for icons called on her. He was a fat, blond American and Maria disliked him on sight. He told her he wanted to buy thirty thousand pounds worth of icons.

But as they talked, he remarked that it was dangerous for David Bruce's daughter to be with Anton, that something might happen to von Kassel, in fact, if he didn't stop seeing her; if he ever hurt her, he might definitely come to harm. Maria thought the man was attempting to bribe her and she speculated that the Bruces were behind it. If Maria found some way of separating Anton and Sasha, the American promised, he would buy her a Mercedes; she could have access to a villa in the South of France; a private airplane would be put at her disposal. He motioned toward the battered old heap Maria was driving at the time. "Don't drive that car," he said solicitously. "It's dangerous."

As Sasha scandalized her family, so Anton did his. Saying he was fed up with Anton, who had a bad character, his father offered one of his nephews the hairdressing salon. He grew depressed and lonely, alienated from his family. Then in Salonika in July 1971 Anton's father hanged himself.

*   *   *

In October Anton promised Maria he would leave Sasha and return to her. "We've been through so much," Maria says he told her. In a week he would be back.

"Why in a week's time and not now?" Maria pressed.

"I've got to give her time. I've got to prepare her for this because she's very emotional."

There had been bitter fights; Sasha was sleeping in the sitting room.

"I can't just drop her," Anton said. "Give me a week."

The day he was to return, Anton came over to tell Maria he couldn't go through with it. Sasha had fainted the previous night and threatened to kill herself. "We had such tragedies last night," Anton's brother Lambros reported to Maria. "All night long there were terrible scenes. Sasha got up and then fainted. Anton became frightened. He thought she was going to die."

Maria already knew of Sasha's hysteria, the emotional extremes to which she was addicted. But where would it all lead? "This girl is stupid," Maria said to herself. "What is she hoping to get out of it?"

That autumn of 1971 Sasha visited the United States again. She seemed girlish and talked like an adolescent schoolgirl about how much fun it was to get dressed up and wear makeup. Sitting in her milk-stained clothes with Sasha's infant namesake on her lap, Julie Clark was taken aback. Sasha insisted she was very happy, enchanted by Anton. All was wonderful. She had only to tie up loose ends with her cabin in Maine, dispatch her Jeep with Terry Graham, and return to London. Later her friends enumerated all the topics Sasha studiously avoided. She never mentioned the gallery or that Anton was married or that he hadn't yet gotten a divorce or that her parents did not approve of how she was living.

On that same trip she met Tom Dolembo in Maine.

"You're getting old," Tom warned. "You'd better quit messing around. You've been at the fair too long. It's time to get serious."

Shaken, Sasha wrapped herself in a defense of self-pity. She couldn't really love anyone, she mourned. It would never happen to her. Then abruptly she changed the subject. She wished to move permanently to Jerusalem. She feared there was only a short time left to her; she had already exhausted her welcome on this planet.

Tom thought her being in London with no sense of home undermined her fragile sense of self. He looked at her carefully and it seemed to him Sasha had lost her spirit. She always had been full of sparkle; her eyes had shone. Now they were dull. The departure of her spirit was like a light being extinguished. He was angry at whoever had robbed her of her spirit.

To Sasha he could only voice these thoughts obliquely: "The eyes grow dull in the newly dead."

By 1972 things were going badly at the New Grecian Gallery. Sasha was left to explain away Anton's lies—the bounced checks, the appointments missed, the promises unkept, even the spurious title. When others voiced their mistrust of von Kassel, she became resentful and brittle. She interpreted each incident—a disagreement about the Macedonian School of icons with John Stuart, the curator at Sotheby's, Claudio Astrologo's complaint about not being paid—as a personal attack upon her lover.

Meanwhile Anton was spending infinitely more than he earned, spending as if he hoped someone would stop him, like the criminal who yearns to be caught. "I want all these dealers to come to me on their knees," he told Astrologo. He lived psychotically as if he could forever escape his creditors and the consequences of bad checks and stolen works of art. Couldn't he always manipulate the law and talk his way out of everything? "You should study and take the exams because you know the law better than any lawyer," Maria once had told him. To a London barrister, Anton boasted, "Open to page so-and-so and you'll see. I know the law; I read the law on my own. It's lucky I also studied economics. I know how to play with money and I know how to play with the law!" Later he would in fact successfully evade all attempts by the English courts to bring him to justice.

Before Sasha's time he had fastened upon a man named Sir Anthony Hooper from whom he swindled thousands of pounds, convincing Hooper, who thought he was a film producer, to cosign a loan with him. When the bank foreclosed, it was Hooper who was left to become a bankrupt.

Sometimes Anton became depressed and played his con

games only half-heartedly. One Mediterranean government was actually ready to subsidize him legitimately in a film project, having learned of his involvement in a documentary called *Jerusalem, Jerusalem*. A message was sent to Anton marked "recorded delivery" (certified mail), but Anton thought it was a summons from the tax people and never went to sign for the telegram. The government, perplexed, sent an emissary to von Kassel's house. At once—unfortunately for Anton— the emissary realized there was no film company located there and the deal was off. Some time later Anton tried to raise money from the Israelis to do a propaganda film. "Has he still got Sasha?" the Israeli producer wanted to know. "Oh, dear," was his reaction when the reply was in the affirmative.

At the New Grecian Gallery Sasha sold forgeries and stolen works of art. When she wrote the catalogues, she couldn't have helped noticing that some of the same icons had been offered by Anton and Maria in the old days and appeared in catalogues of the Grecian Gallery with different dating. There were times when she went to restorer Stavros Milhalarias and asked him to make an icon appear to be of an earlier date. In her elliptic style she would say only, "It doen't look as good as it should."

In March 1972 Sasha told Julie Clark that she had more than once soiled her hands in business. But, she reasoned, since Anton owned the gallery, and she was working for him, she was not herself fully accountable.

She began to suffer from painful headaches. The strain of offering herself up to Anton's world and yet remaining unscathed, of living close to danger as a means of winning her parents' attention, was taking its toll.

Later, to Stanley Frye, Sasha made a blunter admission than she had to Julie: she had been involved in the forging of icons. She didn't speak of Anton, but of a man named Stavros whose brother, Sasha said, painted icons on an island off Greece and brought them to be sold as antiques in London. Stavros, she told Mary Frye, was a person who was important to her. There was also a Syrian priest named Arcadios who often helped obtain icons which "had been buried."

She had arrived bringing Frye the gift of an icon.

"Is that an old one?" Frye asked her.

"Yes."

"Don't lie to me, girl!" Frye boomed.

Sasha went crimson. That she should lie to Stan measured the depth of her fall. And Frye thought, she needs someone to tell her what to do, to set limits. He had attempted to be that figure in her life, taking the place of a parent, but he had failed. Her need to rebel was too strong. If someone is bent on self-destruction, Frye concluded as he stood by and watched Sasha immerse herself still deeper in the icon demimonde, no one can stop them. Meanwhile Sasha chattered in a semi-scholarly manner about the differences among schools of icon painters, the Macedonian from the Russian and the Serbo-Croatian. Frye listened, but didn't bother to ask her what she planned to do with all this new knowledge. He had given up hope that she would do anything worthwhile.

"Good for the bed," Stavros pronounced her, sharing the joke with London's leading icon collector, Eric Bradley. She was a nice girl, but she knew little about icons and no one took her writing seriously.

She participated in the icon "rings" where dealers would agree among themselves on who would bid on particular icons and so keep the prices down at auction. It was whispered that Sasha belonged to a ring with a German dealer named Neufert and an Armenian who went only by the name of Roy. After a public auction, the dealers would auction off the pieces among themselves, sometimes paying off those who had agreed not to bid. The minimum profit they expected was 100 percent. Within such conventions Sasha bought and sold her icons.

Once at a Sotheby's sale in New York a spectacular fourteenth-century Russian icon with Christ and the Virgin on one side and John the Baptist on the other came up for sale. It was estimated at ten thousand dollars, a high price for an icon then. Sitting in the front row, Sasha's competitor Dick Temple heard a secretary pick up a phone and say, "Hello, Miss Bruce, can you hear me? Yes, there's still another nine lots to go."

My God, Temple thought, that means they're buying from London on the telephone. He had planned to bid on this icon himself and had been relieved when, glancing around the room, he had not spotted any serious competition.

Smitten by auction-room fever, and angry at Sasha's seeming willingness to pay any amount of money, Temple bid to about twenty thousand. Yet still Sasha went on bidding until she got the icon. Temple returned disappointed to London.

Three months later Sotheby's called Temple to ask if he were still interested in that icon. Sasha hadn't paid for it, although it was illegal to bid at auction and then not pay. Would Temple be prepared to pay the price he originally bid? Of course he was not and at the next Sotheby's auction he bought the icon for less than the original ten-thousand-dollar estimate. In Sasha's new life, the bounced check, the forfeited promise became almost daily occurrences.

Often now she was sad and self-deprecating. Asked how she got interested in icons, she replied vaguely, "Well, I came across icons through Anton."

At the gallery Sasha produced certificates from Switzerland that authenticated their fakes. The forgeries from Greece were so sophisticated they would elude even chemical analysis, for old colors and varnishes could be collected from an icon in bad condition and used to paint a new one. Varnishes could be cracked by being put in a deep freeze, then repeatedly heated and frozen to simulate centuries of wear. In two hours an expert thief could strip a wall painting from a wall and walk away with it in his pocket.

One of Sasha's forgeries appeared with a certificate signed by the leading scholar in the field. His chemical analysis had pronounced the work an original and only the fact that a restorer named Michael Kailas had watched the forger painting the fake from the original brought the information to light. In this case, neither Sasha nor Anton knew the icon was a fake, and yet they sold it very cheaply, considering that it was supposedly of the fourteenth century.

On one buying trip to Greece Sasha bought a good eleventh-century Saint George, later listed in a New Grecian Gallery catalogue as tenth century. She paid three hundred pounds to a dealer who obviously didn't know what he had. Her ethics did not include informing the man of the price he should get. But who in the icon demimonde would have been guilty of such honesty? Anton never accompanied her on these business trips to Greece because he was a deserter from the Greek army.

In Athens she dealt with a swindler named Manos who had begun with a pushcart and suddenly boasted of an enormous collection. He sold forgeries which he tried to bribe restorers into authenticating. Some thought Sasha must be a tough businesswoman because she traveled around with Manos, who was part of the icon underworld. Mihalarias himself was later accused by the chief of police of Salonika of being "the Professor" who masterminded the theft of two icons, one from the Benaki Museum, another from Rhodes. Stavros Mihalarias had been awarded a medal for bringing the two stolen icons, works of great importance, to the attention of the Greek Embassy; the medal was withdrawn when he was accused of the thefts himself. A dapper, diminutive man with piercing black eyes, impeccably dressed, he rode around London in a Mercedes-Benz or in his 1939 Rolls-Royce with its mahogany and velvet interiors. He had studied at the Byzantine Museum in Athens and had gained the reputation of being the finest icon restorer outside Greece, only to be called by a Greek newspaper "one of the greatest receivers of stolen goods in the field of Byzantine icons which he exports and trades abroad." And yet, Mihalarias's friends insist, the man who denounced him was a convicted criminal serving fifteen years, a man who had himself once brought Stavros a stolen icon to restore, only to be tossed out of his studio.

By the time Anton von Kassel initiated Sasha Bruce into the illegal trade, the stealing of icons had reached epidemic proportions with a triangular route running from Greece to Germany and England. It was well known in London that a diplomat at the Greek Embassy was himself involved in this traffic, graciously assisted by the diplomatic pouch. The Greeks joked that their top secret documents were escorted by saints!

To her friends, Sasha seemed increasingly disoriented. She began to say "it bothered her" that she got the job at the gallery and the opportunity to work with icons only because Anton had opened the gallery and she was living with him. Her good qualifications were of no account.

Once Sasha told Maeve Kinkead that she planned to enroll in London University's archaeology program. Hoping to encourage her to be independent, Maeve said it was a good idea. But, Sasha went on, pursuing archaeology would mean leaving the New Grecian Gallery. She wondered if she could do what she called "the dual thing." But it wasn't in Anton's interest that Sasha go to graduate school and become a professional archaeologist and so she never did.

To David Bruce's daughter, the cutthroat competition she encountered seemed alien. One day, incredulously, Sasha said of Dick Temple, "Look at him! I sent him clients and he didn't even call to say thank you." Whenever she could, Sasha tried to compensate for Anton's lapses. She arranged for Michael Kailas to draft the letter to the Home Office establishing his employment, which Anton had promised and failed to do for him, and then demanded that Anton sign it. One day, quite upset, she took Michael aside and told him that Stavros Mihalarias had come to the gallery and threatened that if Kailas, whom he disliked, were hired to do any more of their restorations, Mihalarias would let it be known these icons were from the eighteenth and nineteenth centuries. Von Kassel knew enough not to cross Mihalarias and fired Kailas at once. But Sasha felt she ought at least to tell Michael why he had been so summarily dismissed.

Even as Anton flaunted his infidelities, she pretended not to be aware that he had other women. He bestowed a Porsche upon the handsome German secretary in charge of publicity at the New Grecian Gallery. Then one night Anton took off with her for a romantic evening in Portugal. This was too much for Sasha; she got on the next plane in hot pursuit. At the last of the New Grecian Gallery openings, she fled before the party ended, leaving the never-to-be-paid-for caviar and smoked salmon behind, embarrassed to be there with a woman with whom Anton was openly having an affair. One night, out with the Astrologos, Sasha slinked off before the meal ended as Anton lavished his attentions on this woman. She was pitied even by Claudio Astrologo, who had often been angry with Sasha for taking Anton's part in his unsavory business practices.

Periodically Anton brought rich, silly women home with him to Charles Street just to show Sasha he could have anyone he wanted. He drove around London in his Rolls-Royce accompanied by women in expensive fur coats, those same women who, to keep up some pretense, might be found desultorily typing at New Grecian Gallery. When Maeve Kinkead came to visit, Anton made a pass at her.

But, after all, Sasha had chosen him because he withheld love. Increasingly she couldn't resist the pleasure of reproducing old family traumas. She had failed to win both her father and Stanley Frye. Unlike her beautiful, elegant mother, or one of those "perfect people" she had envied at Potomac School, she could not win all of a man's attention. She was unworthy and through Anton's contempt she demonstrated how inferior she really was. She didn't want Anton any more than he wanted her. Rather, she had selected him as the agent of her destruction. And what could he, or Michaelides after him, being the kind of men they were, do but comply?

Evidently she found little sexual fulfillment with this man who called himself von Kassel. Marios says when they became intimate Sasha was very much afraid, expecting the same cruelty she experienced with Anton. "He was biting her," Marios says Sasha told him.

Von Kassel could be loving one minute and threaten a woman with murder the next, and against his rages even Maria was helpless. Once Maria says he grabbed her by the throat and threatened to end her life once and for all. He was highly sexed and making love three times a night was not unusual for him. "Why not?" a Greek woman who was sleeping with him at the same time he was with Sasha commented. "He ate well and he didn't have to work."

Greek men control what their women do, Anton told Sasha. When a man enters a room, a woman must get up and relinquish her seat to him. He wouldn't allow her to be alone in the kitchen with visiting friends and would appear every five minutes to check on her conversation. Then he might request her to make telephone calls for him.

Anton often expressed his belief that the best man is the one who has a lot of money regardless of how he came by it. He pushed Sasha to ask her father for money. Then he would pretend he was joking. If he didn't beat her, he was verbally cruel, jealous that she was born into an aristocratic family while he had only a fake title. Occasionally the normally reticent Sasha was driven to complain about Anton. She said she wasn't satisfied with him as a man because he didn't bathe enough. "Typical of him," a Greek woman friend laughed. "Dirty underneath!"

Most of the time Sasha kept up the charade, never admitting she gave Anton money because she didn't want him to seem weak, while his friends believed he would never have stayed with her if it hadn't been for the money. One friend openly encouraged her to leave him. Sasha gave one of her evasive responses. "Oh well, life is like that. It might last one, two, or three years and then someone else will come along." But she couldn't resist adding that Anton was not the man her father was.

Having discovered Sasha feared losing her mind, Anton accused her of being "mad" and "crazy." He tortured her by attacking her parents, knowing how she hated nasty things to be said about the family. A friend remembers Anton made Sasha put fifty pounds in an envelope, hail a taxi, and drive over to deposit it personally in Maria Andipa's mailbox. Meanwhile his first wife back in Salonika was threatening him with legal action since he had never divorced her when he married Maria Andipa. The first wife demanded her dowry back; Sasha paid. And it seemed everyone knew that Anton was still sleeping with Maria at the same time he was living with Sasha. To save face, Sasha took to wearing a wedding ring to Sotheby's and Christie's. When she spotted Maria, she put her hand behind her back.

In February 1972 Maria began a divorce action against von Kassel, naming Sasha as corespondent. Anton came around then and begged Maria to drop Sasha's name from the action. Her father is an old man, Anton begged. Indeed David Bruce did age suddenly that winter. Arthur Schlesinger noticed that he became a feeble old man almost overnight.

Sasha's father will die, Anton told Maria. Often Anton had sneeringly gossiped to Maria about how the Bruces had mistreated Sasha and how she hated them. Now he was concerned. "I'm giving you the flat," he told Maria, referring to the Eaton Place penthouse where they had begun their social climb together.

Maria relented and when the case came up in court, Anton was charged only with desertion. Yet whether through bureaucratic error or dissimulation, Sasha's name still appears as corespondent on the final divorce decree. Then Anton secretly pledged Maria's Eaton Place apartment as collateral on a loan he was negotiating with the Bank of Cyprus and wrote a fraudulent check. Although the bank knew the Eaton Place penthouse was a matrimonial settlement by court order, they promptly evicted Maria.

In letters to her friends back home, Sasha continued to sing Anton's praise, calling him brilliant, marveling that he should want to stay with her, wondering what she could be offering him. In March 1972 she said "Anton and I are happy together." That June, Maria went to the High Court and asked the judge to jail Anton "for having broken his undertakings concerning maintenance of the matrimonial home."

Throughout 1972, Anton took larger and larger amounts of money from Sasha, pleading he was depressed, threatening to kill himself, making her believe something terrible would happen to destroy what they had together should she fail to make her fortune available to him. He was so clever, so practiced in divesting people of their money, that Sasha would not know for years the extent to which he implicated her financially and legally in his schemes.

In August 1972, cashing in her revocable trust, Sasha lent von Kassel one hundred eighty-five thousand dollars.

He salted money away in Swiss bank accounts, traveling once a month to Switzerland.

In December he took her to Jerusalem, the scene of his initiation into the icon trade. It was Maria who had originally introduced him to Archbishop Germanos, head of the Greek Orthodox Church there. Sasha told Annie Borland that Anton was "helping" a Greek Orthodox bishop. This was Arcadios, the link between von Kassel and the monasteries on the Sinai from which icons were systematically being plundered. In Jerusalem Anton allowed Sasha to present herself as his fiancée. He interjected her name into conversations and sent her around so that it seemed they were in Jerusalem on legitimate shopping trips.

Christmas found Sasha with Anton sleeping overnight at St. Catherine's Monastery on Mount Sinai. Outside volcanic peaks loomed. Within resided the finest collection of Byzantine icons in the world. She found the experience irresistible.

She told her friends she and Anton had been invited to

remain at St. Catherine's for months to study icons, if they wished. Reckless criminality was not enough for Sasha—she relished this return to the cradles of civilization—just as the safe and the predictable were equally insufficient. She did study icons in Jerusalem. But there were also wild Jeep rides through the desert, forays to strange, out-of-the-way Coptic and Greek Orthodox monasteries. Her word for it all was "exciting." Freedom was a pallid thing unless it was accompanied by danger. Jerusalem, Sasha pronounced, was among her "bag of tricks" to "avoid facing reality."

They attended a dinner with Archbishop Germanos at which there were fifty guests, half of them known to Sasha as illicit contacts of Anton's, people he was using to smuggle icons out of those monasteries. Once Anton asked her if David K. E. Bruce might not offer Archbishop Germanos a Cadillac as a present.

The trips to Jerusalem began as two or three times a year. Then they became much more frequent. Worried about what his daughter was up to there, David Bruce jokingly threatened to send Arafat a message: "I can send you two more hostages if you like." He begged Sasha not to go to the Sinai where terrorists might kidnap her if they discovered who she was, even hijack the plane she was on. But Sasha was at her most uncontrollable. She began to smuggle drugs as well and there was one nasty incident at the airport in Israel where customs officials opened a cross she was carrying, convinced there were narcotics inside.

On a visit to Cambridge, she presented Wes Profit with an icon she said had been procured in the war zone outside Jerusalem and defended von Kassel's practices by arguing that exquisite works of art were rotting in damp, obscure monasteries; she was negotiating to preserve them.

Bishop Arcadios turned up in London. Anton entertained him in grand style with Sasha's money, putting him up at the best hotel and driving him around in the Rolls-Royce; the bishop was convinced Anton was a millionaire. Back in Jerusalem, Arcadios paid off the monks and lifted more old icons from the monasteries. And then Maria Andipa couldn't stand it any longer. Driven by jealousy, she informed on Arcadios and the game was up. One of von Kassel's former cohorts laughed and said that now Anton couldn't get an icon the size of a cigarette box out of Israel for one million pounds.

By January 1973, with still a year to go with Anton, Sasha was confessing to dreams of rescue, adding with a toss of her head, "I'll be all right." Tom Dolembo wrote her that *he* had dreamed of a shadowy figure huddled up to its neck in a blanket, about to harm her. He reminded her that a few years earlier he had dreamed of a shape darting in front of a car and that had come true in the summer of 1970 when she had rescued that child hit by a car in India.

In February she went to Athens on one of her buying trips, still talking of her love for Anton. She was waiting only for his divorce to be final so they could be married. Loula Kailas invited her to stay at her family's home. But Sasha said she must first call London to ask Anton's permission, since he expected her to stay at a hotel. Once within the house, she made a beeline for the telephone. And only after Anton had granted her request was Sasha able to return to her normal, gracious self. "What a lovely house," she then told Loula. "You won't find such a nice place in London."

During this stay in Greece in early 1973 Sasha spoke of London, not America, as her home. She presented herself to Loula as a simple person for whom money was of no importance, waiting only for Anton's divorce to be final so she could assume the life of a normal married woman. Why had Maria taken so long to give Anton a divorce? It wasn't Sasha's fault that their marriage had failed. "Even if it weren't for me, the marriage would have collapsed." ("The marriage was over before I met Sasha," Anton would also say later, but one could not expect him to remember it otherwise.)

One day in 1973, Michael Kailas, who was still restoring icons for the New Grecian Gallery, came in to find Anton jumping up and down in glee.

"I've got a divorce! I've got a divorce!" he exclaimed.

A few weeks later he proposed to Michael, "I have some girls. Do you want to come out tonight?"

Michael, who was truly fond of Sasha, was rather stunned. "But you're getting married to Sasha. You're living with her. She's a beautiful girl. What the hell do you want other women for?"

"She's all right," Anton said then. "But I prefer other women." He had no intention of marrying Sasha, or anyone else. Marriage was bureaucratic, just a piece of paper.

Maria herself asked him, "Well, are you going to marry her?"

"No, never," Anton replied in his soft way.

In May 1973, Anton stole Sasha's checkbook and forged three checks on her account at the Wilmington Trust Company, which was in charge of her irrevocable trust. These he made payable to the Westminster Bank and to an individual named Spierer. The total was sixty-five thousand dollars. There wasn't that much cash owing to Sasha. Suspicious, her trust officer called her in London and asked whether in fact she had issued those checks, which were about to bounce. Sasha said she had! Wilmington Trust had to grant her a loan against the capital in her trust to cover the amount.

That same May 1973 she had a "therapeutic" abortion, her second.

Summer of 1973 found her in Istanbul. Awaiting Anton's arrival, she passed the time with her brother David, who chuckled as a Greek friend of Sasha's named Yannis Petsopoulos asked how Anton happened to be called von Kassel. Sasha visibly stiffened, then came to Anton's defense. His family was related through marriage to a titled nobleman, she explained. He had the right under tradition to pick up that name. He was neither usurping the title nor doing it to impress anyone.

One morning Sasha announced she must rush to the airport to meet Anton. Eager to make a date with Yannis, she asked him his plans. But he never saw her again on that trip. The minute Anton arrived, they vanished. And Yannis thought: Anton didn't want him to know what he was up to in Istanbul.

Back in London, young David Bruce phoned Barbie Hanson Pierce and asked her to call Sasha. David said he was worried about his sister. He thought she might need a friend.

The final and most elaborate of the New Grecian Gallery exhibitions was called Feast Day Icons. It ran from November 1973 through January 1974. Sasha wrote the most complex of her catalogues, printing the appropriate gospel text beside the icon which it illustrated. Kurt Weitzmann's writings were used for the introduction.

Of a fifteenth-century Entry Into Jerusalem, Sasha wrote: "The palm branch was used by the Jews to welcome people of high rank and was presented to conquerors as a symbol of valor. Christ, arriving directly from Bethany, was hailed by the people of Jerusalem as the conqueror of death. Everywhere are palm branches and the walls of the city are decorated with luxuriant plants. The sense of movement and excitement is all-pervasive as the crowds press forward to greet the Messiah. There is a festive and triumphal quality quite unlike that found in any other feast day icon." In its simplicity and grace her style matches that of her father.

She traveled to Frankfurt and Hanover in November and December of 1973 and again in early 1974 in connection with the Feast Day Icons exhibit which was to open at the Maria Rutz Gallery. She delivered the icons, content to allow the gallery to organize the rest. In 1974, David Irons was in Europe and Sasha asked him to meet her in Berlin. She seemed nervous, exhausted, and deeply relieved to have someone safe to talk with. It was impossible for them to visit together in London, Sasha explained, because Anton was jealous of her friends. She feared the consequences of displeasing him. David thought she feared Anton himself.

There were ground rules for those Berlin conversations, more topics ruled out than ever before. Sasha stayed in an expensive hotel off the Kurfurstendamm, David in a more modest one. When they met, she made David do most of the talking.

According to Marios Michaelides, after Sasha's death he found a note in her handwriting among his papers in which she listed what she called examples of "her shame." One such episode took place in Berlin. At the gallery she met a grotesquely deformed dwarf with a gigantic head, massive hands, and a shriveled trunk. Flaunting his deformity, Sasha picked him up and went about with him to cafeterias. Then she took him back to her hotel where she excited him to the point where he was ready to have sex. Suddenly she disengaged herself and threw him out. But the next day she saw him at the gallery again and this time she took him back with her to the hotel where she allowed the sexual act to take place uninterrupted. She met a German icon dealer and proceeded to enact the same scenario. "I have sunk so low," Marios says Sasha had written. He claims he burned this note and flushed it down the toilet.

By Christmas 1973 Sasha was in deep trouble with unprecedented disasters still to come. The Bruces had failed in every effort to separate her from von Kassel. Late in 1973 they decided to force the issue of Staunton Hill as a means of bringing her to her senses.

Still in great agitation months after the event, Sasha told Terry Graham that Mrs. Bruce had telephoned and demanded that the children buy the farm or it would be sold in ten days. It was, according to Terry, "an absolute ultimatum."

Sasha said she'd panicked. She loved Staunton Hill as much as her father had when at the age of twenty he had told his mother, the indomitable Louise Este Fisher Bruce, that it would break his heart if his parents were to sell Staunton Hill. But Staunton Hill was now in Evangeline's name. No doubt motivated by tax considerations, David Bruce had made an unrestricted gift of it to her in 1970. He had planned to leave the property to his wife in his will, but had changed his mind. The contents of the Mansion House were already owned by the three children.

Sasha had never considered it her mother's farm. It was the *Bruce* ancestral home and the transfer ought to have been between David Bruce and his children. She was certain Evangeline's ultimatum could not have been suggested by her father. As Sasha put it, her mother had said they had to come up with one hundred grand! (That was the value David Bruce assigned to Staunton Hill when he gave it to his wife, the same price which he had paid for it when he'd bought it back from his daughter Audrey a decade earlier.)

During these last months with von Kassel, Sasha had lost track of David and Nicky. She reached David in Taiwan; Nicky was involved with a Scientology group in the Southwest. The thought of Staunton Hill going out of the family made Sasha desperate. David and Nicky had never loved the place as she had, but once she found her brothers, she convinced them to purchase the estate with her. From childhood the three of them had banded together in time of crisis. "As kids we were closer to each other than any of us was to the parents," young David says. From childhood Sasha felt it was her burden to hold the family together.

Sasha and Nicky went to Peking to visit the Bruces for Christmas of 1973. There Sasha found her mother had done wonders with the decor of the jerry-built compound that served the American delegation, despite her having to make do with "mail-order" furniture from State Department catalogues.

But Evangeline Bruce had this "mail-order" furniture upholstered in fabrics she ordered from Hong Kong and Bangkok. She had the main drawing room lacquered a brilliant Chinese yellow; the dining room was papered in silvery gold and there were lush brown curtains. A large sitting room had fur cushions and a fur rug, the ubiquitous Evangeline Bruce plants in every corner.

There was a family conference. With David's agreement in hand, they would purchase Staunton Hill from their mother as of January 31, 1974. The children would be responsible for all expenses and were ordered either to buy two cars belonging to their mother—a 1963 Chevrolet truck and an old Plymouth station wagon—or to sell them for her and remit the proceeds. They were to reimburse their mother for those real estate taxes she had already covered and for insurance policy premiums paid in advance. Their father would continue to pay the wages, hospitalization and medical expenses of the Staunton Hill caretakers, Jamie and Elizabeth Hamlett, during their lifetimes, but his wife would be under no obligation to continue these payments after his death.

Bruce's Charlotte County lawyer, Reginald Pettus, suggested that instead of selling Staunton Hill outright to the three children it should be conveyed to them as "joint tenants with survivorship," so that if one of the three were to die, even though he or she were married, the interest would go to the survivors without any dower interest attaching. Only the last one to own it would have an estate in which the inheritance of Staunton Hill could come to a husband or wife.

It was a brilliant suggestion to treat the property as a trust and it would have saved Sasha's survivors much grief. But Ambassador Bruce decided against joint tenancy. Dryly he wrote a Charlotte County friend he was pleased that the ownership of Staunton Hill within the Bruce family was ensured. He knew any one of the children could not afford to keep up the place alone. Wearily, he then let the matter drop.

The children were united again; but the breach between children and parents had widened.

Anton had suggested that he accompany Sasha to Peking, but she went alone. She may have been relieved to get away from Anton, who some months before had hired thugs from the Cypriot Mafia to burn down the New Grecian Gallery while he was conveniently away in Paris, so that he might collect the insurance money.

The fire was set. Some icons were damaged, but not the best ones. The insurance company was deeply suspicious, for the arson—accompanied by a stabbing—had been rather obvious. Finally, however, they paid. Then von Kassel refused to give the thugs he had hired their 25 percent of the insurance settlement, as agreed.

Now Sasha was involved in a financial crisis of her own: how to find the $33,333 to pay for her share of Staunton Hill. Her brothers had been prudent with their trusts. But having supported Anton in so extravagant a style and having acquiesced in his forgeries the previous May, her own trust was depleted. In January 1974 she did not have $33,333.

After her return from Peking, Sasha made one last voyage to Greece. Because he could not enter his own country without risking arrest, Anton sent her to Salonika to be his emissary at the wedding of his brother George. She arrived laden with gifts including a brooch worth seven hundred pounds for Anton's mother. Seated beside her in the church was a friend of George Hatzinestoros named Marios Michaelides. (In the late sixties George had brought Marios to meet Anton and Maria von Kassel in London, Maria pronouncing him a "nice boy.") To the wedding Sasha wore outlandish platform shoes and a multicolored mididress slit deeply up the side. Marios noticed her.

As Marios talked with a friend about the animal feed business at the reception, he felt Sasha watching him. But it was only the next day at their hotel that they spoke. Both had been scheduled to return to Athens, but on different flights. Turbulent weather led to Sasha's being canceled. She ran into Marios in the hotel lobby and they agreed to have lunch.

Then they flew back to Athens together on the afternoon flight.

She remained in Athens for two days, spending every minute she could with Marios. At night when Marios took her back to her hotel, she cried because they had to separate. They did not become lovers. Strung out and depleted by her struggles with Anton, Sasha was on the verge of collapse. Marios told her he had plans to come to London which had been postponed when he accepted the invitation to George's wedding.

"When you come to London, drop by our place," Sasha said.

Returning to Charles Street, Sasha said nothing to Anton—or anyone else—about having met Marios Michaelides.

Marios delayed his travel to London for a week. When he arrived, Sasha was away in Germany. When she learned that Marios had come to London and had tried to contact her, she began to telephone hotel after hotel from Berlin. Finally she located him one night at one in the morning at the Grosvenor House Hotel.

"I want you to know I'm in love with you," Marios told her.

Sasha agreed to meet him.

He flew to Dusseldorf where Sasha joined him. When he got off the plane, he told her for the first time that he was married—so he says. They spent two days together at a luxury hotel and a day in the countryside. He recalls their lovemaking as clumsy and tentative, but they treated their awkwardness playfully. By the time Sasha flew back to Berlin and Marios to Greece, they had agreed to meet again in Athens on April twenty-seventh, Marios's birthday. She told him she was living with von Kassel; he was ready to defy the code among Greek males forbidding overtures to the girl friends of friends—or friends' brothers. Nonetheless the situation seemed relatively uncomplicated to Marios. He had succeeded in making this heiress, this ambassador's daughter, succumb to his charms. And perhaps Marios seemed to Sasha, even at this first meeting, the very man to extricate her from the mess with von Kassel.

In the winter months of 1974, Anton engineered his most ambitious scam of all. On December 19, 1973, he had entered into an agreement with a London solicitor named Lewis Cutner whereby four hundred thirty thousand pounds of funds belonging to Mark's Trust, a trust set up in the Channel Islands to manage the money of a rock star named Marc Bolan, were to be invested in works of art.

Working through Cutner, von Kassel obtained from Mark's Trust two bankers' drafts totaling one hundred twenty-five thousand pounds, payable to two gentlemen named Fayt and Coulon, from whom von Kassel had undertaken to purchase two oil paintings for Mark's Trust. The paintings were never delivered, for Anton planned to keep them in his possession to be used as collateral in future dealings. He forged the payees' signatures and endorsed each draft in favor of Sasha, and she then signed them as well. The money was deposited in Sasha's bank account. Under Anton's instruction, she then disbursed the money back to him. She cashed the drafts through her bank and afterwards made payments as directed by Anton.

Sasha was obviously duped and could not have been held liable in this swindling of Mark's Trust, except that out of the 125,000 pounds embezzled, Anton gave her $33,333, so that she could pay her mother her one-third share of the price of Staunton Hill. It was with this stolen money that Sasha purchased her part of the Bruce ancestral home.

Of the $185,000 Sasha had lent Anton in August 1972, he still owed her over $150,000—for which she agreed to accept eight icons. They were hung on the walls of the house on Charles Street where Sasha had agreed that Anton could keep them temporarily.

After she met Marios, in the early spring of 1974, Sasha gave a last dinner party at Charles Street. She dressed herself entirely in black—sweater and trousers—her somber costume relieved only by three gold chains. She also wore an amethyst ring, which her father had given her. The atmosphere was formal, yet Sasha was openly sharp with von Kassel in front of their guests. It was a farewell dinner, although Sasha told no one she had decided to return to America for good.

Later people remembered she had been extremely irritable those last months, shouting and swearing at workmen, upbraiding one for lateness with incommensurate acrimony. "I told you to be here at this time and not one minute later,'' Sasha had shrieked, proceeding to swear like a trooper so that the man said later he had never heard such language from a woman. She and Anton were often heard yelling at each other; at other times she seemed to throw up her hands, as if to say, "There is nothing I can do about him." At times she was withdrawn and wouldn't talk at all. Her expression was one of perpetual sadness at the end and she had lost a lot of weight.

She surprised Annie Borland by agreeing to have dinner without Anton. Then her mood was optimistic, even joyous as she talked of Staunton Hill. She was looking forward to taking her dog there. She said she needed rest and was going to "the farm" to straighten things out. The name Anton did not once come up.

The New Grecian Gallery had gone bankrupt and in March 1974, receivers came in. Elvira Cooper, once Anton's assistant at the Grecian Gallery and now working for Christie's, was called in to evaluate the remaining one hundred and twenty thousand pounds worth of icons. One of the receivers commissioned to close the gallery was an attractive woman and as she busied herself, people mistook her for still another of Anton's secretary/mistresses.

On Valuation Day at the New Grecian Gallery both Anton and Sasha were present. This time it was Sasha who did all the talking. She was polite to everyone, but at moments her voice would turn to steel and then she seemed tough and strong. She isn't as sweet as she seems, Elvira Cooper thought.

While Anton hovered weakly in the background, Sasha did all the negotiating. She was calm and too proud, even as the remaining icons were being estimated, to admit that the gallery had in fact gone bankrupt. She offered everyone coffee and saw that the job got done. She said she wanted to keep one provincial Saint George with Elvira valued at eight hundred pounds. But after the receivers took over, this icon too was sold by Christie's at the final auction in Geneva. There were a few fakes in the group, but these Sasha left Elvira to discover for herself.

Although she was in love with Marios, even now as she superintended the bankruptcy proceedings of the gallery, Sasha tried to explain away Anton's failure! "It's because he didn't have enough friends in England," she said. She complained that Dick Temple did things behind people's backs, but because he seemed like a gentleman (in fact his father once listed "gentleman" on his passport as his occupation), people preferred to buy icons from him. She gave the impression that she still believed in Anton and that if he had gotten into trouble, it wasn't his fault.

In April 1974, Sasha arranged for her remaining possessions to be sent home by sea. But before her final departure for Staunton Hill, she flew once more to Greece where she and Marios spent ten days together. Aware of Sasha's presence, his wife Mary sat waiting alone in their apartment, hoping the affair would blow over.

One day Sasha and Marios stopped in a heavily polluted industrial area where a pure blue flame rose from a factory chimney. They sat in Mario's car watching and they spoke of their love as that blue flame, eternal, unalloyed by a speck of carbon.

When Sasha revealed the treachery of von Kassel to Marios, he told her he would give up his flourishing business in Athens and attend to her problems full time. They began to plan a life together at Staunton Hill.

Anton remained for a time in England and so enmeshed himself with the underworld that Maria began to receive calls at two in the morning threatening her life for bounced checks (she had taken up with her baby-faced ex-husband once more). She purchased icons for him at Sotheby's—only for the twelve thousand pounds in German checks that he gave her to bounce. Sotheby's sent bailiffs, stripping Maria's shop of every remaining icon. By now Anton had taken up with a woman named Gillian Rolland-Jones, whom he rechristened Leora.

During the summer of 1977 Anton stole an icon from Michael Kailas. When Michael demanded redress, Anton gave him a bad check. Michael threatened to turn the case over to Mafia thugs. Quickly Anton set up a rendezvous at a bar in Bayswater where Michael found a Greek from Switzerland named Oyanoulis waiting for him. Oyanoulis gave him eight thousand Deutsche marks, the equivalent of the two thousand pounds the icon was said to be worth. This still wasn't enough to cover Michael's expenses, so he had to corner von Kassel and threaten him once more.

"Look, I know you," Michael said. "I was living on the top floor when your father was a hairdresser in Greece, so don't play games with me." Anton came up with another thousand pounds and soon after the icon was spotted on sale at the Temple Gallery. A short while later, unperturbed, Anton contacted Michael again. "We're going to Palestine," he said. "I'll pay you five thousand pounds to go along, copy some icons, and then replace the originals with them."

"Will he go next to North Africa, or to Malta?" Sir Anthony Hooper, who has never recovered from Anton's chicanery, wondered. Twelve people declared Anton a bankrupt, including Charles Churchill, who had financed the old Grecian Gallery, and a clerk of the Bank of Cyprus named Gabriel Michaelides (no relation to Marios), who, in a rage one night after Sasha had gone, broke down the door of the house on Charles Street threatening to kill von Kassel because he had ruined him and his family.

Jailed briefly for fraud in London, Anton convinced Maria to raise the sixty thousand pounds bail and then fled to the continent. Opening a gallery in Frankfurt complete with gold doorknobs, he bought icons only to have his check bounce. This time he landed in a German jail, where he served six months having been caught at the airport with three passports in his possession, one of which was Yugoslav!

"You can get away with bouncing checks in England, but not on the continent," one of his British victims observed, while still another predicted: "If he ever comes back to England, someone will bump him off for sure."

Still later, a London wit, asked how he would go about finding von Kassel, joked, "Just go to the best restaurant in Paris. He'll be there, his Rolls-Royce parked outside."

Five years after Sasha's death, von Kassel had become so fat his belly hung over his belt. His hair was gone, and he had grown an unbecoming mustache so that he resembled, someone said, an East End shopkeeper.

Once more he was plying the icon trade, moving between Venice, Padua, and Paris, "Leora" in tow. Of his days with Sasha he had little to say in his gently inflected English: "That was all five years ago. I've started a new life."

When I asked him about the man who had been indicted for Sasha's murder, Anton said quietly that Marios Michaelides had never been a friend of his. He and Sasha had already separated when she began with Michaelides. Then he added with a little laugh, "Unless you know different."

Von Kassel did want to know what the evidence against Marios was. Told it was largely circumstantial, he became indignant: "What kind of justice is that in the twentieth century?"

Citizen of
Charlotte County

Sasha returned to Staunton Hill that spring of 1974, a child of the sixties dropping out sixties-style to work the land and live a pure and simple life. Going back to the earth, renouncing icons, art, and all concerns of the intellect, she would purify herself after those sullying experiences with von Kassel. She would become "a farmer." Marios, whom she dubbed Farmer Jones in a light moment, would work at her side.

Ambassador Bruce said he was delighted to have one of his children bring Staunton Hill to life again and asked his old friend, Charlotte County attorney Reginald Pettus, to look after Sasha. He hoped she wouldn't become a nuisance. Pettus must treat her as a client; Sasha was to pay her own way.

For many years the ambassador had been unhappy with the handling of Staunton Hill. He'd given the estate to his daughter Audrey as a wedding present on her marriage to Stephen Currier in 1955. But the Curriers had made changes and every alteration was felt by David Bruce as an affront. It pained him when the sycamores he'd loved from childhood were cut down by Stephen Currier and it had distressed him again when the ivy covering the Mansion House was removed, robbing Staunton Hill of some of its dignity. He considered the wood-paneled stables built by Stephen wildly extravagant.

A year before Sasha's return, two large bronze turkey gobblers, grotesque objects, were stolen from the gateposts of Staunton Hill. Bruce had urged a full-scale police action to recover them. The local sheriff succeeded in tracing a suspect to Roanoke. A judge of the Roanoke Municipal Court was then enlisted to locate someone on the Roanoke Police Force to go around to search the premises of all the local junk dealers. A drifter working at a farm not far from Staunton Hill, who dealt in scrap iron, was reported to have moved to Roanoke at the time the turkeys were missed.

But they were never recovered. Mourning these turkeys, regretting he would no longer spot them as he drove up to Staunton Hill, Bruce even tried to buy one hundred fifty acres of land from US Plywood, adjacent to his property, to prevent further such pillaging. But the company refused his offer. It turned out the suspect had worked for them, but although they were aware of the theft, and the sheriff pressed them hard, they refused to file a complaint. Several years later, newly resident at Staunton Hill after Sasha's death, David Surtees Bruce, whose tastes were less given to the decorative than those of his father, laughed and called the outlandish turkey gobblers "well gone."

In June 1960 when David Bruce bought Staunton Hill back from Audrey, the exchange had dragged on with elaborate bitterness. Anxious to have done with Staunton Hill, and dreaming of the paradise they would create in northern Virginia called Kinloch, the Curriers accepted Bruce's offer of $100,000. By the seventies David Bruce feared Staunton Hill would always have to be subsidized—with Sasha and her brothers earning money independently from business or professional activities—which none of the children gave any signs of doing. True "aristocrats," they shunned commerce, unlike their great-great-grandfather James Bruce, who at the age of sixteen had not considered himself above "stepping out of the groove carved by his planter ancestors and entering the counting house of Mr. Colquhoun of Petersburg, Virginia." But Sasha and her brothers lived primarily on their trusts.

Sasha's trust had been so depleted by von Kassel that by the time she dropped out at Staunton Hill, work had become a necessity. Sasha convinced herself that she could turn Staunton Hill into a paying farm by raising chickens and cattle and planting crops like alfalfa. And she believed, as her father had said fifty years earlier, in words that soon would come to seem ironic, that an old family place like Staunton Hill was certain to influence for the better anyone who lived on it.

She was so poor when she returned to Staunton Hill that when she went to Norfolk to collect her household goods and personal effects which she had shipped from England, she couldn't afford to pay the $450 owing in duty. There was $77 due on an "ornate robe," a dress valued at $250. Sasha chose to have it auctioned off. She was relieved to be able to

redeem some pots and pans and her dog Aesop's bowls and
her Beatles records. She wrote Marios they would at least
have music for Christmas.

Until her brother Nicky joined her, Sasha lived alone with
the servants, taking possession of the room she'd had as a
little girl. Sasha's bedroom, unlike every other room in that
house, had no expensive antiques, fine carpets, or paintings,
none of the Chippendale, Empire, Regency, Hepplewhite, or
Queen Anne furniture with which Staunton Hill was otherwise bulging.

There were twin beds painted white, a chiffonier, and a
dressing table adorned with a blue and white floral glazed
English chintz. On the floor was a hooked rug, on one wall a
Currier and Ives print. A bottle had been made into a lamp.

Sasha put on blue jeans and told herself she was joining the
community.

One day she entered the Fidelity Bank in the tiny hamlet of
Brookneal to open a checking account.

"Are you David Bruce's daughter?" the teller wanted to
know.

Sasha made a distant reply. "Yes, I am."

"Well, my name is Marie Harper," the woman gushed.
"My father was Frank Clowdis that worked for your father to
train his bird dogs and horses."

At once Sasha became warm and friendly. "I've heard
about your father all my life," she said. "I want you to come
down and tell me some of the stories about when you used to
live at Staunton Hill."

A simple child of the earth was the way Sasha presented
herself to Charlotte County. Secretly her attitude was one of
somewhat more hauteur. Shortly after meeting Marie, she
wrote to Marios that Marie Harper was "one of the town's
biggest gossips and interested in anything to do with men.
She is terribly upset that almost everyone in town has met
you. . . . I really do not much like her, she is so pushy and
aggressive, but you could deal with her and charm her. The
thought amuses me."

Marie Harper took Sasha to meet her mother, Ethel Clowdis.
Mrs. Clowdis regaled Sasha with stories of the sad-eyed,

reclusive Ailsa Bruce, and of little Audrey and her pony cart. The Clowdises had lived in a tenant cottage on Staunton Hill plantation. One day after Mrs. Clowdis had given birth to one of her daughters, a chauffeured automobile delivered Mrs. Bruce to her door. Ailsa was plainly dressed and she brought with her an aura of melancholy. She took little notice of the latest addition to the growing Clowdis family; mothering seemed to be no more her inclination than social life. And then Ailsa Mellon Bruce startled Ethel Clowdis.

"Mrs. Clowdis, you're happy, aren't you?" Ailsa asked mournfully.

"I certainly am," Mrs. Clowdis said.

And suddenly Ailsa burst into tears, her weeping continuing throughout her visit. "I'll never come to Staunton Hill again without visiting you and your children," she promised as she took her leave. Several times a year there would come boxes of Audrey's hand-me-downs for the Clowdis daughters, little buttoned shoes, winter coats, and one box containing nine cashmere sweaters.

Sasha asked Mrs. Clowdis endless questions about Audrey, saying she would have liked to have known Audrey as a sister. Once she exclaimed, "Oh, if only I had a mother like Marie's!"

Her own mother hadn't been a friend, Sasha confided, and her father was more like a grandfather. She did not like the life her mother lived and her mother was disappointed in her. She told Ethel Clowdis that since she didn't get what she wanted as a child, she'd decided after she grew up to live her life the way she wanted without any interference.

At the moment she had decided to live as she thought the Bruces of old might have done. When the son of the Guthrie family died in an Evel Knievel–style stunt, Sasha baked a cake for them. She took old Mrs. Carter, widow of a family retainer, shopping, and grew closer to the household servants, Elizabeth Hamlett and Emma Elam. One day she cooked a turkey dinner for these two elderly black ladies, refusing to let them do a thing to help her. They were always so nice to her; now she wanted to do something for them.

Sasha visited Emma's tobacco farm and helped her in the fields; she begged Elizabeth to teach her how to cook. She dove into the Staunton Hill pool, betting Marie on who could come up fastest, and in Carroll Holt's grocery store popped a huge gob of raw meat into her mouth. She told people she took no newspapers because she didn't care about what was going on in the rest of the world. She was determined to be accepted in Charlotte County on her own merits—not because she was the daughter of its most prominent resident.

In this spirit she became involved in the local movement to prevent an electric company from damming the Staunton River, on which her great-grandfather had run his steamboat.

Southside Electric made the application, but Sasha knew it was VEPCO, the Virginia Electric and Power Company, which was behind the plan. "You know, anything VEPCO wants, they're going to get through," Sasha warned. For the time being, the local group succeeded.

Deliberately, Sasha befriended people with none of her education or worldliness. A farmer named John Morris pulled her car out of the mud one day with his tractor and after that she cultivated the Morris family, religious Baptists who had yanked their children out of school when desegregation was ordered in neighboring Prince Edward County. She invited the Morrises to Staunton Hill where they stood in awe before all the grandeur, never believing they would ever find themselves inside that house.

Sasha cooked too little stew that night so that she had to collect the plates and remove a bit of food from each to serve the last two people. On another occasion she cooked southern fried chicken for the Morrises because her father loved it and she was practicing for him. This time there were tubs of chicken as well as staggering quantities of fried potatoes, tomatoes, and bananas. Sasha confessed that since there were seven people, she had multiplied each recipe by seven! She asked Mrs. Morris to teach her how to make biscuits. They're just flour, lard, and milk, Mary Morris thought.

Sasha told the Morrises she admired them as a family. She wished she could have come from a close family and sat around the table and laughed after dinner the way they did. It must be so nice to have a family that's young and does everything together, Sasha said. She recounted how David Bruce had always tried to shoot a wild turkey while secretly resorting to the freezer. "He never did get one," Sasha said fondly.

Nick was at that dinner and Mrs. Morris asked him, "What is your father doing now?"

"I don't know," Nick replied, "I really can't tell you."

One Sunday the Morrises were invited over for roast beef. Sasha said enthusiastically, "Once a week we would have a meal like this with the family," and Nick added, "Yes, this does remind me of having a family dinner." (David Surtees Bruce has remarked on the absence of family ties in his early years: "The children grew up on their own.")

Sasha announced then that she and this Marios whom she planned to marry would have a baby right away. She would be very close to her own children. Nick said he planned to be a terrible uncle. He would spoil them all and let them do whatever they wanted.

"That's why she had us down there," Mrs. Morris said. "She was looking for love. Somebody to love her."

Later when they met Marios, the Morrises felt he didn't want Sasha mingling with them because they were poor. Indeed Marios was fond of quoting David K. E. Bruce on the subject of Brookneal. "There was a time they were offering to sell me the whole town of Brookneal for two thousand dollars," Bruce is supposed to have said. "Did that include the people?" Marios asked. "Yes," Marios contends Bruce replied. "That's why I didn't buy it."

When he met Sasha Bruce, Marios Michaelides was twenty-eight years old. He had a bleeding ulcer, was a chain-smoker, and was prone to severe nonstop migraine headaches. He would eat no vegetables or fish, only beef; his favorite dinner was Scotch and steak. He refused to eat at all if the food did not meet his specifications. Already he was obsessed by the stock market, his ambition to corner the commodities market in cotton. And his humor bordered on the macabre. "Kill anyone you involve in an accident," Marios would say, "otherwise he'll bother you for life!" He was volatile, hot-tempered, and unschooled, as cynical and sarcastic as Anton. Much later Nicholas Bruce would compare him to a Doberman pinscher slightly out of control, like a wolf.

Marios Michaelides was born on April 27, 1945, the middle of three sons. His elder brother, Eugenios, would join the family raisin business, his younger brother, Nicholas, became an electrical engineer. His mother had been a neglected child whose stepmother was her nemesis. Marios talked of her as a Cinderella who rose above her early unhappiness. For Marios she was the epitome of the lady—kind, loving, and even cultivated, as well as a splendid cook, pure, and a saint. Her favorite child, however, was Eugenios.

Mario's father was a merchant, the owner of a factory that processed sugar from currants. He had come to Greece after being expelled from Turkey and had made and lost his fortune several times. He was a man of peasant mentality who believed that the woman you married should be strong and healthy so she could produce robust children. After the war, he lost everything, only to start the business up again with some success. But any prosperity accruing to the family came to an end with the death of George Michaelides in 1967.

Marios studied at Athens College, a preparatory school for sons of the moderately wealthy, where he was a troublesome, unruly student. Corporal punishment was permitted and he was subjected to frequent beatings by the masters. He never went on to university. Mary Lewis Michaelides says that although he told people he had been a colonel in Cyprus, a flier attached to the Greek secret army, he was in fact rejected for military service, failing the psychological examination required of all recruits. He told Mary he had feigned insanity in order to get out of serving in the army. But after he was indicted for Sasha's murder, he recalled failing that test and cried fearfully, "They could prove I'm crazy!"

Exempt from the army, Marios went off to London, his ostensible goal a General Certificate of Education at the Kensington School of Languages. A few years later he told his intended bride, Mary Lewis, that he had attended the London School of Economics; diligently she added this lie to her wedding announcement which was printed in the Tennessee *Maryville-Alcoa Times*.

Marios had no interest in higher education. Subsidized by the family, he lived in London like his playboy compatriot von Kassel and grew addicted to gambling and fast cars. Once he hit a man and injured him; somehow he got out of this scrape and was cited only for the speeding. It was during this time that George Hatzinestoros brought Marios to call on Maria and Anton.

When his family could no longer support him in high style

in London, Marios returned to Greece where, he says, he went around to bakers' shops trying to convince them to buy the fortified flour which became the center of the diminished Michaelides family business. He pictured himself during this period pathetically trudging through the market with heavy sacks of flour on his back.

He broke labor laws and was sentenced in December 1971 to fifteen days imprisonment for not reporting the excess working hours of his truck drivers to the police.

Rumor had it in Athens that Marios mistreated and beat a woman who complained about him twice to the police. But the case was never brought to court and there is no official record of the incident.

One night at a party an Englishwoman engaged to one of his Athens College classmates introduced Marios to Mary Lewis, an American teaching fifth grade at the Ursuline Academy in Athens. "Who is he?" Mary later asked about this dynamic young man. She was told he came from a wealthy family, a fact then only slightly out of date, for it was recently that the family fortunes had completely crumbled. When Marios told Mary his family was nearly as rich as the Onassis clan, she believed him.

Two years Marios's senior, Mary Lewis was a naive young woman from Tennessee, where her maternal grandfather had started the Parks Belk chain of department stores. She had a brother who was a professor of economics at the University of Alabama at Birmingham. Her family were respectable middle-class people, liberal-minded, if provincial. Bored by the South, by the University of Tennessee, and by sorority life, Mary had ventured to Athens, knowing no Greek.

She found Marios unlike any of the men she had known in Maryville. He was cosmopolitan, full of life, quick-witted, funny, and even brilliant. Once he told Mary he could make one of her friends fall in love with him and then could turn around and make her hate him. Mary scoffed. But Marios accomplished this feat. Mary was passive by inclination and lacking in self-confidence. Inclined to be overweight and wearing her brown hair short, she was not pretty. But she was a sweet, good-natured, loyal person. When she met Marios, she was like an empty vessel waiting to be filled up.

Mary was twenty-nine, slightly overripe for a southern bride, when she married Marios Michaelides, aged twenty-seven, on July 11, 1972, in Knoxville, Tennessee, at the St. George Orthodox Church. The bride wore white satin and organza. The groom's family did not attend.

Back in Athens, Marios mysteriously failed to introduce his new wife to any of his relatives. He told her his grandfather had been a banker in partnership with a tycoon named Andreottis and had owned the property on which the Grande Bretagne Hotel now sits, only to lose it. He said he had grown up in a mansion worth millions which was now rented out to a shipbuilder's family. He told Mary he had bought a ship and, until he lost it, had been carrying concrete between Athens and Crete. He said he and his brother Eugenios had their own huge flour mill. He presented himself to his new bride as a clever young entrepreneur, thwarted by older people threatened by his competitiveness who drove him out of business.

In fact there had been a home outside Athens, but it was hardly a mansion, and George Michaelides had to sell it after the Communist uprising. There was no huge factory somewhere beyond Piraeus. Marios was penniless. His brother Eugenios had opened a tiny storefront business which made additives for bread dough and Marios was accepting an allowance from him. He was so ashamed of his family's reduced circumstances that he never told his mother and brothers that he had gotten married.

It was only after Sasha's death that Mary finally met Eugenios. When she told him of Marios's stories of the fabled wealth of the Michaelides family, Eugenios threw up his hands in horror and said, "He's absolutely crazy. He doesn't know how to behave himself." Then he rushed home with such violent chest pains that his wife had to call in a doctor.

There were times as she waited for Marios to join her at Staunton Hill when Sasha's facade cracked and the dark emotions surfaced. The night after the southern fried chicken feast a storm came up and Sasha demanded that everyone go out and watch. She said she loved thunder and lightning. It was a bad storm, but it delighted her and she was not afraid. Danger still held its attractions.

Every day she plunged herself into frenetic activity. "When I'm depressed, I do something physical," she said. She busied herself compulsively. Covered with dust, she tried to catalogue the Staunton Hill rare book collection. She painted the walls white, vowing to remove "everything that had been Mummy's." She supervised the renovation of the tenant cottages, selecting wallpaper, having hot water heaters replaced. And she had from her trust only the five hundred dollars a month the people in Wilmington were allowing her.

She studied Greek or drove aimlessly about the countryside in her 1972 green Ford Torino; one day she drove the thirty-five miles into Lynchburg three times. At a dinner she ate nine quail at a sitting because quail were a great favorite of her father. Drunk at a party she stood on her head and rolled in the grass. She was lonely and often invited Diane Morris or Marie Harper to spend the night with her at Staunton Hill. Diane thought Sasha liked her because she never asked any questions. Like an actress, Sasha could behave like whomever she was with, Diane noticed.

And always Sasha was in a hurry, driving seventy miles an hour or more down the winding back roads of Charlotte County, hitting the brakes when she had to. At a barbecue she arrived in a dress only to drive back to Staunton Hill to change into slacks at such lightning speed that it took her only twenty minutes to go back and forth the fifteen miles. Marie Harper's son Allen dubbed her Rachel Petty, after Richard Petty, the stock car racer. After she amassed a collection of speeding tickets, she tried to slow down.

She was often depressed and her despair was exacerbated by the isolation she had chosen. There was no one of her education or sensibility, no one with whom she shared a past, with whom she might have discussed her troubles. She had mastered the civilization of Mesopotamia, studied Chinese, and grown up in Europe, she had sailed to Byzantium. How could she not have found the half-deserted towns of Charlotte County "devoid of the ridiculous," as she put it? She invited some locals to dinner and wrote Marios she had giggled at the thought of his having to sit through such a meal. "I *am* good," she mischievously judged herself.

One morning she even visited the local sheriff whom she asked to find her a .22 pistol. He gave her a tear-gas cannister to keep near her bed those nights she slept alone at Staunton Hill, when she was beset by nightmares. "That tear gas was so powerful it would make you cry for the rest of your life," Marios said later.

Tongue-in-cheek, Sasha inquired whether there had been any race riots in Brookneal. "Not yet," the sheriff said, as if he eagerly awaited such an event. He told her he had pursued a drunk to the marshes "where there was thirty niggers if there was one." His talk was completely unmediated by conventions of respectable terminology, Sasha noticed. She admired his collection of confiscated moonshine and when she left, he gave her the large plyboard figure of a man she would later use for target practice and which would be discovered at the spot where her body was found.

When she departed for America, Sasha believed her troubles with von Kassel would soon be settled. This was not to be the case. Mark's Trust began to pursue her through their solicitor, Lewis Cutner, claiming the sum of 125,000 pounds since she had countersigned those forged bank drafts for von Kassel and accepted $33,333 of the money. The prospect of further scandal terrified her.

She was determined, however, not to have been cheated so monumentally by von Kassel and on May 9, 1974, she managed to make him sign a letter agreement stipulating that the eight icons with which he had promised to repay her for the $185,000 loan she had made him in August 1972 were her personal property which neither he nor any third party could remove from his house. This agreement also stipulated that an additional $62,000 he owed her would be repaid in four installments. Strangely she still seemed to trust him; she was incapable of accepting that von Kassel was not a man to honor an agreement, verbal or written. She had no chance whatsoever of securing those eight icons once she left them in his custody.

Confused and scared, plagued by the debt to Mark's Trust, Sasha visited Maeve Kinkead that May 1974 and asked her, "If you had these debts, what would you do? What way out would you take?"

"Pay them back," Maeve answered.

At least her life was not entirely bleak, Sasha told Maeve. She had found a good and simple man. Her dark eyes were shining, her spirit became effervescent, as she described Marios.

It was a story like a fairy tale in its grid. Marios had rescued Sasha from Anton and soon they would be married.

That Marios was already married Sasha treated as no obstacle at all. He had told her he'd never loved Mary; he'd only married her because they had been seen together around Athens so often that it was expected of him. She sent passionate love letters to Marios at his and Mary's apartment and Mary found one as she was sending a suit to the cleaner's. "Is Marios there?" Sasha would ask when Mary answered the phone. There were no preliminaries, no introduction, and never a message or a name. Somehow Marios was never at home when Sasha called, but she kept right on telephoning.

Mostly, of course, she communicated with Marios through letters. His love-name for her was Goat, the submissive, bleating domesticated creature, although it was much more *he* who was the goat-god Pan of Greek mythology, disguising his hairy black goatishness with white fleeces to seduce the fair Selene. He made her dependent on him, calling such dependence "natural." To ensure his control he encouraged her to talk about how unhappy her childhood had been, how she was denied the love he would now provide. He set himself against the Bruces and even insisted on calling her Alexandra since Sasha was what her parents called her. Attacking Mrs. Bruce for the amount of money she spent on hairdressers he cried, "You could definitely feed half of Biafra with it!" The ambassador he took to calling a "sly fox."

Weary of the struggles with von Kassel, on edge as she feared the encroachment of Mark's Trust and the publicity which would so pain her parents, she gave herself up to Marios. By that spring she was calling him husband and he was calling her wife. He joked about his nondescript physical appearance and praised her for having escaped notions of masculinity fostered by American films. She was wise to have rejected the fake glamour of the diplomatic community; he would provide "something more peaceful."

He had discovered soon enough Sasha didn't think she was beautiful and so he told her she was one of those women whose looks improve with time. She wasn't a classical beauty, but she had a certain air. He invented a game in which he would ask, "Who is the prettiest woman on the earth?" so that she would be obliged to answer that she was. Her self-acceptance was dependent upon his whim.

When it served his ends, however, he also knew how to confirm her low opinion of herself. "The other woman is better than you," he'd taunt her, referring to the plain, sweet Mary Lewis.

From the start, he seemed to have figured out that Sasha's great obsession was winning the love of her mother. She could be most effectively controlled if approval were *withheld*, if she were kept on tenterhooks. Even as an adult Terry Graham still talked with wonder of how when she and Sasha were children Mrs. Bruce could be approving one minute, a best friend to her daughter, then seemingly as cutting as a knife so that you never knew where you stood. Marios evidently decided to adopt a similar tactic. Sasha could best be managed if she were thrown off balance.

The key was the shame of her time in London. And so he invented the absurb mythology that he was the aristocrat and she the peasant slave who must raise herself to his high moral level. He convinced Sasha that she had sacrificed her honor and her reputation with von Kassel, that she had injured the good name of the Bruces. She began to fear she would never outlive her shame, just as the "faux pas" of Nancy Randolph, her grandfather wrote in his *Recollections*, was still talked about a century later in southern Virginia "as if she were the only woman of the gentry class in that part of Virginia who had ever stooped to folly." William Cabell Bruce had lamented the "excessive sensitiveness to every point of personal honor or dignity" which beset the "quasiaristocrats" of Southside Virginia. "If a Southside Virginia woman of the dominant race became involved in scandal," he remembered from his youth, "the fact was not forgotten as long as she lived."

Returning to her ancestral home from the license of those years in London when she had smuggled icons and drugs, Sasha took such views to heart. Marios was right. She had been made "impure" by her criminal and sexual escapades with von Kassel. Her mother did not help, Marios said, by phoning her at one point when an item about Sasha and von Kassel appeared in the London press, advising her that if newspaper people called, she should refuse to talk with them. According to Marios, Evangeline used the word "embarrass-

The Bruce family in 1961.
(Alfred Eisenstaedt, Life *magazine,* © *1979 Time Inc.)*

St. Tim's Latin-American summer
(Sasha, second row, center).

Sasha in St. Tim's yearbook.

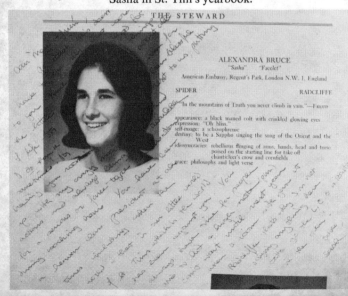

THE STEWARD

ALEXANDRA BRUCE
"Sasha"   "Facelet"
American Embassy, Regent's Park, London N.W. 1, England

SPIDER   RADCLIFFE

"In the mountains of Truth you never climb in vain."—FREUD

appearance: a black maned colt with crinkled glowing eyes
expression: "Oh bliss."
self-image: a schizophrenic
destiny: to be a Sappho singing the song of the Orient and the
          West
idiosyncrasies: rebellious flinging of arms, hands, head and torso
                poised on the starting line for take-off
                chanticleer's crow and cornfields
grace: philosophy and light verse

Sasha at Wendy Wisner's debutante party, 1965.

Sasha at Wendy Wisner's wedding, 1970.

Anton Von Kassel.

Maria Andipa.

Sasha in London, 1974, with Barbie Hanson Pierce.

Sasha at the Bruce home in Washington, D.C.

Marios in Athens.
(Enrico Ferorelli/Wheeler Pictures)

Sasha at Staunton Hill, 1974.

Marie Harper, David K. E. Bruce,
Priscilla Jaretzki, Nicholas Bruce.

Mrs. Bruce and Hans Gleisner at the Phipps wedding.
(*Tim Jenkins*/WWD)

Staunton Hill, aerial view.
(*Stanley Tretick,* Life *magazine,* © *1979 Time Inc.*)

The tree at Staunton Hill
under which Sasha's body was found. *(Lynda Jones)*

ing.'' If that was the case, it could only have driven her hypersensitive daughter to further hysteria, paralyzed as she was with shame.

Mario's own mother would not receive her because of her sordid adventures with von Kassel, Sasha was told. She was lucky, since she was not a virgin, that he should bother with her at all. *His* mother was a sainted figure; *his* parents had enjoyed a perfect love. He had great misgivings about allying himself with such a woman as she. Sasha must now do exactly as he said.

Late in the spring of 1974, Sasha invited Terry Graham to Virginia. She longed to share the trauma of her last days with von Kassel and her blueprint for a future with Marios with her best friend. Marios was still in Athens. The two women would spend the weekend alone at Staunton Hill, a place where they had shared many happy childhood memories.

When Terry drove up to the Mansion House, Sasha was waiting for her outside. She was nervous, more jumpy than Terry had ever seen her.

''Marios is here!'' Sasha said quickly. ''He called up and just flew in.'' Her words ran into each other. ''It's the first time he's ever been to Staunton Hill so you and I are not going to have as much time together as we thought.''

Something is amiss, Terry thought at once. Sasha was on edge and at his beck and call. At one point as the three were engaged in conversation, Marios abruptly rose and demanded that he and Sasha retire to their bedroom where from his manner it was clear that what he had in mind was sex. Dutifully, Sasha followed him, leaving Terry by herself. And Terry wondered then whether Marios was doing strange sexual things to ensure his power over Sasha, what sexual aberrations he might have had in mind.

Marios tried not to allow the two women a moment alone, but once he had to leave the property. For these two hours Sasha seemed more like her old self. They sat in the little cottage adjacent to the main house and talked. Sasha filled Terry in about what happened in London, the times she and her mother were at war with each other. She spoke of how desperately she wished to be accepted by Marios's family. He was one of three sons of the wealthiest milling family in Greece, Sasha said, a family run by a matriarch who was very strong and who disapproved of Sasha because of her sordid relationship with von Kassel. Now she must be purged of her wrongdoings. That she was not "pure" was why, when they were in Athens and Marios visited his family, Sasha had to remain alone in the purgatory of her hotel room.

She had done "bad things," Sasha told Terry. Now she wanted to be a clean person, worthy of being Marios's wife and of bearing his children. But to achieve her end, Sasha went on, she must isolate herself at Staunton Hill and have no further contact with family or friends. Only in this way might she free herself from her terrible past.

"Well, I can see some of this," Terry said carefully. "But, Sasha, I don't think it's a good idea for you to isolate yourself from your friends. These are people who have known and loved you all your life. You can get some very distorted ideas if you don't maintain some continuity with people from your past."

She dared not go further, although later she would regret not having been more emphatic. It seemed to Terry then as if Marios, fearing Sasha's family, the power of the Bruces, had created the myth of her being a tainted woman, insisting he would marry her only if she were completely isolated.

There were unpleasant arguments during meals as Elizabeth Hamlett served her famous Brunswick stew. Marios was provocative and insistent, gesturing with his arm outstretched, his lips curling in a sardonic smile. Women are happiest when they take care of their men, he said. They have no place in the working world. His face settled into his chin in repose and he lit a cigarette, waiting for his words to take effect. Terry, who had become a marine biologist, defended career women. But Marios spoke as if there were something dirty, sexually decadent about that idea. It was woman's place to stand behind her husband.

He bragged about grain mills he owned in Greece, as well as one in Tennessee. He was going to build a flour mill at Staunton Hill, the biggest grain mill south of Washington. He and Sasha then began to discuss among themselves how they could arrange for the financing of this mill. Terry listened, incredulous.

(A year later Marios did attempt to borrow $125,000 from a local Charlotte County bank supposedly for this flour mill. The banker agreed to lend him the money on the strength of his connection with David Bruce. But as an afterthought he decided to consult Reginald Pettus.

"We'd better ask him for some security, to put up some stocks," Pettus recommended.

"What do you mean by security?" Marios demanded of Pettus when he was told the loan was in doubt.

"You'd better put up some stock for it."

"If she [it was now Sasha who was making the loan] has to put up stock, she can get the money anywhere."

"That may be true," Pettus said, "but we don't want to lend it unless she puts up some stocks."

"We don't want to talk to you," Marios said venomously then. "Maybe we can loan *you* money. We can loan you OPEC money, all you want, a million dollars. We have all we want.")

After lunch Sasha and Marios sat on the porch drinking bourbon and shooting with a pistol at the target in the shape of a human figure provided by the sheriff. Marios was teaching her how to shoot, Sasha said. They each sat with a glass of bourbon in one hand and a pistol in the other. Later Terry reminisced about their trip to St. John in the Caribbean during college when she and a young man had joined Sasha and Bear Barnes. Casually she referred to the good time they'd all had, her way of reminding Sasha of the past they'd shared, which was not without joy.

Marios flew into a rage. He called Sasha away from the table and insisted she throw Terry off the property. Throw her out! Marios insisted. She has insulted me.

Was it a game for Sasha? Terry wondered as she drove off. Was it like smuggling Byzantine icons with von Kassel? Or shooting at a target while drinking bourbon? And to all these games Sasha was pledging her complete loyalty, punishing her parents in the cruelest of ways—by punishing herself.

"I won't be in touch with you," Sasha told Terry as she left.

"I think you ought to think twice about that," Terry replied. "I don't think it's such a hot idea."

Returning to the Mansion House, Sasha told Marios that Terry had agreed—isolating herself was a good idea. "Your old friends are a gangrene," Marios told her.

Terry left believing Sasha planned soon to marry Marios. She hadn't been told that he was already married.

*   *   *

That May, while Marios was in Athens, Sasha visited Stanley Frye in North Carolina. She told him she owned a priceless iconostasis, a standing screen with doors that separates the altar from the congregation in the Greek Orthodox Church. It was carved of cypress with niches into which icons were fitted. One tier alone held twelve icons for twelve holidays. "It belongs to me," Sasha said. "It's in Europe."

"Send for it and we'll build a Byzantine church here!" Frye promised. He thought he could still help her rebuild her life. The iconostasis, one of the eight icons left in the custody of von Kassel, represented the promise of a fresh future.

"Could we?" Sasha asked wistfully.

That summer of 1974 was not all target practice and picnics with water goblets filled to the brim with Jack Daniel's. Sasha had come home to work and she poured her energy into her farming projects. Marios lacked a permanent visa and could only visit for two or three weeks at a time. But through the mail he involved himself in every detail of Sasha's enterprises from the chickens to the feeder lot to the alfalfa field. During one visit the two of them took a "short course" in the raising of chickens at the Virginia Polytechnic Institute at Blacksburg where they were taught how to make feed from chicken feathers and how to handle the manure, which would be their biggest problem.

Although friends scoffed at the idea that Staunton Hill plantation could be maintained by chickens, and everyone in Charlotte County knew you couldn't make any profit out of chickens with as few as Sasha had because the feed cost as much as what you'd get for the eggs, she went to work in earnest, beginning with twenty-five hens which she called her "ladies." Trying to be a "scientific farmer," she pored over charts during the unbearable heat, writing to Marios for advice about what size cages she should buy or how much land she should have cleared for the alfalfa. Wandering alone through the cavernous house, she sat in the room she had shared with Marios and pretended that a "cool peace" was descending upon her. She opened the closet and took out his sneakers. They are forlorn without their master, she thought.

Meanwhile she studied feeding and watering, egg collecting, egg grading, and fluctuations in market prices so diligently that Pettus reported to her father that Sasha had good business sense, seemed cautious, and no doubt would invest wisely. She decided she needed at least two hundred thousand dollars in capital to run her operations. Her goal was thirty thousand hens. In June she had "the farm" legally incorporated as "Staunton Hill Farm, Inc., an agricultural operation." She kept the books herself.

On another level it was all a game. She saw onion grass growing behind the house and said she didn't want to be a gardener because that was so "bloody English." "When I grow up," Sasha said, "I want to be a farmer!"

Marios filled her head with talk of amino acids and proteins and told her to mail him photocopies of charts put out by the Department of Agriculture which he would then examine with his computer. She flattered him and told him the feed people in Virginia spoke of "essential amino acids," just as he had done. She would not decide between the Southern States and the Ralston Purina brand of feed until he gave his opinion. If "black shadows" pursued her at night, the next day even more compulsively would she immerse herself in details of "clutches" (eggs laid on successive days), figures of egg production, and articles on how control of light might eliminate "winter pause," the time when hens do not lay any eggs at all. At such moments she seemed in control, intelligent, and effective. Most people in Charlotte County who met her concluded that she was stable and cheerful, not depressed at all.

Marios turned up at Staunton Hill again. On this visit he told the Morrises that he didn't work inside the family mill in Athens, but in an outside office with the books and so would be useful to Sasha only with the record keeping. He told others "our time in Virginia is not a playboy's life. Working in chicken shit all day is not a playboy."

One night the Morrises invited Sasha and Marios to dinner, but they didn't turn up. Marios answered Diane's call from the Mansion House. The water had stopped up in the chicken coop. Sasha was down there cleaning it out. Other calls brought the same response. Sasha hadn't come back. She was still trying to unclog the pipes. If the drains were clogged, why was Marios sitting up there in the house while Sasha was cleaning out the dirty chicken water? the Morrises wondered.

* * *

For her alfalfa field Sasha hired a man named John Howard Marshall to clear pastureland; he was to pay her for the lumber he took away. But he chopped up the land in an unsightly mess. Then he blabbed, "Sasha wanted to be paid right at the end of every month," obviously enjoying the tenuous financial circumstances of a Bruce. The magnificent vista entering Staunton Hill that had once been David Bruce's pride was spoiled.

Sasha asked John Morris to fertilize the cleared field, but by the time he arrived, she had shoveled the fertilizer out of her truck and into the spreader herself. "Aren't you afraid you're going to injure yourself with overwork?" Morris asked her.

"No, I'm doing this for exercise," Sasha answered.

With the help of Emma Elam's son, she sowed her alfalfa. But either birds or insects devoured the seed, because it never came up.

Her third project was to set up a feeder calf operation. She would buy two hundred small calves, weighing three hundred pounds each, and feed them from an automatic feeder. Then she would put them back on the market at one thousand or two thousand pounds. Marios talked of computing profits and costs on his computer, while the local farmers looked at each other and decided Sasha didn't know what she was doing, figuring out farming from a book! She drove to the stock markets in South Boston and learned it would cost between eighty thousand and ninety thousand dollars to install a feeder lot.

The feeder calf operation never got started, however. Sasha was not scheduled to come into any real money until her thirtieth birthday, when she would receive between two hundred and three hundred thousand dollars. This was money which had no connection with the irrevocable trust depleted by von Kassel. But she could not get her hands on it until May 1, 1976.

Fussing over her "ladies," singing "Good Night, Ladies" to them at night, Sasha tried to keep her mind off the continuing ugly aftermath of her affair with von Kassel. In early July he sold six of the eight icons he had agreed were legally hers for forty-eight thousand pounds. Later he disposed of the remaining two. These transactions proceeded through Lewis

Cutner, who purchased them for Mark's Trust and then sold them to a gallery owner in West Germany named Schmidt (Smith) with Cutner providing a false warranty as to "true ownership."

Cutner said only that the icons had been purchased by Mark's Trust; he did not demonstrate that title had been acquired. In fact, the icons belonged to Sasha, having been stolen by von Kassel. Since Mark's Trust at least theoretically received financial gain from the sale of the eight icons by von Kassel, Sasha would have had a substantial counterclaim against them—provided Mark's Trust knew the icons belonged to her. But her lawyers told her Mark's Trust could *not* have been expected to know of her arrangement with von Kassel.

Mark's Trust sent Sasha a letter saying that in order to avoid embarrassing publicity, she must arrange for them to be paid more than a hundred thousand pounds—with interest.

In July she visited the Fryes again, bearing Greek cheese, pistachio nuts, and olives. She brought with her as well her photograph album which contained pictures from her archaeological digs. Marios was so jealous that he didn't want them in the house, she explained. Nothing of her former life must remain. But the pictures meant a great deal to her and so she wanted to leave them in the safekeeping of the Fryes.

She told Stanley Frye that Marios had refused to introduce her to his mother because she was an American. Ashamed, she left out the part about her sordid past.

"That can't be true," Frye said.

"How do you know?"

"I know Greeks. My first wife was Greek. I know the Greek way of thinking."

Frye's voice rose. He was genuinely alarmed.

"How do you know they even exist?" he pursued. "How do you know this man is what he says he is?" Sasha had told him Marios's brother had a flour mill in Alabama and his father a currant business in Greece.

"How do you know it's true?" Frye demanded. "Have you met the brother? The father? The mother? Marios is not a Greek name! What priest baptized him? In what church? What is the background of his father and mother? Michaelides is a common name, like Smith!"

Frye was surprised to hear Sasha use the phrase, "the game of money," and it seemed to him she had become materialistic. She told Frye she and Marios wouldn't be able to get married until they had enough money to go into business and Frye became even more alarmed.

"Don't you know where the money will come from?" he demanded.

"No," Sasha said.

She admitted Marios had told her, "Unless you put up your share, I won't marry you!" Clearly he had his eye on her future inheritance.

"You're a fool! A dunce!" Frye said angrily.

"Stop. I'm trembling," Sasha pleaded.

"Go ahead and tremble," Frye shouted now. "You're headed for a real disaster, Sasha."

"Please don't say that."

And then she told the Fryes she was getting trained German police dogs to guard her at Staunton Hill.

"Why?" Frye wanted to know.

"To protect me. Marios says I need protection."

"Did you ever need that before? Why now?"

"Marios thinks I do."

And she told the Fryes she carried a gun and a tear-gas cannister in her purse.

Indeed Marios had frightened her. The icon demimonde was on her trail, he said. He drove her to such hysteria that one day when a car innocently entered Staunton Hill property, she began to scream at the top of her lungs, "That's private property! Can't you read the sign?" She told a friend she wanted her privacy, but Marios had planted the idea that the underworld lowlifes from the Cypriot Mafia, whom Anton had hired to set fire to the New Grecian Gallery and then refused to pay off, were after her. He made her believe she was unsafe at Staunton Hill and ordered her to check her gun before she went to bed every night when he was not there.

On August sixteenth, Sasha began proceedings for the recovery of the sixty-two thousand dollars which Anton had forged on her account at Wilmington Trust and which he had promised on May ninth to repay in four installments. At first she sued only for the first three installments since the fourth was not due until August thirty-first.

* * *

Back in Athens, Marios bragged about the mansion where he lived in America, so that his family wondered why he didn't help them out financially since he was apparently so rich. He made considerable efforts to prevent the Bruces from discovering how poor they were. Slyly he told Sasha to ask her father to do a financial check on him. He told her she should tell her parents, it's unheard of for somebody to want to marry your daughter and not to find out who he is.

A Chase Manhattan Bank representative called him in Athens and said he'd like to ask him a few questions regarding his financial situation.

"I don't discuss such matters on the telephone, but contact my bank," Marios said haughtily.

When Chase reported to the Bruces that although Marios had no debts and no problem with bad checks, he was virtually penniless, as well as being "a very difficult person," David Bruce confronted Sasha. Stoutly Sasha defended Marios, as he knew she would. "Well, his money is all tied up in OPEC," she said.

Longing for family, Sasha invited her teen-aged Currier nieces, Andrea and Lavinia, and her nephew Michael, whom she barely knew, to Staunton Hill that summer of 1974. They arrived from Kinloch accompanied by their own horses, complete with special feed and a horse trainer. Proudly they carried a saddlebag with the name of their mother, "Audrey Currier," inscribed on it.

Before the Curriers arrived, Sasha called Stanley Frye and asked if his daughters might join the group at Staunton Hill. "No," Frye said, remembering her trip to Nepal in 1970, "because you're on drugs." Crushed, Sasha made no defense.

The carefree family group roamed the outdoors. Once they were refused admittance to a Brookneal restaurant because they were not dressed appropriately. Nick always wore stretched-out T-shirts with a pocket for his cigarettes. Sasha rarely put on a dress.

That summer Sasha and Nicky shot at the gray torso-shaped target with pistols.

On Labor Day weekend Sasha seemed happy as she entertained a young male friend visiting from England. Marios was in Greece, but Sasha organized a picnic, producing a big ham and a three-bean salad. Although she had very little money, there was always ample food and drink at Staunton Hill. At the Holts' grocery store she stocked up on what she said were Marios's favorites: Hershey bars with almonds and dried apricots, figs and peaches.

That Labor Day Sasha became quite rowdy. Someone got stung by a bee and she poured bourbon on the bee sting. She took her English friend around to see the local plantations, especially Greenfield, telling him she was interested in old houses herself. Afterwards she warned Marie Harper not to tell Marios about her guest because he would be very jealous.

On September third, through her English solicitors, Sasha began proceedings against von Kassel for the recovery of the eight icons, or their equivalent value.

In the early fall she visited the Fryes for what would be the last time. Having driven all night, dressed in old pants and a shirt, she arrived at 4:30 A.M. Then she climbed up into an old apple tree and waited for the family to wake up. On this visit she took back the photograph album she had left with them in July, although she did not tell the Fryes that Marios had now calmed down sufficiently for these emblems of her past to remain at Staunton Hill.

She drove her car recklessly on the wrong side of the road, racing around the hairpin curves of the Great Smokies with Frye yelling, "Sasha, if you don't stop driving so fast, I'm getting out!" She had hoped to bring Marios to the Fryes for their approval, but they were not enthusiastic. This time she did not even mention the idea. By now Frye was certain Marios was sinister. He was frightened for Sasha, she seemed so susceptible to mind control, but he felt there was nothing he could do for her.

"*Yavas Gel!*" he called in Mongol as she drove off. "Take it slowly! Don't rush into anything!"

But she was obsessed by Marios, obsessed by what she had made of him and she could admit no voice but his. "I can't live without him," she told Maeve Kinkead. She took a perverse comfort in his pathological possessiveness, as if this were proof that he cared for her.

Marios was the man she loved and wanted, Sasha told herself. She believed she needed to be controlled and she allowed herself to experience the way he took over her life as fulfilling. In her extenuated fantasy life he was her rescuer. She promised she would always be there for him. When she told him about her fears and depressions, Marios complained that she was being "unpleasant."

"Haven't you always told me to tell you everything I felt, to hide nothing?" Sasha countered. Then he would ease up on her for a while.

They were in a contest as to who loved whom more, Sasha said, and she was "the miserable winner." She told him she was certain she would love him still even when she had grown old and withered. When he was in Greece, she said, she got her only comfort from her "white, no-good bastard child," her dog Aesop. It was too dangerous to tell him she had found comfort among the people in Charlotte County.

At night as she fell asleep, she pretended to feel his back pressed against her. The nightmares increased. She begged that at the end of the "long black tunnel" of her depressions she should find *him*. He must reach out to her too if he needed her. And still he held back.

She called herself his "loving wife," describing their love in terms of mutual self-annihilation. In this fantasy there would be no place where she ended and he began. When he had a minor automobile accident in Virginia on one of his visits, she was upset that she had been so close geographically and yet had felt nothing. She used phrases like desiring "to melt into him" and "obliterating herself." No fate could take him from her, Sasha insisted. Thinking of him, she would begin to tremble, as she had literally trembled when Stanley Frye challenged the veracity of Marios's boasts. The blood rushed to her face; her heart beat faster.

Into their love talk entered the element of danger and risk, which had attracted her since college. Early on Marios had said, "We've never had a fight. You don't know what pleasure is!"

"I'll give you hell," Sasha now returned. "What hell it will be, you and me!"

If Marios called unexpectedly from Greece, she fell into such a frenzy that she could barely speak. Knowing he was still living with Mary, she "cursed" her jealousy. "Another one will guard your sleep," she whimpered. At other times she told herself she was thankful he was being well looked after. But it rankled that he was back with his wife in Athens. Then she blamed herself, cursing her heavy debts and "civilized life" itself which demanded that she restrain her mad passion and her jealousy and the anger of whose origins she had little idea.

One day she sat down and calculated their time together. It had been ninety-two days and eighty-two nights, although it was difficult to know, Sasha mused, whether she should count one Sunday in July when he was in Tennessee, for on that day she had seen him in the morning, but not at night.

Despite her pleas that she loved him, Marios kept up his attacks, contrasting the fallen Sasha with what he expected, what his family hoped of the woman who would be his wife. She took to calling herself not only "goat" but the "creature" he had adopted, pitiful and unworthy of his strong feelings of love and pride, of his sense of honor. She told him she wouldn't blame him if "his continual discoveries of how low she was threatened to explode his dream of the life they could have together." As he was leaving for Greece on one occasion, she begged him pathetically to consider whether he could in fact live with such a person as she.

He did love her, Marios insisted. But what had happened to her in London made her represent everything he despised. When they fought, he threw von Kassel in her face. He accused her too of not standing by *him* and telling her parents how important he was to her. He engineered a struggle with the Bruces in which she was the prize. And he would accept from her nothing short of a repudiation of her family.

Sasha promised to change. At her lowest moments, however, she doubted whether Marios could ever wholly forget what she was. But how could she hope to redeem herself, she pleaded, when he continually threw her transgressions in her face?

"Marios needs to conquer," she told Marie Harper. She confided a vicious remark Marios had made: "I could make it with your mother."

Appalled, Marie thought, If he's her choice, he must have more than I can see. He must have one *that long*.

For Sasha's unsophisticated neighbors in Southside Virginia it was impossible to understand why so clever, gentle, and beautiful a person should have awarded this small, dark Greek with his little mustache, sullenly chain-smoking as he stood aloof from her friends, so much power over her.

Money and property took on an importance for Sasha they'd never had before. At Marios's instigation in late 1974 she hired her father's Washington antiques dealer, Michael Arpad, to evaluate the contents of Staunton Hill. She got Nicky to give her "almost blanket authority to sell some of the furniture for a year or two," telling the locals only that she was having the contents of Staunton Hill appraised "for insurance purposes."

Marios found Arpad "oily." As for his assistants, Marios raised his arm in an obscene gesture. But the appraisal of the contents of Staunton Hill which David K. E. Bruce had given to his children as an undivided gift in 1970 went forward with Marios eager for the results. That American furniture is good even if it's only 75 percent authentic, he thought.

On October fourth, Marios opened a bank account at the Fidelity National Bank in Brookneal with a ten-dollar deposit, listing Staunton Hill as his address.

Meanwhile, Sasha's attempts to recoup her losses from von Kassel in the English courts slowly moved forward. On October twenty-eighth she obtained a judgment against him for forty-eight thousand dollars, representing the first three installments of his defaulted repayment of the sixty-two thousand dollars he had forged on her Wilmington Trust account. The issue of how to collect damages from the wily von Kassel had still to be faced.

That October Sasha visited her mother, newly returned to Washington from Peking. She did not announce her arrival and Mrs. Bruce turned pale when she saw her daughter. She had received a letter from Sasha telling her of Marios's decision that she isolate herself completely at Staunton Hill breaking all contact with family and friends.

"I thought you weren't going to be allowed to see me for a while," Mrs. Bruce told her daughter when she regained her composure.

"Marios has relaxed the rule a bit in your favor," Sasha answered.

They talked for hours. Sasha told Mrs. Bruce of her great good fortune in having found a man with whom she came first. He had never cared for anyone or had a relationship with anyone except a girl to whom he was engaged when he was nineteen, Sasha told her mother. She wanted Mrs. Bruce to accept Marios, whom she planned to marry. Marios's criticisms of *her*, his strong sense of morality, were what she liked and respected most about him, Sasha said.

Mrs. Bruce confided she had been struggling with how to approach her daughter and Marios. Now that she was convinced of the kind of man he was, she rejoiced for Sasha. She told Sasha she even respected his negative feelings about their family.

Evangeline Bruce then said she blamed Sasha herself for not explaining to Marios the conflicting demands of husband and children which she had faced. She had never given enough serious thought to her role as a mother, Sasha later said her mother told her.

The subject of the London episode arose. Mrs. Bruce questioned the wisdom of Sasha's permitting Marios to blame the Bruces for not separating her from von Kassel. "Don't you understand?" Sasha told her mother then. "It's much easier for me to have him blame someone besides myself and not put it all on me. As soon as we're married, I'll be able to straighten it all out."

Mrs. Bruce defended herself. She told Sasha nothing short of physical removal from von Kassel would have worked on someone as stubborn as her daughter who, in addition, had her own money. Open hostility might have pushed Sasha immediately into marriage. She admitted she did not have the love and trust built up from childhood to make her daughter realize that her disapproval was for Sasha's own good, Sasha later recounted.

Mrs. Bruce told Sasha she felt the joy of a mother whose daughter had found a good, wise, loving man. She joked that she was even jealous of her daughter. Now she wanted to meet Marios and would even go to Athens if Sasha would go with her. Sasha, gratified, answered that Marios must first read a letter Mrs. Bruce would write to him. Her mother replied she would respect Marios's wishes.

Sasha and her mother drew closer. She believed that Mrs. Bruce was hesitant to intrude upon her happiness; she hoped

Marios would give her mother a chance. She told Marios later that Mrs. Bruce's reactions were so loving and full of warmth for him that her heart went out to her. Mrs. Bruce had said Sasha's feeling for Marios was the happiest thing she could have heard.

But the Bruces were not to remain in America long. By November 15, 1974, David K. E. Bruce had been appointed United States permanent representative on the Council of the North Atlantic Treaty Organization, succeeding Donald Rumsfeld. He was seventy-six years old. On November twenty-fourth, they departed for Brussels.

Thanksgiving 1974 found Sasha alone at Staunton Hill. She invited the Harpers and the Holts to dinner. That morning in Brookneal the florist, who also sold newspapers, stopped Marie on the street. There was an article about Mrs. Bruce in one of the papers. Would Sasha like to see it?

Marie brought the article with her to Staunton Hill. But when she handed it to Sasha, she threw it violently on the floor, muttering, "Bullshit. Bullshit!" Marie brought butter beans and string beans from her freezer. There was turkey and squash and homemade cranberry sauce. The article lay discarded on the floor all that afternoon.

When her guests departed, Sasha sat down and multiplied out the number of layers of chickens which could be put in a cage of a certain size by the price of eggs; then she computed the mortality rate of a given density of chickens in a cage. Along with an Anderson Box Company leaflet on cages, she mailed her calculations to Marios. She was certain *he* could design something even more efficient, Sasha wrote. She asked him to inquire in Greece about chickens that laid more than one egg a day. These would indeed be "miracle birds," Sasha joked, "better than the goose that laid the golden egg," that mythological creature which would later become Marios's code name for her.

She kept on with her chickens and one week the "ladies" produced eleven dozen eggs. She told them thankfully she would now keep her promise and play soothing music in the barn. With Elizabeth Hamlett, she packed and washed the eggs herself. There was an outbreak of Rocky Mountain spotted fever and so to avoid getting ticks on herself, she drove down to the chicken coops. Every night there was a ritual deticking of Aesop, who gently herded renegade hens back into the barn. She spent hours raking the wood shavings around the barn floor to prevent them from getting damp and so encouraging the diseases to which chickens were susceptible. Her ladies, Sasha said proudly, showed no tendency toward either hysteria or cannibalism.

Each week she paid her earnings to Southern States, the feed company, and once she "impressed herself" by putting one hundred dollars in cash on the counter. The ladies had produced 425 eggs in one day! Cold weather was approaching and then Sasha hoped to be paid eighty cents a dozen. During a storm she lost a sack of feed and this upset her since it was worth thirteen dozen eggs. Every penny counted. And always in her letters to Marios she made certain to stress her helplessness and dependence. She mailed him a photograph of the old dairy barn at Staunton Hill and told him to think of his goat spending her days in the last stall.

The price of eggs dropped. Alarmed, Sasha found herself earning only sixty-five cents a dozen. Not one to give up, she scouted for new markets: another grocery store in Brookneal, a small restaurant. She was disappointed that Carroll Holt was taking only half her eggs, although he was buying ninety to one hundred dozen a week. Sasha insisted on delivering them herself, picking up the heavy crates and carrying them into the store. "Sasha, leave them out there. I'll pick 'em up," Holt called out. But Sasha insisted. Once as she lugged the egg crates into Holt's grocery, Marios stood beside the car waiting, as if carting eggs were beneath him.

She dealt too with a professional egg man, a huckster named C. O. Stevens, who took her eggs and sold them in a neighboring town. If she could locate one more market, Sasha calculated, she would be safe. At home she set up a roaring business in cracked eggs, selling them at thirty-five cents a dozen to Buss, John, Emma, Elizabeth, and their friends. Jamie Hamlett's sister, a nurse, drove over from Charlotte Courthouse to buy eggs from her.

After six months the chicken business failed, joining the alfalfa field and the feeder calf project—all aborted, quixotic efforts to retain her fragile hold on life.

After Thanksgiving, Sasha both dreaded and looked forward to Marios's impending Christmas visit. The labors with the chickens had exhausted her physically with little return.

Marios had ordered her to stop calling him in Athens. She began to knit him a sweater for Christmas. "For anyone you love, it means so much more if you knit it yourself," Sasha said. But she had to start it over five times and finally reconciled herself to allowing the many mistakes to remain. She woke up crying in the middle of the night and didn't know why.

Late in November she mailed Marios a postdated check for his air fare back to America. She warned him not to allow the check to reach her bank until December or it wouldn't clear. Despite her trepidation, she counted the days until his scheduled arrival on December fifteenth.

Marios's return continued to trouble her, however. In letters she begged him to be kind to her when he came. He must help her avoid angering him, at least for the first week or so after his arrival. She could not stand it if they had a fight right away. I am a very little goat, she pleaded. She told him she went down to the mailbox every morning with a beating heart. She was his woman, but she needed his reassurance to conquer the demons that gathered around her in his absence. Bombarding him with letters, she wrote she feared being murdered in her sleep; she wanted so much to go on with life in the present, forgetting the dark times of the past. She hoped Marios would forgive her, that he would get over his obsession with her purity so that they might live in peace. Awakening from what she called "horrific dreams," she wrote these letters at four in the morning. She whispered his name, "Marios—Marios—Marios," as she lay in her bed at Staunton Hill and tried to telephone only when she could no longer stand the horror of separation. But the bad dreams destroyed her peace and threatened all her hopes. If only she could reach out and touch Marios, she convinced herself, everything would be all right. When he did come to the phone in Athens, she thanked him for reassuring her. She had conjured up so many monsters pulling them apart.

"Better to die than to live apart from my man," she told him. Chillingly prophetic to the day, she feared she would not last another ten months! Now she awaited only the moment he would hold her pressed to him so that they would be one, the day when they would never again be parted. She drew breath only in anticipation of the time when every night would bring them perfect peace. She called him now her "adored Master," her "sun" and her "God." Did he love *her*? Did he know how much in love with him she was? I doubt it, goat said.

At times she tried to rise above her doubts. Should he be so lucky as to be able to afford his own ticket to Staunton Hill for Christmas, Sasha said (she had sent him a full month's allowance of five hundred dollars), he should use her money to eat a meal at Tudor Hall, a well-known Athens restaurant, with the woman of his choice. But only on the understanding, Sasha went on, that this woman be either his mother—or Mary. After talking to him on the phone one day she said she felt so light and giddy she burned something she was cooking. "Obviously I am in love," Sasha said with a return of her old self-mockery.

Only piecemeal had she revealed to Marios the extent to which von Kassel had implicated her in his crimes. With each revelation he lashed out at her anew. Only because he was strong, he said, was it possible for him not to be contaminated by bending down and reaching out his hand to her. But his decision "to take on her shame" always had a condition. She had to tell him everything. Once he asked her if she still had the eight icons left in Anton's care. He thought they might be sold and the money used to pay off Mark's Trust.

"Yes, I've got them," she had said.

"You have every right to sell them," Marios urged, no matter what she had promised Anton. But it became apparent that not only did she not have access to the icons, but that Anton had shipped them to Germany and sold them there. Late in 1974, Marios discovered that von Kassel was now threatening to expose her part in the arson at the New Grecian Gallery and subject the Bruce family to public humiliation unless Sasha desisted in her law suits against him. She had told Marios nothing about the arson, the deal with the Cypriot Mafia, or Anton's reneging on his debt to them.

Over the telephone from Athens, Marios exploded. He was canceling his Christmas visit! He never wanted to see her again! The relationship was over! That night Sasha had planned to go out to dinner with the Harpers. At seven they sat waiting until Sasha called in tears.

"I've got to go to Greece," she said. But she went by way of Brussels, where she had promised to visit her family—

leaving so hastily that she had to instruct Nicky to telephone the Bruces and tell them she was coming. But he forgot and so had to call at the wrong hour, getting his father out of bed. The Morrises were with him as he apologized over and over again, "I'm sorry. I'm sorry."

As soon as she arrived in Brussels, Sasha fell into her mother's arms. Her sobbing was uncontrollable. Marios had left her forever, she cried. He never wanted to see her again. She no longer wanted to go on living. "I'm going to Athens tomorrow," Sasha told her mother. "I don't know his family and he doesn't want me to see them, but somehow I'm going to find them and find him and do anything to bring him back!"

"I'm coming with you," Mrs. Bruce said.

"No, I have to do it alone," Sasha told her mother.

She spent that night trembling in her mother's bed.

The next morning she telephoned Marios. He questioned her closely about the blackmail, accusing her of lying to him. "Here is another thing I don't know about," he claims he said. "If I don't know what we're in, we're through."

Sasha began screaming and finally said, "Okay, I'll explain." It was then that she disclosed the details of the arson. "It's the truth, it's the truth," she cried. "I can't remember. I can't remember. I'm not lying." But it was apparent that Marios had not forgiven her because her mother noticed she was still crying when she hung up. "I'm going anyway," she told Mrs. Bruce.

She cried as she boarded the flight to Athens. After she was gone, Marios called back and Mrs. Bruce told him what flight Sasha had taken. "Well, I'll meet it and come back with her to you," he said. They returned that same night, Marios having arranged that they make the trip via Rome. Sasha was not permitted to meet Marios's family in Athens.

Back in Brussels, according to Marios, Sasha told her father that Anton was trying to blackmail her by revealing her part in the arson. He had telephoned Staunton Hill and told her, "If you go to court, I'll implicate you in the arson. If you dare to sue me, I'll make it known you were an accomplice!" And he'd have some frightening Cypriots call her, too, threatening to expose her and see that she landed in jail.

David Bruce remained calm. Knowing he was dealing with a petty swindler, he would not take von Kassel's threats seriously. "You young people don't know what real blackmail is," he said lightly, trying to defuse the situation. He recommended to Sasha his own London law firm, Goodman, Derrick, and told his daughter that one never gave in to blackmail. Ignore them, David Bruce said.

This meeting of Sasha, Marios, and the Bruces was highly charged. At one point Marios confronted Mrs. Bruce. Why hadn't she extricated Sasha from von Kassel? he demanded. Mrs. Bruce told him Sasha had been an adult with her own money while she was in London; there was little the family could have done.

As they were leaving and in front of Sasha, Mrs. Bruce made a request of Marios. "Please don't criticize her so much all the time," she said. "I think it's very hard on her. Don't be so hard on her. Be a little bit kinder."

"Thank you," Sasha said sweetly, gratefully, to her mother.

The Christmas season approached. Sasha permitted Marie Harper to conduct a fund-raising tour through Staunton Hill mansion. Marie cracked jokes all along the way with Sasha grinning her approval from the sidelines. Pointing to a portrait of Sarah Seddon Bruce, Sasha's great-grandmother, Marie wisecracked, "This is a portrait of Sasha's mother," as Sasha exploded with laughter. An etching of a family of monkeys hanging in one of the bathrooms became the five Bruces. Wearing an elegant black pants suit with flared legs and a silver belt, Sasha attended the Fidelity Bank Christmas party with Marie.

Marios arrived on December eleventh.

On December twenty-third, in London, Sasha obtained a judgment against von Kassel for the eight icons or their value, which had been assessed as the $185,000 she had lent him in 1972 minus the $33,333 he had repaid.

That last Christmas of her life, she gave her brother Nicky an icon of Saint Nicholas. Marios received the sweater Sasha had labored over—a local woman had to complete it, but it was still too small. Sasha had begun another.

On Christmas Eve they dropped in on the Harpers. Sasha came laden with gifts: a desk set for Tanya, Marie's daughter, jeans from England for both Marie and Tanya. For Sasha, Marie had a locally made corn-husk doll depicting Sasha in jeans and a shirt (like the one of Marios's she often wore) holding a basket of eggs. "Look what Marie had made!" Sasha cried. But Marios was aloof and unfriendly all evening.

When Sasha went down to the basement to give Marie's son Allen his Christmas present, a book on quail and pheasant, Marios trailed after her, not wanting her out of his sight for a second. He found Sasha examining Marie's canned goods. How is it possible to can tomato juice? Marios wanted to know. In Greece you can't keep canned things. It's impossible.

To humor him, Marie patiently explained the principles of canning and told him she and Sasha planned to raise a garden together next spring. Marie would teach Sasha how to can fruits and vegetables. Sasha lifted the cut lid off a can of tomato juice with her fingernail and Marios, appeased, drank some.

Sasha seemed despondent that Christmas Eve as she sat on a little stool and had a drink. You'd better eat something, Marie told her, and so she sat down at the kitchen table. Marios barely nibbled at his food. Sasha grew increasingly tense.

At one point Marie casually reached over and touched Marios's head. It was so hot it almost burned her hand. A few days later in the Brookneal drugstore the three had a Coke together and again Marie impulsively reached over and touched his head. Again it was like fire.

"When I touch a person's head and it's that hot," Marie said afterwards in her melodramatic style, "I remember it."

A Divorce
and a Wedding

In January 1975, Sasha and Marios went to London to refute
the claim of one hundred twenty-five thousand pounds being
made against her by Mark's Trust. They visited the offices of
Gordon Dabbs and Company where Sasha furnished state-
ments of her dealings with von Kassel. That January the High
Court of Justice in London assessed Sasha's damages against
von Kassel for the eight icons he'd stolen from her at seventy-
five thousand pounds.

Leaving their hotel room at Claridges one day, Marios
deliberately left a hair in his passport. When it was gone on
their return, he went to the American Embassy and reported
that a Cypriot terrorist group was out to get them. Marios
says both his passport and a comb were stolen. When David
K. E. Bruce was told about the incident, he replied, dryly, "I
don't like that about the comb." This meant, Marios
conjectured, that "the old fox" understood immediately that
the theft of the comb was dangerous because it had Marios's
fingerprints on it!

Marios now insisted that the telephone number at Staunton
Hill be changed and unlisted. And indeed there were those in
London like Maria Karantinou who believed that the icon
thieves would kill Sasha before they let her talk; they would
never let her go.

Frightened by Marios into believing that Mark's Trust
could seize her share of Staunton Hill at any moment, Sasha
returned to Virginia to sell her portion of the real estate to her
brother Nicholas. The price was $33,333, what each Bruce
child paid their mother a year earlier. On February tenth she
went to see a Charlottesville lawyer recommended by Wilmington Trust named Leigh Middleditch, Jr. Sasha retained
her share of the contents of the Mansion House. But by now

Marios had convinced her that no assets should be in her name lest the threatened judgment against her in the English courts come through. Back in England, Leighton Davis, her new solicitor at Goodman, Derrick, absolutely disclaimed any liability she might have for the 125,000 pounds stolen from Mark's Trust by von Kassel and let the matter rest.

On February thirteenth, Michael Arpad delivered his appraisal of the contents of Staunton Hill. In Arpad's final summary, the fine arts were evaluated at $667,385, breakables at $86,325, and the furniture at $496,591. The total was $1,163,976, a far cry from the $100,000 at which David Bruce had assessed their value four years earlier.

The quantity of fine eighteenth-century Chippendale alone was prodigious. An American Chippendale chest stood in one of the bathrooms; in the "help's" dining room were an early American Sheraton sideboard and a $2,000 banquet table. One Chippendale chest in Guest Room No. 3 of the New Colonnade was valued at $19,000, while discarded in the cellar sat a set of six Hepplewhite armchairs covered with needlepoint "made by the Huguenots in the French taste"; these were undervalued at $12,000. They had been Ailsa's chairs.

In his own handwriting next to many of the entries in Arpad's book-length appraisal, David K. E. Bruce in pencil marked "undervalued." Certainly this was true of the two paintings by Thomas Sully, one an heirloom portrait of Sarah Seddon Bruce evaluated at $5,000, another, an oil of an Italian water girl listed at $4,500. A European subject by Sully, Marios knew, even an imitation of an Italian painting, would be worth much more than a painting of a member of the family.

On February twenty-fifth, in Marios's absence, Sasha formally conveyed her share of Staunton Hill to her brother Nicholas; the deed was dated February twenty-fourth. Nicky never bothered to have it recorded.

When two days later Marios returned to the United States from Greece, he put the deed away for safekeeping.

After he convinced her that no property should remain in her name, Marios began a campaign to persuade Sasha that "they" should buy Staunton Hill from her two brothers. There was no guarantee that in three years Nicky or David might not want to use the place differently, Marios said. Perhaps they would sell on the condition they could always come for visits.

Late Friday afternoon of March twenty-first, Marios appeared at the Fidelity Bank in Brookneal with a suitcase containing $35,000 in cash in denominations of hundreds and twenties tied with rubber bands. He dumped the cash onto Marie Harper's counter.

"What'd you do, rob a bank?" Marie wisecracked.

"No, we sold a few eggs," Marios returned.

Marie counted the money. Marios deposited it all in his personal checking account. On Monday morning he returned and asked for a cashier's check for thirty-five thousand dollars. Then he and Sasha went to Washington where Marios intended to convert the money back into cash.

But no District of Columbia bank was willing to cash the Brookneal check. Finally they tried the Herndon Bank at Dulles Airport, an affiliate of the Fidelity. The cashier phoned Marie in Brookneal and asked her to describe both Sasha and Marios.

"Does he wear glasses?" Marie was asked.

"Not unless they're sunglasses on top of his head," Marie answered.

There they were—the ubiquitous sunglasses as well as the little mustache and the small physique—everything checked out. Sasha came home. Marios took the money and flew to Europe.

Still no word came from Mark's Trust in reply to Goodman, Derrick's disclaimer of Sasha's liability in von Kassel's scam against Mark's Trust.

On March twenty-sixth, two days after Marios's departure, Sasha borrowed twenty-five thousand dollars from her brother David, promising to repay it at the rate of one percent per month.

"What's the money going to be for?" David wanted to know.

"For some investments we want to make," Sasha replied vaguely.

Not even bothering with a written note, David agreed. The

money was advanced from Wilmington Trust and placed in Marios's brokerage account, for he had begun to do business in stocks through a Lynchburg firm called Anderson & Strudwick.

Now Marios had to get free of Mary, for marriage had become Sasha's obsession. Marios would settle down, everything would change, if only they were married. Marios too was in a great hurry. Aware of how urgently Marios wanted his freedom, Mary decided he could have his divorce—for a price.

Calculating that she was already in her mid-thirties and looking her age, Mary decided her chances for remarriage were remote. In exchange for a quick divorce, since she had always wanted a child, Marios must first make her pregnant!

Marios considered her proposition and was desperate enough to agree, figuring he could explain it all to Sasha later. Meanwhile he told Sasha that his frequent trips first to Athens and then to Maryville, Tennessee, were necessary because there were difficulties about the divorce.

Immediately Mary visited a gynecologist and compiled ovulation charts. Month after month during the winter and spring of 1975 she tried to become pregnant while the divorce and Marios's marriage to Sasha hung in the balance.

On April fifth Sasha paid TWA $773 for a round-trip ticket between Washington, D. C., and Athens. On the twenty-second Marios returned to the United States on his visitor's visa.

April twenty-seventh was his birthday. Sasha drew him a card, a message of yearning expressing the precariousness of her hold on life and her doubts about any future she might share with him. At the edge of a gigantic cliff stands a pretty black and white goat looking out over the sea. White birds fly across the water, beckoning the goat over the edge toward freedom, oblivion, and death. Behind the goat, on the mountainside, is a cave in which another goat sleeps, oblivious of its companion. This is goat-husband, safe in his shelter.

Below on a tranquil beach strewn with flowers sits a plump white rabbit, drawn as big as the she-goat, its back to the sea; it too is safe from harm. Both are unaware of the lonely goat standing at the edge of the cliff poised to jump. Does the she-goat believe husband and bunny will be protected only if she jumps into the swirling waters below? The bunny on the beach may be Mary Lewis, fat and complacent, the unwitting obstacle to the she-goat's survival. The sea is tumultuous, the rocks below a dangerous abyss. The white rabbit gazes in the opposite direction as the male goat sleeps on, indifferent to the she-goat's pain. She threatens to jump should succor not arrive. Was Sasha saying that if Marios failed to relent, the responsibility for her death would be his?

In a world that was flat, Sasha said one day, she and Marios would sail over the edge and return home.

On May first, her twenty-ninth birthday, Sasha wrote a check to The Village Gunshop for $172.71.

That last spring of Sasha's life Carroll Holt took the young couple fishing on the Staunton River. "Damn it, I'm caught," Sasha cried as her hook inevitably snagged on the river bottom. She was no more skillful at fishing than at cooking or knitting or photography, where in every picture she took her finger would appear.

Sasha bought Marios a sailboat and they went fishing for sunfish on Smith Mountain Lake. They also took flying lessons at Lynchburg Airport. On his application for student pilot status dated May 13, 1975, Marios reported he already had three thousand hours of time as a Greek pilot!

Sasha admitted on her application that she was prone to dizziness and fainting spells when she stood up fast. She had low blood pressure, a herniated diaphragm, and an ulcer.

Sasha passed the written test for the permit, but Marios flunked. He explained later that he was an excellent flier, but had only failed the written part. (He bragged, too, that he had a black belt in karate.) They asked their teacher to fly over Staunton Hill and discussed aloft where they would build their private landing strip. Sasha paid for everything.

The local people continued to dislike Marios, while he asserted they were mean-spirited. "You can be condemned just for your accent," he declared. He insisted on being alone with Sasha, driving to Lynchburg, cooking, reading the *One Thousand and One Nights* or the fairy tales of Oscar Wilde. Out in company she carried his cigarettes and would light one for him at his request.

Frantically she continued to seek his approval. One evening Marios glowered at her without comment. She noticed finally that he didn't have a knife at his place setting. At once she raced into the kitchen to correct her error. "He gets upset if everything isn't perfect," she explained to Diane Morris. Back in the dining room, she said apologetically, "Marios wants me to be the perfect hostess. That's all right. I'm learning."

When people couldn't understand Marios's English, Sasha repeated what he said. If someone told a joke, she looked quickly over at him to make sure he was laughing, too. She worried that he wouldn't eat the food her neighbors cooked. "He's a Greek, but he's very Americanized," she explained. "He only likes hot dogs and hamburgers."

At times Marios became loquacious. He told Diane's boyfriend gasoline cost well over a dollar a gallon in Europe, so Americans shouldn't complain. He said he owned a horse ranch with expensive horses on it in Gatlinburg, Tennessee, which he visited once a year, and pastureland with more horses in Greece. When John Mullin, a summer neighbor, was underwriting the Coors Beer Company account, his wife Susan said she had heard enough about Coors Beer to last her a lifetime so persistently did he return to the subject. But Sasha encouraged him. "No, Marios is very interested," Sasha demurred. "Marios is the Fixx beer heir!"

In New York, Marios kept a commodities account with Merrill Lynch, always playing the margin. That summer he installed a telex at Staunton Hill.

At the Mansion House bitter violence raged between Sasha and Marios. "Everything I do is wrong," Sasha screamed. "We have a job to do," Marios says he told her. "How can you help someone if you don't talk things over?" She hated to be told she was wrong and made wild accusations if he had a different opinion about what course they should pursue.

He insisted that Goodman, Derrick were no good. They needed lawyers capable of dealing with von Kassel on his own level. Lord Goodman had too many aristocratic pretensions. But these were her father's lawyers and Sasha wanted to keep them on. If your father would just lift his finger, Marios sneered, curling his lip, he could clear up everything!

He discovered she made a call to someone in Miami about

selling icons and blew up, accusing her of keeping her contacts with the demimonde. He threatened to leave her. He would never marry her. She would never be acceptable to his family. And all the while he was struggling to get Mary pregnant.

The strain of Marios's attempts to isolate her from her family and friends exacerbated Sasha's hysteria as the quarrels continued. She took tranquilizers, fistfuls of Tylenol. She banged her head against the wall in frustration while Marios looked on coolly and said he knew she was deliberately provoking him because in her twisted mind fighting meant reassurance.

He called her a whore because she hadn't been a virgin when he met her. Mary Lewis was a finer person, went the recurrent motif. When, as a result of his calculated taunting, she flew out of control, he hit her, ostensibly to bring her to her senses. She threatened to throw herself down the long curving staircase—architect John E. Johnson's "floating staircase," that glory of Staunton Hill—and thereby end her life. Bruises rose on her skin, welts on her arms. Meanwhile, Marios was teaching her how to use a .22 Walther. "In that area if you don't know how to use a gun, you're considered a freak," he said later as justification.

She was not permitted to call her mother. When she wanted to telephone the Bruces, she had to do it collect and only when Marios was out of the house. Still vicious about her family, he talked of going to Washington himself and making overtures toward her mother. When she said, "I represent everything you despise," he didn't contradict her. She had transferred her need to be forgiven onto Marios; he behaved as if his survival depended upon his punishing her and punish her he did.

One night Sasha was awakened by a sound like the click of a gun. She put on the light. Marios was not in the room. She opened the door to find him in the hallway pointing a gun at *her*. Later she minimized the incident. They had both heard a noise, she said. Marios had reached for the gun.

Frank Clowdis died on Sunday, May eleventh, Mother's Day of 1975. When Sasha heard, she called Marie at once with her condolences. "I'll try to bake a cake and bring it over," she promised. She wanted to see Ethel, too. "I'll be over in a little while," Sasha promised. She never appeared. Marie called Staunton Hill and was told "Sasha has food poisoning."

At eight in the evening, Marios found Sasha in one of the rooms with an empty bottle. She had taken twenty Valium which she found in the cabinet of her father's bedroom.

He bundled her into the car and drove as fast as he could in the direction of Lynchburg. Virginia State Trooper King stopped him for speeding and called Evan Burleigh Vassar at the Gladys, Virginia, rescue squad.

In the ambulance Sasha was semiconscious. "Why did you take pills?" Vassar asked.

"I was having trouble with my husband," Sasha said. Later Marios claimed that on the way to the hospital a delirious Sasha confessed to countless infidelities, occasions on which she had been unfaithful to him in his absence.

At Lynchburg Hospital, Sasha told the attendants, "I want to die. Let me die." Her stomach was pumped. She remained overnight. The doctor, a woman, was required to direct that Sasha have a psychiatric examination, but Sasha refused and managed to persuade the hospital not to record the incident as an attempted suicide. The written report reads only "wanted to sleep, not kill herself." The doctor found Sasha "alert" and "oriented." She made her promise not to overdose again or she would be placed at once under psychiatric observation. They paid the eighty-dollar bill and left that Monday, the twelfth. Marios claims that on the way back to Staunton Hill he suggested they both see a psychiatrist to help them understand themselves better and that Sasha nearly jumped out the car door at the prospect.

A week later Marie Harper spent the night at Staunton Hill with Sasha.

What could you have eaten that gave you food poisoning? Marie wanted to know.

"Marie, it wasn't food poisoning," Sasha said. "I took an overdose. I'd been having problems with Marios."

One night late that spring when Marios was away Sasha had a long talk with her brother Nicky. First she extracted a pledge that he never repeat a word of what she was about to tell him.

Marios knows every way to inflict pain, Nicky later reported Sasha told him. He twists my arm; he burns my flesh with cigarettes; he tortures me. He knows countless ways of making me "scream in pain." So as a Radcliffe freshman Sasha had said that the crimson trees of Vermont made her "scream in disbelief," and later had told David Irons she was making her life with Anton von Kassel because he made her "scream with laughter." The motif of the unanswered scream runs through Sasha's life.

He beats me for not being pure, for not being a virgin, she told Nicky. He's jealous I've been to bed with other men before him; he tortures me to make me tell him every detail of my past. This was the continuous ritual of their life together, Sasha told her brother, Marios extracting from her, by force if necessary, every nuance of her relationships with men before him. If he felt she was holding out on him, he would use any means of extracting the information, even burning her arms with cigarettes.

It was during this talk that she told her brother of her May eleventh suicide attempt.

Like everyone else in Charlotte County, Nicky had known nothing about Mary Lewis. Now Sasha told him about "the other woman" from Tennessee. If we were to get married, she told her brother, Marios might stop being jealous and everything would change for the better. Marios continually threatened to leave her. "I'm going back to Mary Lewis, I like her better than you," he would say. Always he threatened to return to Mary Lewis.

The Mother's Day suicide attempt of course disturbed Nicky and he asked Sasha whether she would ever attempt suicide again. Never with a gun, she replied.

He threatened my life, she now told her brother. He said he could kill me and make it look like suicide. This was his response to what happened on Mother's Day.

Later Nicky would remember her words, "Never with a gun," and wonder if she were worried that this was how Marios would carry out his threat. Was she warning the family that if she were shot, it would not have been by her own hand?

Sasha and Nicky even discussed the possibility that Marios was lying about everything and was just a fortune hunter. Maybe von Kassel himself had set up that meeting between Sasha and Marios in Salonika.

"It couldn't have happened that way," Sasha insisted. They had noticed each other at the wedding. But they wouldn't have seen each other again if Sasha's plane hadn't been fogged in the next day. It was a coincidence that she had to return to the hotel and spend the rest of the day in Salonika. And it was only then that she met Marios again. So she couldn't see how anything could have been set up.

I don't want to live without Marios, Sasha said. If he left me for good, I wouldn't want to live anymore. She had to believe everything Marios told her. It was the last chance she was giving herself. She *had* to believe him.

Nicky decided to leave Staunton Hill as soon as he could without hurting Sasha's feelings. There had been drinking and quarrels. If Sasha took Nicky's side, Marios would lose his temper and accuse her of disloyalty. He made Nicky feel as if he were intruding. Normally reserved, Nick grew despondent and ill at ease. Maybe if I get out, they'll get along better, he thought.

Marriage will change Marios, Sasha kept telling herself. It will make him less jealous. It will allow him to trust me more. On May twenty-fourth Priscilla Jaretzki visited Sasha at Staunton Hill. Marios was away on one of his "business trips."

He's wonderful, Sasha told her godmother. She confided that Marios was very jealous of her and had isolated her from her friends. But she approved. She said Marios didn't want her to wear blue jeans because it was not proper for ladies; she spoke of how they were learning to fly airplanes. They would be married in Greece, but live at Staunton Hill. Sasha would have lots of children. She did not reveal her fear that because she had two abortions, she might not be able to have any. Sasha managed to convince her godmother that she was happy.

On May twenty-eighth Sasha issued a check to Marios's brokerage firm in Lynchburg, Anderson & Strudwick, for stocks in the amount of $9,906.93. They were directed to purchase, in the name of Alexandra Bruce, two hundred shares of Northwest Airlines, one hundred shares of Ford Motor, and three hundred shares of Strother Drug. On June seventh Sasha sent another check, for $9,949.50, to purchase one hundred shares of Heck's, four hundred shares of Johns-Manville, and two hundred shares of Rucker. Then on June seventeenth in a handwritten letter, she ordered Anderson & Strudwick to transfer all these stocks she had purchased to the name of Marios Michaelides. In her letter she included his social security number.

On June ninth Mary conceived her baby.

Diane Morris was graduating from high school that June. Sasha was amazed to find the living room table of the Morris house piled high with gifts. She had no idea that high school graduation is celebrated as a major rite of passage in Charlotte County.

Sasha said she found the custom strange. "Education is for your own benefit," she said. "It's doing you good. Why do people here think you should be given a gift for it?"

Playfully, she then complained about not having been sent one of Diane's announcements. What would Diane like as her present from Sasha?

Diane looked over at her mother. "They were millionaires," Mary Morris would say later, still surprised at having been befriended by Sasha and Nicky, "and we were nothing."

Silently Mary Morris shook her head.

"Nothing," Diane said.

"How about a piece of luggage?" Sasha asked. "I'd love to give you one of mine." But as spring stretched into summer, Sasha's growing problems precluded her remembering Diane's graduation gift.

Sasha continued to place all her hopes in marriage. Marios was so hysterical, she told herself, because he was insecure, uncertain of her, frightened of all the forces that might still separate them. On June twenty-fourth she purchased a dress at Saks in Washington, D. C.

The following day, June twenty-fifth, Marios accompanied her to Wilmington where they called on Vice-President C. H. Hackman and Trust Officer A. Smith of Wilmington Trust. The subject was the status of the trusts of which Sasha was a beneficiary and the amount of income flowing from them.

Marios presented himself as a business tycoon and an expert in the stock market. He literally pounced on Sasha's investment portfolio, scrutinizing every item. Then he began to question the wisdom of some of the stock issues. He noticed one of the companies was an oil concern in Canada which he thought was about to go bankrupt. But when he challenged this investment, he came up against a stone wall. "We're going to stick with an old friend," Marios says the Wilmington people told him.

From his briefcase Marios produced such stock guides as *Standard & Poors*. He attempted to convince Hackman and Smith to invest Sasha's money in some of the issues he preferred. The predecessor trustees selected the investments, undoubtedly with Ambassador Bruce's approval, Marios was told. The selection of investments had been made before Wilmington Trust took over. They let him know his questions were superfluous and could barely contain their annoyance. But Marios had accomplished his end; he had managed to familiarize himself with at least some of the details of Sasha's trust.

On the first of July, Sasha deposited one thousand dollars received from "silver sold to Arpad" in her account, taking advantage of what she called the "*almost* blanket authority her brother Nicky had given her over the contents of Staunton Hill." "I can even at my discretion sell some of the furniture," she had told Marios. Silver had not been mentioned.

The Fourth of July weekend of 1975 found Marios in Tennessee still trying to impregnate Mary, not aware that he had already succeeded. On the fourth, Sasha wrote a check to take care of "Tennessee expenses." She waited impatiently for Marios to get his divorce.

Her friends still had not abandoned Sasha. In July Steve Blodgett began a frantic effort to reach her, calling first Washington and then Virginia. At Staunton Hill a woman answered and told him Sasha was not at home. "I know she's there and I want to talk with her," Blodgett insisted. Feeling like Heathcliff, he called five times. Each time he was told "Sasha isn't going to talk to anyone."

Finally Sasha came to the phone. "I've really screwed up," she said. "I've really messed everything up."

Blodgett would have rushed to Staunton Hill, but visits

from friends were now strictly forbidden as the marriage day drew near.

Sasha purchased Marios's wedding present on July fifteenth, paying $11,207 for a 12-cylinder chocolate brown Jaguar which she registered in her own name. The car was bought from the Bradley Sport Car Center in Richmond. It was a 1974 model bought at a discount and evaluated at $13,331 for insurance purposes. It was insured in the name "Alexandra Bruce" with "Michaelides" appended below.

Marios tried out his new Jaguar driving to a dance in Chase City organized by Susan Mullin's mother. Marios had resisted attending, but at the last minute Sasha called and said "we're gonna go." She wore a silk blouse and a long skirt. On the way home they followed the Mullins along the back roads. But as soon as they reached a point he recognized, Marios pulled out from behind them and sped off.

On July sixteenth in London, where it is possible to declare another party a bankrupt, bankruptcy notices were issued by Sasha against von Kassel. She joined a list of other claimants including a bank called Coutts & Co.; Maruice Walker, a trader in fine fabrics; Harris Nyman & Co., solicitors; Charles Churchill, who had bankrolled the old Grecian Gallery; and the ill-fated Gabriel Michaelides.

On the eighteenth Sasha visited a Richmond gynecologist named Erika N. Blanton. She told Dr. Blanton she was to be married in three weeks. Blanton found a slight vaginal fungus, but nothing else wrong. Sasha requested the birth control pill she had been taking in England and using for years. Dr. Blanton furnished her with a prescription. Another appointment was scheduled for November fifth.

On July twenty-first Sasha and Marios drove to the Clark Brothers Gun Shop in Warrenton where Marios sold a rare L. C. Smith Grade 2 8-gauge double-barreled shotgun (only twenty-eight were ever manufactured) from the Staunton Hill gun collection.

The check for four hundred dollars was made out to Marios alone; he had done all the negotiating.

Earlier he had approached a free-lance gun dealer named

John Stephen Meador about selling him two guns, an 8-gauge double-barreled Baltimore shotgun and the L. C. Smith. On his visit to Meador, Sasha waited outside in the car. Marios explained he wanted to sell these guns so he and his girl friend could have enough money to get married. He promised to return later with the weapons but never did.

The same day he sold the L. C. Smith, Marios and Sasha drove to Charlottesville, that town designed by Thomas Jefferson where even on the hottest days of summer tall shade trees extend shelter. Their appointment was with lawyer Middleditch, who had represented Sasha when she sold her share of the Staunton Hill real estate to Nicky. Was Sasha reminded of her father, who in his book about the first sixteen Presidents had written a description of Jefferson that sounded like a Rembrandtesque self-portrait?—"The man himself, with his complex character, intelligent curiosity, thirst for knowledge, gentleness, charm, serenity of temper, sweetness of affection, and amazing catholicity of interest was more fascinating than his achievements, significant though they were."

Perhaps this was also very close to Sasha's view of David Bruce. Now, having failed her father again, she was too proud, too bitter, and too hurt to come to him and say, I have been mistaken. Meanwhile Marios worked as rapidly as he could.

And so the two of them opened the door to the handsome, well-appointed offices of Leigh Middleditch on East Jefferson Street. On that late July afternoon, Sasha seemed to know exactly what she wanted. She told Middleditch she planned to be married "within a few days." She had already worked out the language of her will.

Middleditch was troubled by the wording upon which Sasha insisted: "Provided I am married to Marios G. Michaelides at the time of my death and he survives me, I give, devise, and bequeath all my tangible personal property to my husband (and wherever in this Will I refer to 'my husband' I mean Marios G. Michaelides)."

Middleditch did not know Sasha well; he had never met Marios before. But such wording was highly unusual and Middleditch felt obliged to advise her against it. It read as if in exchange for the favor of his marrying her, she was to pledge all her assets to her future husband.

Sasha, however, was adamant and Marios himself exerted some pressure. All Middleditch got out of him was his Greek address and citizenship data. Marios did not tell Middleditch he was at that moment still married to Mary Lewis.

Sasha's executor was to be—Marios G. Michaelides, again provided she was married to him. Should he default, his brother, Eugenios G. Michaelides, whom Sasha had never met, would be executor.

Although Marios discussed Sasha's trust funds with Middleditch, the irrevocable trust was not mentioned in Sasha's will. The line of inheritance there had been determined separately, although Marios, believing he was soon to be heir to all of Sasha's property, did not know that.

Between the twenty-first and the thirtieth, when the will was executed, Marios had one more errand to accomplish. He had to divorce Mary.

Mary now says she wasn't sure she was pregnant but agreed anyway, so desperately did Marios plead his case. They tried first for a Tennessee divorce, but learned "incompatibility" was not a ground for immediate divorce in that state. If the ground was that "husband had offered such indignities to wife's person as to render her condition intolerable," this would have resulted only in a 'limited" divorce. Neither would be entitled to remarry until an "absolute" divorce was granted. And time was of the essence.

The Virginia courts were closed to them because there was a six months residence requirement. Adultery *was* a ground for divorce in Virginia, but incompatibility was not; Marios says he was anxious that Sasha not be named as a corespondent in a divorce action a second time. The real point, however, was that remarriage in Virginia would have to be postponed four months.

A Knoxville lawyer advised them to try Haiti. In Alabama, where Mary's brother lived, they found a lawyer named Maurice Bell who specialized in "quickie" Haitian divorces. The ground could be incompatibility.

Mary and Marios arrived in Port-au-Prince on July twenty-fourth. They shared Room 42 at the luxurious El Rancho Hotel in Petionville, tucked twelve hundred feet above the harbor in the Boutillier Mountains. And they registered as

Mr. and Mrs. Michaelides, omitting the "Maryville" portion of their address on two occasions; the registration book reads "211 Mountain View Boulevard, Tennessee, U.S.A." On their arrival, Marios made a collect call to Staunton Hill.

On the twenty-fifth, Mary appeared before a woman magistrate seated in an empty room at a nondescript table. She showed her passport for identification and signed a petition alleging "incompatibility of character." Then the couple returned to their room at the El Rancho. As soon as Mary's back was turned, Marios called Sasha on the telephone.

Pregnant now, Mary was ill for part of the trip. They remained in Haiti until the twenty-seventh. On that day Mary called her parents. But the Lewises were told only that she and Marios had gone on a vacation. Later Mary would say she consented to this "secret divorce" in Haiti "just to please Marios." By then the police had traced all the calls from Haiti to Staunton Hill, adding up the costs along with the Michaelideses' extra meal and beverage charges.

The will was signed on July thirtieth, the same day that Sasha and Marios had their premarital blood tests in Lynchburg.

On August first Sasha and Marios flew to Monterey, California, to visit her brother David. Marios's objective was to persuade the brothers to sell their shares of Staunton Hill. But secretly he continued to insist to Sasha that it was dangerous for any assets to remain in her name. Nicky would be easy to manage, Marios thought. It was David he had to convince.

Almost from the moment they saw David, the conversation was about Staunton Hill and why it would be wise for the brothers to sell their interests in the place to Marios and Sasha.

David resisted, but finally felt he could not refuse his sister. It would have been too selfish. The place was so important to her and he didn't care much for it at the time at all.

David raised the issue of the twenty-five thousand dollar loan he had made Sasha in March. Had the money been well invested? He did not immediately mention that she hadn't begun to pay him back, although she'd promised she would.

"Yes," Sasha said. "It's making some money for us. I'm sorry we haven't started paying you back yet, but we will very soon." She offered no details about how the money had been invested. David still believed the money had been invested in her name.

Back in Brookneal, Sasha told her friends, "I couldn't stand the fussing and the arguments. It was a mistake to go." But she didn't blame Marios.

On August fifth Marios wrote a letter to Anderson & Strudwick in which he directed that all the shares which had been transferred from Sasha's name to his in June now be *registered* in his name as well. That same day an important visitor arrived at Staunton Hill. It was Stephen Massey, a dapper young Englishman, head of the new rare book division of Christie's in New York. Sasha had written to him of her wish to put up for auction some of the most valuable items in her father's rare book collection. She didn't tell Massey that the books were owned *jointly* and in an *undivided interest* by herself, David, and Nicky.

On the afternoon of Tuesday, the fifth, Massey arrived to appraise the books. When he departed on the afternoon of August seventh, he was under the impression that Sasha was in high spirits. He knew she was to be married in a few days.

On August sixth, while Massey was going over David Bruce's rare book collection, Marios arranged for a loan of fifteen thousand dollars from the Fidelity Bank in Brookneal, which he secured with his Rucker and Fabergé stocks. The money was deposited in his account the following day. Sasha guaranteed the loan repayment and prepaid the interest of $230.70.

They were married on August eighth in a civil ceremony at Charlotte Courthouse. None of Sasha's friends attended, neither Marie Harper nor old friends like Maeve Kinkead. Only a few weeks earlier Maeve had called to ask if Sasha had set a date for the wedding. Sasha sounded as if she were in trouble; her gamble was turning out badly. Maeve asked what was going on.

"I'm just leading a simple life," Sasha said.

"Sasha, are you all right?" Maeve asked.

"I'm fine."

Although Sasha didn't forbid Maeve to attend the wedding, she said nothing about an invitation. There was a long pause. Then Maeve said, "I hope the day of your wedding is as beautiful as you are."

Maeve decided to wait until Christmas before seeing Sasha. It appeared Sasha was now trying desperately to bring Marios and the Bruces together. Her message to her friends seemed to be: "If you care for me, stay away."

Originally they had considered a Greek Orthodox Church in Lynchburg for the wedding. At that time David and Evangeline Bruce were vacationing at the Mas d'Artigny in St.-Paul-de-Vence. When Sasha told her father she was sorry he couldn't be present, Marios says David Bruce quipped, "Never mind. I'll come to your next wedding." They had also considered having the ceremony on board the *Queen Elizabeth II* on which they were sailing on their honeymoon, taking the chocolate brown Jaguar with them. According to Mrs. Bruce, she was to go to Staunton Hill in August for the civil ceremony. However, Marios advanced it by a week, insisting it take place before Mrs. Bruce could arrive.

The ceremony was performed by old Edwin Hoy, clerk of the court of Charlotte Courthouse, in a building said to have been designed by Thomas Jefferson. Marios produced a copy of his divorce decree from Mary, which was in French. Deputy clerk Vernia Keller at first thought it was Spanish. Sasha had to do the translating.

As she left Brookneal for her honeymoon, Sasha promised her friends she would return for Christmas. Then they would celebrate traditionally, traveling from house to house for all the courses of Christmas Eve supper. She arranged for the Bradleys and their daughter Daphne Piester to do the books and keep Staunton Hill going in her absence. They would visit Marios's family in Athens, remaining in Europe for three months.

Marios drove the chocolate brown Jaguar to New York without incident. They stayed at the Plaza Hotel. A day or two before the *Queen Elizabeth II* was to sail, they visited the Totteridge Bookshop on Madison Avenue which specialized in rare books.

In the absence of the owner, Oliver Twigg, they were greeted by his assistant, Alan Feuer. The "shop" was one small elegant room on the third floor of a twelve-story building housing other book dealers as well. Feuer sat at a desk in front of a window draped in crimson velvet. Marios and Sasha were seated in front of him on two small Queen Anne armchairs. Sasha's chair was so angled, however, that she half-faced Marios. She looked at him as often during the conversation as she did at Feuer. The pale yellow walls were lined with old and seasoned books in rich bindings. The floor was covered by an Oriental rug.

In so expensive an environment Sasha and Marios seemed out of place. He wore a Lacoste-type pullover, she a gray skirt and blouse. Both looked rumpled. Feuer took note of their thin gold wedding rings. It was only when Marios began to describe "their" book collection in detail that Feuer realized he was in the presence of people of means.

Greeks come in two varieties, Feuer thought, wretched and poor or very rich. Michaelides must be the second son of a rich Greek family, he decided. Tall and flat-chested, Sasha seemed definitely unimpressive. It did not enter Feuer's head that hers was the wealthy family who owned the rare books. As a special military liaison for the American Air Force in London in the sixties, Feuer had once been entertained at the American Embassy. He did not recognize Sasha as Ambassador Bruce's daughter.

Marios did all the talking. Occasionally he turned to Sasha for confirmation of a detail and then she would back him up, no matter what he claimed. He did not know the books well enough to be specific; Sasha was better able to recall the titles. But Marios knew enough to tell Feuer he was considering disposing of complete first editions of Gould's bird books.

Feuer sat up straighter. The Gould bird books, he knew, were worth between fifteen and twenty-five thousand dollars a set at auction.

"Are the books in New York?" Feuer asked.

"No," Marios answered. "They're in Virginia."

"Would some sort of fee arrangement be acceptable?" Feuer wanted to know. He was well aware that his employer, Oliver Twigg, could not afford to purchase such books outright. Marios said yes. The books could be taken on consignment.

He spoke of "we" and "our," not of "my" library as he went on to explain that there were in fact *two* libraries. They had so many duplicates they wanted to sell because an *uncle* had also collected books.

A Letter from Italy

Feuer's suspicions still were not aroused. It wasn't unusual for rare book collectors to have two copies of a book, or even of a first edition; at one time J. P. Morgan had owned three copies of the Gutenberg Bible.

Feuer said Twigg had to appraise the books, and that he could come to Virginia. Perhaps they could find a client who would buy certain books right off. Marios and Sasha stayed and chatted for an hour, seeming to Feuer like an old married couple, no longer particularly intimate. They did not mention Stephen Massey's visit. Marios left his name and the telephone number at Staunton Hill. They were off to Greece now, but would call on their return.

"Goat needs husband more than husband needs goat and goat will prove it one day," Sasha wrote in a note to Marios aboard the *Queen Elizabeth II* which sailed for France on August twelfth. She had been delighted when Marios informed the ship's staff that he would be bringing his pet goat on board with him. Dutifully they had mailed out literature describing the regulations for keeping a pet in your cabin.

Her wedding ring had been inscribed "Marios 8–8–75," and her hope remained that marriage would transform Marios. Now she dedicated herself to convincing him that she truly loved him and that he need fear nothing from her desire to be reunited with her parents.

The honeymoon was disastrous from the start. Either at the Plaza, or as their luggage was being handled by dock personnel, Sasha's jewelry was stolen, including a ring given to her by her mother. They notified the ship's officer as well as the insurance company that handled the Staunton Hill policies. But the jewelry had not been insured.

Aboard the *Queen Elizabeth II*, Marios told Sasha that

Mary was pregnant. She was hurt that he hadn't told her as soon as he knew. To have told her on her honeymoon seemed a calculated push toward the edge; Sasha could scarcely have been heartened that the "other woman" who is "better than you" had become pregnant with her new husband's child. Mary later thought Sasha need never have found out, so reduced were her resources of information, so completely had Marios cut her off from everyone.

They landed in Cherbourg on the seventeenth of August. At four in the morning on the eighteenth, Marios was driving the Jaguar in Châtillon-de-Michaeille. Passing a truck on a curve, he moved into the left lane as a Fiat suddenly appeared right in front of him traveling in his direction. Marios slammed into the Fiat. Both cars were totaled, although luckily no one was seriously hurt.

Sasha and Marios proceeded to the Hotel de la Paix in Geneva where she tried to activate her insurance company to send money to replace the Jaguar at once. She signed the accident reports "Alexandra Michaelides-Bruce," since she was the policy holder. She said she had paid thirteen thousand dollars for the Jaguar, nearly two thousand dollars more than the actual figure.

Until she was paid, Sasha bombarded the insurance company in New York with daily calls. She demanded cash, insisting the trip would be held up until a replacement car was purchased. She needed cash because she had no banking connections in Switzerland. No mention was made of Marios's Zurich account, although on August twenty-first he called the Fidelity Bank in Brookneal and had $10,007.80 cabled to his Swiss bank account.

Finally Winterthur Accident & Casualty paid her $12,500. In court Marios was fined 250 francs. Then on August twenty-ninth, a Jaguar XJ6 was purchased through British Leyland in London for about $9,000. Registered in Sasha's maiden name, it was delivered to the couple directly at the Hotel de la Paix. The car was serviced in Athens on September twentieth.

The original plan of driving through France and Italy and then ferrying to Athens had been interrupted by the accident. A mood of doom prevailed, although Marios would later insist there were some high moments. In Geneva, he says, an Iranian student asked to buy them a drink. "I can't tell if you're husband and wife, or lovers, if you just met or know each other a thousand years,'' the man said. At which point Marios bought the drinks. In Zurich, someone heard Sasha ask Marios for a cigarette and said "Let me hear you do that again."

But in Greece Sasha was miserably unhappy. Marios continued to lie, saying his mother did not approve of her because she knew they slept together before they were married. He kept her segregated in a luxurious $1,500-a-month apartment he rented on a one-year lease next to the Royal Palace. Sasha had carried many books and objects with her on the ship, planning to set up a real home in Greece and she tried to decorate the rented flat. But very soon it became a virtual prison to which she was in effect confined all day.

He would leave in the morning for his mysterious "work," returning late in the afternoons when they'd do their marketing. They'd eat dinner at home. Sasha's disgraceful past life still made it impossible for him to introduce her to his family, he said. The business in England so embarrassed him that she couldn't meet his friends either. Frequently Sasha begged Marios to stay home, saying she was afraid to be by herself.

Returning to America, Sasha was more despondent than she had ever been. She begged Marios to believe she was worthy of his trust, that she was his completely. He must protect her against the chill of her own doubts. All she wanted, Sasha pleaded as the honeymoon drew to its close, was to follow him everywhere. If only he would accept her, she would be the wife he wanted. If he would stay with her, she would not disappoint him.

But the marriage had changed nothing. Still he withheld himself and punished her while she struggled for his love. She flattered him. He was worthy and good, he was "ruler of all her wishes and desires," and still it was not enough. She begged for his protection, she a small dumb goat whom he must crush, press against himself. If he would put her in his pocket and keep her close to him, she would be content.

Far away from him, Sasha said, and she meant it, there would be no air to breathe, no life to live. If she wanted to live at all, it was because of him. Life was wonderful, Sasha cajoled him, only when a small and dumb goat was loved by an adored master. She lived and breathed with one thought in mind: to love and be loved by her glorious husband. She was the happiest wife in the world, Sasha insisted on that return trip, whenever Marios took her in his arms. This little goat, she said, has found all the answers to life in her husband. He must not be jealous. She found only him interesting. She was a true, loving wife. He must not doubt her.

In London process servers were unable to serve von Kassel with the bankruptcy notices issued by Sasha's lawyers on her behalf in July. On September twelfth, while she was in Greece, an order for substituted service was granted. The bankruptcy notices stated that unless von Kassel paid Alexandra Bruce what he owed her within seven days, she was entitled to declare him a bankrupt. Since there was no imprisonment for debts in the United Kingdom, all she could do was prosecute him for having obtained pecuniary advantage by deception.

Von Kassel finally received Sasha's bankruptcy notices in September. Jailhouse lawyer that he was, he at once had a summons issued to set aside these judgments and to enter appearances, a clever delaying tactic. His summons was scheduled to be heard on November seventeenth.

Sasha's grim mood was unmistakable to those who knew her when she returned to Staunton Hill from Greece in early October, having cut her honeymoon short. Believing she had been rejected by Marios's family, she was now determined to be reunited with her own. A proper church wedding in the presence of David and Evangeline Bruce might give her marriage meaning and break the isolation under which she suffered.

Delighted, the Bruces agreed to give Sasha a wedding in Washington on the fifteenth of October. Sasha proposed that the ceremony take place in the little chapel at St. John's, where she had been confirmed. Marios pretended to be in favor of the idea. He told her the long white bridal gown would be symbolic of her purification, a new beginning. At last she was at the point of being liberated from the degradation of the London episode.

Only the immediate family were invited. Mrs. Bruce wrote to the guardian of the Currier children, requesting his help in rounding them up for the ceremony. Somehow they weren't available. Neither was David Surtees, who was too far away.

Arrangements were made with a florist and a caterer. The wedding gift from the Bruces to Sasha and Marios would be the very grand service of crested silver purchased by David Bruce's mother, Louise Este Fisher Bruce, in Europe at the turn of the century.

On the evening of the fourteenth, the family gathered at a restaurant for a prenuptial rehearsal dinner. According to Marios, there was a small dispute at the table about some wedding detail. Sasha wanted it one way, Mrs. Bruce another. Sasha wished her father would support her in her objection, but, typically, he didn't. Marios claims Mrs. Bruce offered Marios and Sasha the money to purchase Staunton Hill. Since her son David was ungenerous and likely to strike a hard bargain, Mrs. Bruce is supposed to have said, she and the ambassador wanted to help. Marios says he refused. He would find the money on his own.

Mrs. Bruce says the only talk of Staunton Hill occurred when Marios invited her to come and stay anytime.

While David Bruce and Mrs. Bruce's cousin, Paule d'Oberndorff, chatted about wines, Mrs. Bruce turned and said, "Marios, it's just one thing that bothers me that I really do want to take up with you. Why didn't you let Sasha meet your family in Athens? I think the situation is terrible for her."

"I don't wish to discuss it," he said quickly. He must have been enraged that Sasha had betrayed him, informing her mother of the intimate details of their life together.

Nicky had arrived from Staunton Hill with Elizabeth Hamlett, bringing the mail, which included a letter to Sasha from her aunt in Italy that was strongly critical of her behavior toward her mother. According to Marios, it attacked both Sasha and Marios for criticizing Mrs. Bruce after she had sent Sasha to the best schools and made every effort to raise her in a warm, loving family. Marios claims the letter said that Sasha was no better than "a common whore." She had brought shame and dishonor on them all. The letter is also said to have accused Marios of turning Sasha against Evangeline.

"We all know what Marios has done for me. There is no one who is going to attack my husband," Marios claims Sasha said.

Sasha's aunt had also written that she would have given Sasha her own bridal dress if she thought her niece was entitled to wear white. According to Marios, in Sasha's hearing, Mrs. Bruce agreed with the spirit of this criticism, indicating she was upset that Sasha had decided to wear a white bridal gown for the wedding, because after all, she was not a virgin.

Marios says he replied, "I don't want to listen to this. I promised my wife I would marry her in a white dress, and I will."

According to Mrs. Bruce today, there was no such altercation about Sasha's wedding dress. Nor was there anything that should have been upsetting to Sasha in the letter. It was decided at the dinner that Sasha should go out the following day and buy a wedding dress, which she did.

In any case, there was a white silk wedding gown with a long lace train and lace trimming on the front and bottom. Sasha wore it to the grave.

Marios contends Sasha was devastated at being told she did not deserve to wear a white dress. Maeve Kinkead says Sasha was always driven to the worst of her impulses when her mother became judgmental. Now she was told it would be better if she were to wear a suit to her wedding. It was Sasha's family, Marios insists, who would not allow her to forget her criminal days with von Kassel and the icon demimonde.

In their room at the Bruce mansion, according to Marios, Sasha became hysterical as her hopes for a happy resolution of the antagonism between Marios and the Bruces were dashed. She screamed and Marios hit her hard across the face, "slung her," in his words. He had found his excuse. "There isn't any point staying in this house," he said. "I'm not going to put up with this. We're getting out of here."

Sasha wrote a note to her father in which she said she feared Marios wouldn't be able to take much more. She slipped it under his bedroom door, enclosing the offending letter from her aunt. At two in the morning Marios dragged her out of the house, both of them vowing never to return. There would be no religious ceremony, no rapprochement with the family.

"I'm not going to have any more contact with Mummy," Sasha told friends on her return to Staunton Hill. "It's terrible." Both her parents and Marios had turned on her. She had never felt more alone. It seemed to make Marios very nervous that Sasha blamed him in part for the break with her family and this upset her even more. She became alternately depressed and angry. The warfare between them accelerated.

On October fifteenth, the day the formal religious ceremony was to have occurred, Sasha was spotted in blue jeans with Marios leaving a movie theater. The film was *Once Is Not Enough*.

The Bruces sent the heirloom silver on to Staunton Hill in the custody of Nick. It was to be the last time he would see Sasha and Marios together. Nick watched as they played a strange, chilling game. With an eerie smile on her face, Sasha kept asking Marios what he had done with the gun, the automatic she usually kept in her room for protection. What have you done with the gun? What have you done with the gun? Sasha chanted. Where have you hidden it? Then they both laughed. Later Nick would wonder whether he'd been treated to a dress rehearsal of the last hour of Sasha's conscious life.

Marios now began to organize the purchase in his own name first of the Staunton Hill real estate and then of the furnishings and fine art. On October twentieth he made Sasha ask Leigh Middleditch to work on deeds and promissory notes. Staunton Hill was to be solely in Marios's name to avoid her assets being attached, although as Marios himself would later admit to the police, they had stopped making payments on her London indebtedness several months before, and since the previous February Mark's Trust had been silent about their claim against her. No doubt he planned to pay off the promissory notes out of the big inheritance coming to Sasha on her thirtieth birthday in May. The price was to be $105,000. On October twentieth an eight-minute call was made from Staunton Hill to Wilmington Trust Company. It seems that Sasha was even trying to arrange for Wilmington Trust to divert a portion of her trust directly to Marios after a period of time, making him a beneficiary in his own right. Late that night a call was placed to David Surtees Bruce in Seattle which lasted ten minutes. Middleditch proceeded to draw up the papers.

Even as she engineered this exchange of the Bruce children's ancestral home to Marios, Sasha withdrew from him, becoming secretive, evasive, and confiding little. Without telling Marios she gave away all her best clothes in late October, loading down the maid Emma Elam with pant suits, dresses, shoes, pocketbooks, and jewelry for her daughter. Twice Sasha visited Dr. John Campbell in Brookneal. Once she complained she had a hernia and asked for a B-12 shot to relieve her pain. She told Dr. Campbell she couldn't fall asleep at night. He prescribed a mild sedative which she had refilled once at the Brookneal Drug Company.

Those who knew her found her actions increasingly erratic. The Carter family had occupied a Staunton Hill tenant cottage rent-free for nearly twenty-five years. Now Sasha told them they would have to pay over two hundred dollars a month. When Mike Carter told her they couldn't afford it and would have to move, she became very upset.

Late in October Sasha appeared on the streets of Brookneal with the first of two black eyes. To explain this one, she told Marie Harper she'd fallen down the stairs.

Meanwhile, Marios redoubled his efforts to enrich himself. He telephoned Oliver Twigg in New York, inviting him to Staunton Hill to appraise the books. Cautiously Twigg said he could take such expensive books only on consignment. Marios rambled on about color plate natural history books, complete sets of Gould, complete runs of the Golden Cockerel, Nonesuch Press, and Ashendene Press books, and rare editions of *Gulliver's Travels* and *The Canterbury Tales*. From a collection of twenty-five thousand volumes, he wished to dispose of ten thousand.

"I'll drive down with my wife some weekend," Twigg said.

A few days later Marios called again. "We're in a hurry," he said. "Could you come down on Thursday, November sixth? You'll have to fly because we're leaving for Greece. We have no free weekend. We're expecting people both the weekend before and the weekend after."

Twigg wasn't the only book dealer Marios called. On October thirtieth, Stephen Massey made his second appearance at Staunton Hill. Rare books had been his obsession since he was eighteen and he was fascinated by the Staunton Hill collection. Decorous and circumspect, he asked few questions. Sasha had originally represented that she was the owner and Massey was too interested in the books to think anything about it.

As he organized them for sale at auction, Massey couldn't have known the importance not only of these particular books, but of libraries in general to the Bruce family. The Baltimore house in which the ambassador grew up had three libraries, one for the children. David Bruce read *The Iliad* at age seven, beginning *The Odyssey* as soon as he was done, then going on to Macaulay's *Ode to Horatius*. At eight he instructed his mother visiting Boston to bring him some good books, having discovered nothing would please her more. At twenty, he begged his father not to part with his Baltimore library since he wished to consolidate it with the collection at Staunton Hill.

"Be sure to exempt the books!" he ordered his parents when he heard Staunton Hill was to be sold. And in the late 1930s and early 1940s he donated libraries to ten poverty-stricken rural Virginia counties. They were financed by Ailsa'a Avalon Foundation, except for the one in Charlotte County which was his personal gift. He once remarked that libraries were "one of the few institutions that never did anybody any harm."

In the Staunton Hill drawing room Massey may have paused before the oil painting of the first Bruce to come to America, attired in Charles II dress heavily adorned with lace. This ancestor had come from Scotland as a tutor and a learned man to serve as secretary to Governor Spottiswoode of Virginia, Bruce told his children; his purpose had been to teach Virginians to read and write and hate the English! Two centuries later three of Charles Bruce's sons became authors; his son-in-law Thomas Nelson Page, famous for *In Ole Virginia*, wrote many stories while he lived at Staunton Hill.

It was the library of a man who had loved books all his life, one redolent of Bruce tradition, that Stephen Massey now began to dismantle.

Massey observed that while Sasha had seemed in high spirits in August, now she was troubled and tired. He played Ping-Pong with Marios, whom he rather liked. On Saturday afternoon, November first, Sasha was absent. Marios claims he and Massey went to Lynchburg to rent a car at the airport. When they returned, Sasha was nowhere to be found. After Ping-Pong, Marios searched again for Sasha. He expected her to be in the library, but instead she was upstairs sleeping. Beside her was a suicide note. He had difficulty in waking her and thought she must have taken ten sleeping pills, which she had obtained from her Brookneal doctor. He claims he dragged her to the bathroom and forced her to drink a lot of water in an effort to flush the overdose of pills from her system. He says Massey witnessed this. Massey denies it, pointing out that he would hardly have been privy to such an intimate scene. Marios also says Sasha flung herself down the staircase that weekend—one of his explanations of how she got her black eye—but this did not happen in Massey's presence.

According to Massey, Sasha came downstairs late in the afternoon on Saturday and said she had taken a sleeping pill because she'd had a sleepless night. She was drowsy, but the three prepared dinner together. The talk was of London and of books. Massey noted that Marios loved Staunton Hill.

It was after Sasha tried suicide on that first weekend of November, Marios says, that he hid the .22 Walther under his bed.

By six o'clock Sunday morning, the second of November, Massey had loaded his rented station wagon with the finest volumes in David Bruce's collection and was on the road. He didn't see Sasha that day at all. No written contract had been drawn up. For insurance purposes the books Massey took with him were valued at $44,930. They included a nine-volume folio of *English Caricatures* evaluated at $8,000 and an Audubon and Bachman *Quadrupeds of North America* ($1,500). There were two volumes of Bodoni's *Manuale Tipografico* worth $2,600. But the gems were Elliot's *Birds of North America* ($7,000) and Elliot's *Family of the Grouse* ($8,500)—and a Gould *Birds of Great Britain* in five volumes, alone estimated at $15,000.

Sasha waited that Sunday for a moment when Marios was out of the house. Then she opened her address book and dialed the number of Mary Lewis Michaelides in Maryville, Tennessee. They had never met, although once Mary had caught a glimpse of Sasha at the Athens airport. By now Sasha knew that Mary was five months pregnant with Marios's child.

Her tone was apologetic. She spoke so softly that at first Mary couldn't hear her at all. But there was an obvious note of desperation in her voice. Mary wondered whether Sasha was calling because she had found out about her pregnancy.

"I'm sorry to bother you, Mary," Sasha said. "But I feel that Marios is so unhappy here. I was wondering if you could invite him to Tennessee for a while. He's so unhappy. Maybe he could stay with you until he settles down."

"What's the trouble?" Mary asked. At that moment she felt genuinely sorry for Sasha.

"He just doesn't seem to be very happy."

Sasha would neither explain nor beg. She must have known it was dangerously treasonous for her to be calling Mary at all. Knowing Marios, Mary must understand how drastic a step this was.

"I'll try," Mary promised. "But it will depend on Marios." She wondered if she was about to get her husband back, if her baby would have a father after all.

Mary had more questions, but then her mother came into the room. Mary still had not told Mrs. Lewis that she had divorced Marios that past July, let alone that he had remarried. Abruptly she ended the conversation.

The last week of her life Sasha stayed out of Brookneal. There was a fresh black eye. She told Elizabeth that she had fallen down the stairs. Elizabeth was convinced that if she had, Marios had pushed her. By now Elizabeth hated Marios. He was just there to get everything Sasha owned, to beat her out of all her money. He was out to get what he could.

On Monday, the third, Sasha canceled Wes Profit's impending visit about which Marios had known nothing. When she invoked her "problems," Wes knew that meant her separation from her parents and what had happened in Washington at the aborted second wedding. It was the old trouble. She still wanted rapprochement while Marios kept pressing her to cut all ties.

Sasha visited Meg Tibbs's cottage on Tuesday, November fourth, looking for particular books of historical interest among the nearly one thousand stored there and belonging to the Staunton Hill library. It was then that Meg asked her about the black eye and Sasha gave the explanation of a gun having kicked back while she was out on the shooting range.

*   *   *

On the same day Sasha called Middleditch again. Now she requested that he arrange the conveyance of the personal property at Staunton Hill from herself and her brothers to Marios. Marios would own not only the real estate, but the furnishings of the Mansion House which Michael Arpad had estimated at $1,163,976. Concealing the Arpad appraisal from Sasha's brothers, Marios proposed to pay $40,000 for each of the children's one-third interests, abiding by the old $100,000 appraisal, the figure David K. E. Bruce had used only five years earlier when he gave the contents of Staunton Hill undivided as a gift to his three children.

To convey the real estate was simple. But although Middleditch did not challenge the $120,000 figure, he was concerned that he lacked a tax base for the furniture and contents. He thought he'd better obtain this information from Ambassador Bruce or Wilmington Trust before going ahead. Sasha pressured him to get this information as quickly as he could. That night of the fourth of November she called her brother David in Seattle, pushing vigorously to persuade him to convey his share of Staunton Hill to Marios.

At 3:50 P.M. on this Wednesday the fourth, Sasha also called her brother Nicholas in Portland. They spoke for twenty-six minutes. She sounded terrible.

"What's wrong? Why do you sound so bad?" Nicky asked his sister.

Sasha told him she had taken pills again. Nicky let it pass, thinking Sasha meant she had taken some aspirin for one of her headaches.

"Nothing's changed," Sasha told her brother. To Nicholas this meant Marios was still beating her, still trying to extract details of her past love affairs, still threatening to go back to Mary Lewis. Nicky didn't know what to do. Marios frightened him sometimes. But now he was far away. Like Mary Lewis, he could do no more than register the urgency, the cry for help in Sasha's call. It was confusing since all the while Sasha was urging him to go forward with the plan to sell Staunton Hill to Marios.

Still that same day, the fourth of November, Sasha received a call from her godmother Priscilla, who was in North Carolina with her companion Rainer Esslen. Priscilla suggested that Sasha and Marios meet them in Richmond for dinner on Thursday night. Sasha said they had a prior commitment.

Perhaps then she saw what she had to do. She would invite them to Staunton Hill for the weekend and so once and for all break her forced isolation. She loved her godmother. It may have seemed that fate had provided her with someone to help her in this hour of trouble and confusion. Priscilla could provide a bridge back to her mother and the world she had lost.

The deeds transferring Staunton Hall from Nicholas and David to Marios were dated by Middleditch November first. He would pay Nick $69,900 with 8 percent interest, due on June 1, 1976, a month after Sasha's thirtieth birthday. David would get $34,900. Meanwhile Marios would mail the draft deed and a check for one hundred dollars to each of the brothers. They were to sign the deed, have it notarized, and return it to Leigh Middleditch. Once Marios signed the notes, the deeds would be recorded at the Clerk's Office in Charlotte County.

David Surtees Bruce later said he thought they were selling Staunton Hill to both Sasha and Marios, but the language of the deeds and the correspondence is unmistakable. Perhaps the brothers had accepted Marios's claim that given the troubles in England, it was best that no property be in Sasha's name. They did express concern that Marios might turn around and sell Staunton Hill right away. Marios then agreed on a buy-back provision, granting them an option to repurchase provided they pay for improvements and operation of the property to be determined by a certified public accountant hired by him. He said nothing about the property being owned by himself and Sasha together some time in the future.

On the fifth of November, Sasha herself called John Herdig, who was in charge of the trust department at Wilmington Trust and was also counsel for the bank. She asked him how to establish the valuation basis for the furnishings. He told her he'd have to call her back. But when he did, Marios grabbed the phone and said he'd take the message. Herdig told Marios that Wilmington Trust didn't have a tax-base figure to assist in structuring the sale of the contents of Staunton Hill from the Bruce children to him.

Worried, Middleditch wrote to David K. E. Bruce in Brussels on the same day. He said he was writing at Sasha's request. She had instructed him to prepare various instruments conveying Staunton Hill to Marios alone because of the possible impact of the pending English writ, the judgment against Sasha supposedly about to be won by Mark's Trust. Middleditch repeated the notion that it was wise that no property remain in Sasha's name. Then he raised the question of transferring the property from the Bruce children to Marios. What was the tax impact of such a transaction? Would they realize taxable income? He needed to know the basis of David Bruce's original decision to evaluate this property at one hundred thousand dollars.

Middleditch urged the ambassador to hurry with his answer. Alexandra and Marios had extensive travel plans. It would be helpful to them if he could forward this information before their departure for Greece at the end of November.

David Surtees called Marios and told him he and Nicholas wanted to show the papers he had sent them to a lawyer in Seattle. They had decided to sell, but were going to make sure it was legal first.

Mike Carter stopped Sasha on the Staunton Hill grounds on November fifth and told her his grandmother had said she wasn't going to move unless Sasha herself told her to do so. Sasha became distressed. Mrs. Carter loved the Bruce family. Sasha knew she could never tell old Mrs. Carter to leave. Mike himself was sure the demand for such exorbitant rent could only have come from Marios.

That night the telephone rang at Mountain Hermitage in the Great Smokies. Mary Frye answered. There was no voice at the other end, an unlikely occurrence in that rural outpost. Later the Fryes would wonder: could it have been Sasha in search of Stan, pleading for help, struggling to stay alive?

All that last week Elizabeth watched sadly as Sasha settled into the deepest of her depressions.

On the sixth of November, Stephen Massey drew up his summary of the books he had taken from Staunton Hill together with their insurance prices. He listed the owner of the books as Mr. Marios Michaelides, his address: Meleagrou II, Athens TT 138, Greece. That same day Marios borrowed fifteen thousand dollars from the Brookneal branch of the Fidelity Bank. The loan was guaranteed by Sasha.

Thursday the sixth was Emma Elam's day to clean house at Staunton Hill. When Emma arrived, only Sasha was at home. Emma looked at Sasha and her heart sank. She forced herself to look again at the dark, blue-black bruise around Sasha's eye. All day Sasha kept pulling her sunglasses on and off. Sometimes she'd attempt to conceal it. At others she'd defiantly flaunt it for all to see. When she passed the ornate Victorian mirrors in the downstairs hall, she'd pause and examine her black eye. Emma pretended not to notice for fear of hurting Sasha's feelings. She waited for Sasha to mention it. But she didn't.

Sasha was even more nervous than usual today, even giddy, Emma thought. She was always high-strung, but usually she was cheerful. She liked to help Emma with her tasks, even with the ironing. Emma sometimes thought she was memorizing how to keep house.

But today Sasha was somber, preoccupied. Together they made up one of the guest rooms. Their guest would be staying the night, Sasha said. Then she disappeared and didn't help Emma anymore.

Mid-morning Marios met Oliver Twigg at Lynchburg Airport. Twigg didn't understand the nervously belligerent man sitting beside him in the car. He knew only that he didn't like him.

Marios told Twigg a telex had been installed at Staunton Hill so he could get stock market reports. He mentioned his father and brother.

"What business are they in?" Twigg asked politely.

"Investments," Marios said.

He drove very fast. "I don't have to worry about speeding tickets," he bragged. "The sheriff knows me and my family. My father-in-law is very well known in the area."

Twigg had no idea of the identity of the father-in-law.

"My father-in-law is quite influential," Marios went on. "He has two places around here. I bought Staunton Hill from my wife's family and he lives on the other property. It's similar in size but with a smaller house."

They entered the long approach to Staunton Hill. Twigg

noticed that many trees had been hacked down, leaving a barren, butchered field.

"It's one of the improvements we're making," Marios explained. He called the work "landscaping." "We have more than ten thousand acres of woods."*

They reached the circular driveway and the Mansion House. In the yard a handyman was talking with a tall, slender young woman with thick, unruly black hair and a dusky rose complexion. She wore trousers and a sweater. When Marios introduced them, Sasha said hello quietly. Twigg blanched as he saw the pronounced blue-black bruise in the center of the socket of the young woman's left eye. Relatively fresh, he thought. But she was beautiful anyway. He admired her long, elegant hands which seemed to go on forever.

Twigg stood holding his briefcase, the only luggage he had brought since Marios had told him he wouldn't be remaining overnight.

"I'll show you to your room," Sasha offered sweetly. "Do you want to get your suitcase out of the trunk?"

"I haven't been invited to stay for two days," Twigg said stiffly. He was annoyed. It would be a grueling day followed by the 7:06 flight back to LaGuardia.

"If anyone comes all the way down here, I'd think they'd spend the night," Sasha said, as if it were Twigg's fault.

"Well, it hasn't been offered," he answered, "so I'm going back tonight." His English reserve prevented him from saying more.

As she served him coffee in the living room, Sasha laughed merrily and didn't seem self-conscious at all about her black eye. Twigg admired the room, the painting of a greyhound and setter by François Desport, the Chinese export hunting bowl, and other works of art.

"Staunton Hill is a trust house," Marios said proudly. "It can never be torn down."

He demonstrated that he knew a great deal about the value of David Bruce's books, even those worth only a few hundred dollars. Twigg asked him where he'd learned so much about rare books.

"I haven't been doing much else in the last few months,"

---

*The estate at the time consisted of 273.3 acres.

Marios said. "I got some catalogues, looked up auction records, and began to figure out prices."

Then he made an unexpected announcement.

"Some have been shipped off to Christie's!"

And so Twigg discovered that the best titles—the Elliots, the Audubons, even the Golden Cockerel, Nonesuch Press, and Ashendene Press books—were gone. He flushed with anger. Taking inexpensive books on consignment was a waste of time since most of the commission would go to paying shipping expenses. Worse, Marios now revealed he was against any consignment deal at all.

"I can't send you expensive books on consignment with no guarantee as to what price you'll get," Marios said. He wanted a percentage of the appraised value of each book in advance.

"I can't handle a purchase deal, especially not on the books you have in mind," Twigg said testily. Hadn't Feuer made this clear? He had been brought all the way down to Southside Virginia at his own expense on false pretenses.

The weather was fine, the temperature in the sixties, although there was too much humidity for Twigg's taste. For want of anything better to do, he began to examine the books. Some he was told were not for sale. They wanted to keep a set here, a set in Washington, and another set in Greece, Marios said. Sasha told Twigg she had begun to catalogue the collection. But when he examined her notes, he discovered a scant thirteen pages of childishly handwritten names, a sketchy, unprofessional, and useless job.

"I'll send you a more complete list in a week," she promised. Her plan was to begin work on a comprehensive catalogue right away.

Elizabeth cooked lunch, hobbling about in the kitchen on her crutches. Sasha did the serving. They sat at the mahogany dining table surrounded by the inevitable hunting scenes in print and porcelain. In this room as well were two busts of Roman statesmen. David K. E. Bruce had donated similar ones to the Charlotte Country courthouse in the thirties after buying them at auction from the estate of a Vanderbilt who had once thrown him out of her house after he playfully decorated each emperor with a man's hat during a poker game. (Later, inclement weather forced their removal into the courtroom itself to preside over what Charlotte County hoped would be the murder trial of Mr. Bruce's son-in-law.)

The conversation began pleasantly enough. Marios told Twigg it was Sasha who had baked the pecan pie. It was Twigg's favorite American dessert. He had never tasted better pecan pie. Twigg remarked on the lovely views afforded by Staunton Hill. Then suddenly he found himself in the midst of an unpleasant argument. Marios had launched into a heated attack on Sasha's ancestors as brutal slave owners.

Staunton Hill was built by slaves! he pronounced.

Sasha and Twigg found themselves allies as they worked hard to convince Marios that slavery had to be placed in its historical context. Sasha argued pointedly and with considerable energy. She wouldn't be intimidated. Even the opening of *segregated* public schools in 1870 was a revolutionary event for Charlotte County. A written test and educational qualification determined suffrage well into the twentieth century.

Staunton Hill was always known as a place where blacks were treated well, she said. The former slaves of her great-grandfather Charles Bruce stayed on after the Civil War, working for wages. An elderly black woman was supposed to have been asked by the Reverend Morgan Dix why the former slaves didn't leave Staunton Hill. The reply was "None eber leahs de marster cep'n de daid."

(But she neglected to recount how James Coles Bruce, half-brother of Charles, a virulent racist, had written to Charles in 1863 that he should "put (his) wife and children on the smallest amount of food, kill dogs and old negroes, if necessary, to keep our army alive." Charles Bruce owned five hundred slaves and had trained a Confederate artillery company on a Staunton Hill field he named Waterloo.)

Slavery continued even now at Staunton Hill! Marios claimed. Sasha agreed it was wrong, but argued that you had to bear in mind that slavery began hundreds of years ago and all white people in Charlotte County of the planter class had been slave owners. Twigg mentioned the civil rights work of the Curriers whom he'd met when he worked at the rare book division of Brentano's; they had been his customers.

Sasha didn't permit the argument to dampen her good spirits. She was looking forward to the visit of her godmother Priscilla the next day. She and Twigg had coffee and more pecan pie. Marios went off somewhere.

Around three in the afternoon a telephone rang somewhere in the house. Sasha and Twigg were deep in conversation and evidently didn't notice that it had been answered.

The last thing Marios expected was for Mary to be calling him at Staunton Hill.

"What do you want?" he demanded. Nervously Mary came to the point. She was inviting him to come to Tennessee for another visit; he had already made one five-day trip to Tennessee since their return from Greece.

Immediately he was suspicious. He knew it was unlikely that Mary would take such action on her own. "Why are you calling? Who put you up to this?" he insisted. He pressed and pressed. Faced with his rage, against which she had always been helpless, Mary finally admitted that Sasha had called her the previous Sunday requesting that she invite Marios to Tennessee to "settle him down."

"Alexandra has called here and she wanted me to invite you back," Mary admitted. "I don't know what the problem is, but I just felt sorry for her and I wonder if there's something wrong or something."

She faltered. Marios was furious and wouldn't discuss it. He refused at once to go to Tennessee, remaining noncommittal about what could have prompted Sasha to call Mary behind his back. Before she could even ask him why he was unhappy, he had hung up.

Marios now began to move angrily about the house, in a rage and not caring whether Twigg noticed it or not. He knew he would never see Twigg again. Coming downstairs, he began to pace back and forth on the terrace, visible to Sasha and Twigg through the window, as he ostentatiously demanded their attention. Finally he came inside the house and demanded that Sasha come with him at once. Sasha excused herself and followed. Bewildered, Twigg decided to occupy himself with the books until it was time for the drive back to Lynchburg.

Sasha was gone for close to an hour. When she returned, she was markedly quieter—and very sad. The three had a last drink together. Marios asked Twigg an unusual question during these final moments of his visit. What happens in book deals if it is discovered later that books sold to innocent purchasers by dealers were found to have been stolen?

Twigg answered that the purchaser would probably get good title anyway. The dealer would have a hard time getting the books back from someone to whom they had been sold in good faith. In most sales of rare books receipts weren't even considered necessary.

Nothing would happen, Twigg unwittingly reassured Marios. Possession would mean everything.

It was getting late. Twigg was afraid he might miss his flight. "We ought to leave," he said.

"There's plenty of time," Marios insisted more than once. Then he drove eighty miles an hour all the way to Lynchburg, obviously enjoying Twigg's discomfort.

Murder or Suicide?

Marios had reason to fear Sasha's reunion with her god-mother on November seventh. Priscilla had been there for her since she was a little girl. She had attended Sasha's gradua-tion from Potomac School and when Sasha was at Radcliffe, she urged New York–bound friends to look up her "cool" godmother. She knew Priscilla would love to see them.

Priscilla was scheduled to arrive with her friend Rainer at five. There were many chores to be done before then. The wines for dinner had to be selected and the silver polished. Sasha was going to bake her famous chocolate cake. It was to be a festive occasion, Sasha at her best, showing Priscilla—and herself—that no matter how many defeats she had suffered, she had come through. All the hospitality Staunton Hill had to offer would be marshaled for Priscilla's visit. Marios could do what he liked about it.

Of one thing Sasha seems to have been certain on Novem-ber seventh, this Friday. The old game of isolation, separat-ing Sasha from those she loved, was finished. She didn't know what would happen between her and Marios, but he would have to accept that she was going to meet his family when they returned to Athens on November twenty-seventh, as they were planning to do. And she would no longer be separated from her own.

She had already packed her china, silver, and linens for this trip to Greece. Now there were storage bins to be built. On this morning of Priscilla's visit, Buss Baker would be helped with the carpentry by John LeGrand. Sasha liked old John and often drove down the back road to pick him up when he didn't have a ride to Staunton Hill. One day when he had a cold, she ordered him to wear a scarf. "How can I work with a scarf around my neck?" John said. Later his wife Mary told anyone who would listen that Sasha was "the best white person I know. She's just like a black person."

Sasha put on her blue jeans and went down to the basement at eight in the morning to tell Buss and John that today she wanted them to repair the old workbench and then start on the storage bins. She remarked that she planned to sell some of the furniture and had been negotiating with Ruth Bailey, the Brookneal antiques dealer, to sell some items from the house. Sasha chattered on pleasantly. She was planning to spend winters in Greece and summers at Staunton Hill.

Elizabeth Hamlett worked energetically to finish polishing the silver before she had to leave for Brookneal where she had an afternoon appointment at the hairdresser's. She thought Sasha had been down in the dumps, depressed, and just not herself all week. She was glad Priscilla was coming.

Sasha went down to her father's wine cellar to choose something appropriately grand and came back with a fine champagne. She arranged flowers dramatically around the drawing room. The best present she could give her godmother was to show her how well she had set her life in order.

During the morning Sasha talked cheerfully on the telephone with Paule d'Oberndorff, her mother's cousin, who was at the Bruce mansion in Washington, but would be joining the group at Staunton Hill. At ten thirty Sasha called a woman in Brookneal and promised to do her a favor; Sasha would meet her in town around one o'clock. At eleven she came into Marios's room to give him a telephone message. Anderson & Strudwick had called and said that a transaction Marios had ordered had been accomplished. Sasha told Marios she was planning to call her London lawyer, Leighton Davis, to find out what had happened yesterday, November sixth, when Anton was scheduled to answer her suit against him in court.

Marios claims he was working on his "finances" in the study all morning and that he took a call from Wilmington Trust concerning whether he and Sasha should file a joint tax return for 1975.

At eleven fifty Sasha was in the basement chatting with

Buss and John. Then she said she was going back up for
lunch. A few minutes later, just as Buss was about to drive
Elizabeth to Brookneal, Marios came down to the basement
and asked the two men if they'd seen Sasha. They'd just seen
her, they said, but they didn't know where she went. "I'll
help you look for her after I drive Elizabeth to Brookneal,"
Buss said. How Marios hounded her steps that day!

At noon Buss drove Elizabeth to Brookneal, leaving old
John LeGrand as the only servant at Staunton Hill with
Marios and Sasha. Before going on to her hairdresser's,
Elizabeth stopped at Holt's grocery store. Sasha had given
her a list of additional items to be purchased for the gala
weekend. While Elizabeth stood chatting with Cleo Holt, the
telephone rang in the store. It was Sasha adding to her list of
groceries. She asked Cleo a detail about the baking of the
chocolate cake and seemed reluctant to hang up. Cleo thought
this odd. Sasha had perfected her technique of baking chocolate cake. Why would she need advice? But Sasha sounded
fine otherwise and Cleo, brushing aside her misgivings, went
about her business in the store.

Buss left Elizabeth at the hairdresser's, agreeing to pick her
up at four o'clock. Then he returned to Staunton Hill to go
back to work.

At one o'clock Sasha reached Leighton Davis in London.
Davis told her she'd been mistaken about the date. Von
Kassel's summons was scheduled to be heard not on the
sixth, as Sasha had thought, but on November seventeenth.
She was mildly distressed, but the case had been dragging on
for a year and a half and so once more she said she'd be
patient.

Marios asked Sasha what happened. "I'll tell you later,"
he says Sasha told him. Then she went off. He told the police
he last saw her at eleven but the Staunton Hill telephone
records indicate that the call to London was made at one
o'clock and Marios admits he talked to Sasha after that. This
was, of course, also after he told Buss and John at noon that
he couldn't find her.

❖   ❖   ❖

Between two thirty and three, Marios reappeared in the basement and again asked Buss and John if they'd seen Sasha. Buss repeated he hadn't, not since ten minutes to twelve when he went into Brookneal.

"You must help me find her," he told Buss and John. "I haven't seen her for four hours!"

Marios sent John outside to look for Sasha—it was then that he appeared at Meg Tibbs's cottage.

Buss felt funny. "Maybe she's at some of the houses down on the farm. You ought to go down there and see. You done checked every room in the house?" he asked Marios.

Marios said he had disappeared again. This was when he, too, knocked at Meg's door and she wisecracked, "What'd she do? Leave you?"

Buss was suspicious when Marios "came back too quick." He thought to himself, Well, he ain't half checked down there.

"Let me go down there and see for myself," Buss said. Checking at the Carter place, he asked if Marios had been there. Old Mrs. Carter said, no, he hadn't. Buss came back and asked Marios again if he'd checked all the rooms in the house—he thought there must be fifty or sixty. When Marios said he had, Buss answered, "Well, let's go over them again." They searched the house, but they couldn't find Sasha.

It was now almost four o'clock. Buss said he had to go to Brookneal to pick up Elizabeth. "If she ain't here when I come back, I'll get Elizabeth to call the courthouse and get the sheriff," Buss said.

"All right, all right," Marios answered.

After a while Marios returned to the basement where John was back at work. "I bet she done kill herself," was John's recollection of what Marios said.

Although Marios knew that Buss was in Brookneal and wouldn't return until about five o'clock, he demanded that John "go get Buss! I need him to help me look for Sasha!"

"How can I get Buss without a car?" John asked him. I'm not about to walk eight miles to Brookneal, he thought to himself. He was seventy years old and not well.

"Go and find him!" Marios insisted.

Afraid to cross him, John walked out onto the Staunton Hill grounds, pretending to be following orders.

Between four and five o'clock the following events occurred:

Buss left just before four to pick up Elizabeth in Brookneal

At some point between four and five Marios claimed he discovered Sasha's body under the gnarled old cedar and banged on Meg Tibbs's door crying, ''She's killed herself. She's dead! She's dying! Call the doctor!'' Meg made the call to the Rescue Squad at 4:50.

But at 4:09 from Staunton Hill Mansion House Marios telephoned Anderson & Strudwick, his Lynchburg stockbrokers, and ordered the sale of some of his stocks. The proceeds were to be deposited directly into his Zurich bank account. Either he had shot Sasha—or had found the body—or, at the very least, knew she was missing when he took the time to make that call.

When Buss and Elizabeth drove up to the gates of Staunton Hill, John was waiting for them. Buss found this odd. ''What's done happened?'' he asked.

''Sasha laying down there at the pool. They say she's dead,'' John reported.

In the yard Buss found Marios running around frantically. ''Buss, I found her. She's dead, she's dead, she's dead,'' Buss remembered him saying. It was not yet 5:15, when the rescue squad would arrive. Buss knelt down and caught hold of Sasha's hand. Her hand was warm. ''That woman ain't dead,'' he said. Then he had a thought. He checked to see if any of the Staunton Hill screens were loose. Someone could have shot at her with a rifle from the office building. But the angle was wrong. It didn't happen that way.

It may be that sometime after one in the afternoon, having exhausted all her chores, Sasha was seized by her old shame and depression. She knew it would not escape Priscilla that the gamble on which she had staked everything had failed. Having called Mary for help, having invited Priscilla, Rainer, and Paule to Staunton Hill, she had thrown away the old script. She was no longer the imperfect sinning goat struggling to purify herself for Marios. But what remained?

Now Marios's fear that he would lose her would lead him

to even more erratic behavior; there would be more violent interrogations. There was no getting rid of him, certainly not now that the prospect of his owning Staunton Hill was so close. He would remain, undermining her sanity, harassing her, torturing her, knowing, as she had told Nicky on that spring night, every way to make her scream in pain. On that hazy, rainy November afternoon, Sasha may have wondered why she had ever chosen him at all.

They had their games about the .22 Walther; she knew that Marios had "hidden" it last weekend under a bed in his room that nobody slept in. Someone had sawed the barrel down to the slide so that it was only three and three-quarters inches long. Sasha slipped the silver pistol into her pocket. It was already fully loaded.

She knew now she would do anything to prevent Marios from owning Staunton Hill. She no longer owned any of the real estate. If she were dead, there would be nothing he could do. This was why the Saturday before, when Marios and the rare book man Stephen Massey were in Lynchburg renting a station wagon in which Massey would cart away the choicest volumes from her father's rare book collection, she had swallowed all the pills Dr. Campbell had prescribed for her.

The decision to shoot herself today has come upon her suddenly. There are no more chores to be done. The appointment in Brookneal seems trivial in the face of her despair. She feels as if she were suffocating, so overwhelmed is she by the waste, the futility of all her efforts to live an upright life, her having chosen not one but two men who represented everything she despised.

What lies ahead of her? Sasha wonders on this dreary November afternoon. What would prevent her from again hurting her parents and all the people on whom she has brought only disgrace? She feels as if she has exhausted her welcome on this planet, an old feeling for her now revived. Staunton Hill, the home of the Bruces of old, is about to pass from the family. She will shoot herself if only to free the Bruces of Marios.

If she were to tell all this to Priscilla, it would only distress her godmother. What could Priscilla do for her now? And how could Priscilla free her of Marios? No doubt Marios would insult her godmother, try to cow her into submission, taunt her, and conjure up images of the Bruces as heartless parents who bore children only for show, to enhance their public image. Sasha would die of shame.

This morning Priscilla's visit seemed a goal, the end of a long race in which Sasha would be returned to her old self. But too much has happened. There is no starting over. Priscilla would take note of her black eye; she might even glimpse the bruises that crisscross her body. She would think, my goddaughter has sunk so low.

Perhaps Sasha understood as she wandered outside in the rain that the ferocity of her need for Marios only revealed her compulsion to destroy herself, that she chose him so that she would be driven to this moment. She may have realized at last that she had never loved Marios Michaelides, but had been obsessed by a struggle to convert a man incapable of love into caring. She had chosen Marios precisely because he could never love her. He would always confirm that she was worthless, the feeling with which she felt most at home. Taking advantage of her weakness, knowing how to cultivate her most self-destructive tendencies, what did he know of love?

Perhaps she even wished that he might have accomplished this last act for her and saved her from having to do it herself. Her parents would at last be relieved of a daughter who had been only a burden, a blight on their exemplary lives.

She knelt then, perhaps, by the old stone wall to accomplish her final purification. Her brother David would call her the strongest of their generation, the child most like their earliest known American ancestor, Charles Bruce of Soldier's Rest, born in 1732, "a man of great vigor of intellect," according to his contemporaries.

She had long been troubled by Phil Graham's suicide. Arguing that she killed herself, Marios would later call attention to how affected Sasha had been by Graham's death. He had been forgiven for the hurt he inflicted on those closest to him, Sasha had said of Phil Graham, using terms that seemed to bear upon her own life. But "the bitterness of those he had hurt could not be washed away and the full horror of the harm he had done closed in upon him. He took his own life soon after."

She, too, felt worthless. "Knowing you are doing the wrong thing for months corrodes a not-too-solid bank of self-respect," she had said a decade ago. Even at nineteen she had despaired: "It all comes to the same thing when you're shot. Death equalizes everything."

It was all too difficult to explain, she would not leave a suicide note. She'd never trusted words anyway, as she'd told Wes Profit so long ago.

But there is something else. Leaving behind not a word for anyone, she punishes all those who never loved her enough. Could it have escaped her that by leaving no explanation she was shouting for all to hear that whoever pulled the trigger, the possibility remained that Marios had killed her? She had told Nicky she would never try suicide with a gun. Let Marios be accused, let him answer for his unkindness to her, his secrets about Mary's baby, his insults toward her parents, his greed.

"I feel that she held the gun and I think he was the murderer," her mother would tell the police two years later with great emotional distress. If Sasha pulled the trigger, Marios guided her hand. The light had indeed long ago vanished from her eyes, this girl who so undervalued herself and who was now faced with her last unequivocal defeat.

She held the gun in her left hand, pressing it against her right temple, triggering it with her left thumb, stabilizing it with her right hand. Filled with despair at this last moment of consciousness she can no longer distinguish, she literally does not know, whether it is Marios's finger which is pressing the trigger—or her own.

But one may imagine another scenario for this rainy November day. Sasha felt a new strength, buoyed by her godmother's Tuesday call and impending visit. She had argued vigorously yesterday with Marios over the racism of the old Bruces. So what if her great-grandmother Sarah Seddon Bruce kept the only copy of *Uncle Tom's Cabin* in the house locked up in her wardrobe so that its contents wouldn't poison the minds of her children! Nor had she been intimidated by Marios's rages over Mary's call inviting him to Tennessee, which he knew had been inspired by Sasha. That tactic didn't work. But she was glad to have tried it—she saw it now as a step toward health.

She would enlist Priscilla in her cause. Priscilla would be a comfort. Sasha knew now that the life she envisioned for herself at Staunton Hill was incompatible with Marios's possessiveness, his lies, and his violence.

No longer would she listen to his accusation that she was bad and impure, to his absurd insistence that she was "the cause of his shame." No longer would she be separated from family and friends. The "dark tunnel of her despair" was behind her. She saw Marios now not as she once did, as "the strong man who was reaching out his hand to her," but as the weakling that he was.

She had had enough of assuaging his fears, of his endless interrogations about her relationships with other men, of his frantic jealousy. She was tired of his obvious attempts to control her by making her feel bad about herself, sick of his efforts to make her believe her parents never loved her. She will no longer be his prisoner.

Violence had become their sole means of communication since the aborted Washington wedding. The beatings intensified. The only way he could possess her now was to kill her even as Priscilla got into her car and began the two-hour drive to Staunton Hill from Richmond.

Marios had to be unsettled by Sasha's efforts to free herself from him. The notes she left around the house, even the one beginning "mou Husband mou," begged him to set her free. He had to have been terrified when she approached Mary, the "other woman [who] is better than you." Now Priscilla would be told if not everything, then a great deal.

In this scenario Sasha plans to tell Priscilla enough so that Marios will be prevented from owning Staunton Hill. She knows she cannot rid herself of him alone. But allies are on the way. She will get practical advice so that Staunton Hill will not be lost to the Bruces.

Once she has made this decision, Sasha is calm. The silver, the wine, the flowers, the cake—all represent elements of an independence day feast. Sasha is once more a Bruce, a person who faces the consequences of her actions. She even has time for a charitable errand as she agrees to go to Brookneal after one o'clock.

The quarrel that began in Oliver Twigg's presence after Mary's call has not abated. Sasha confronts Marios. She tells him she will talk to Priscilla and get help in disengaging herself from him. She is sorry the marriage has failed. She'd hoped that the legal bond might have calmed him down, made him more secure. Hadn't she even agreed to help him purchase Staunton Hill—contents and real estate—so that he would not feel so threatened? But nothing has worked.

Marios is terrified. Her family is so powerful—they could arrange a divorce in a minute. He has never met Priscilla—he doesn't know what to expect. Once more he would be an impoverished adventurer with delusions of grandeur, a nondescript Greek with an eye for foreign women. But how would he ever land another Sasha Bruce, that "golden goose"?

But the will still stands. He would have preferred that the transfer of Staunton Hill to him—including the $1,163,976 worth of furnishings for which he was paying $120,000—have been completed. But he is Sasha's heir and executor provided they are married at the moment of her death. She with all her history of suicide attempts—hadn't he even once told her, "Someday I could kill you and make it look like suicide?"

Perhaps they began their quarrel indoors and continued outside. But a laboratory check revealed no bloodstains on the Staunton Hill carpet which the police had examined.

In this possible scenario he removes the Walther, Hitler's favorite weapon, from its hiding place and faces her. The quarrel grows more heated. And perhaps Sasha with the hauteur of her class taunts him, daring him to send her on her way. "Shoot me, shoot me," she may indeed have sung in his face. "I don't want to live anyway. At least not with you." The edge to her voice suggests it is sexually gratifying for Sasha to so taunt this violent man; her erotic fantasy is at its height as she goads the man she desires even now into killing her.

"It couldn't have been premeditated," Marios would say later, as if he were admitting he did shoot her, but in a spontaneous outburst and not as the result of a plan. "Even if I killed her, it couldn't have been premeditated." Certainly as they faced each other at that last moment he was out of his senses. For a colder, cleverer man would have made a last attempt to win her, bearing in mind that thirtieth birthday inheritance of several hundred thousand dollars due in May.

It may have been that Marios then fulfilled the role for which Sasha had chosen him: that of her killer. Needing to be punished, she selected someone whose sense of himself as a man depended upon sadism. He may have complied, knowing the high piercing sound of the .22 Walther would go unheard. With Buss and John, or only John, in the basement and Elizabeth safe in Brookneal, there would be no witnesses. He may have looked her in the eye and put the gun to her head. And she may have stood there compliant and let him do it, as he knew she would.

If he did in fact shoot her, he would have had to hold the pistol slightly upward against her right temple so that there would be a contact wound and it would look like suicide.

Once Sasha fell to the ground on the soft bed of needles, he might have begun to improvise. He knew enough to fire only once. What to do with the murder weapon? He carried it away with him. And then, unthinking, and so he would not have an accident, he put the gun on safety, in a position to be fired again. When Meg Tibbs ran off to get that large quilt to cover Sasha, he took the opportunity to slip the gun under her body, which was why Meg found no gun when she drew the first flimsy blanket up around her friend. He forgot to take the gun off safety, not realizing that a person with a gunshot wound in the head would be incapable of putting the gun in a position to be fired again.

The isolation into which he had forced Sasha would help him now. The Bruces didn't known Staunton Hill was to have been solely in his name: Sasha had told her mother only "we want to live here and it's impossible—this thing of sharing it between the three of us. We'd like to buy them out." The Bruces knew nothing about her will.

He would later tell the police that she had an unhappy childhood, that she and her brothers "had no family." He counted on David and Nicky's estrangement from their parents and believed they would back him up. Invoking Sasha's many suicide attempts, he would tell the police "how somebody can reach a stage that doesn't care anymore." He would be charitable when he talked about his wife. "Unhappy people are not crazy," he would say. "Maybe they act in a different way but they are not crazy."

On November ninth, the day Sasha died, Marios immediately called Mary Lewis in Maryville, Tennessee. Why don't you come back here? Mary invited him at once.

Entitlement

The Bruces returned to Europe immediately after Sasha's death. Once the guiding spirit of a United European Army, Bruce had to suffer being lectured by Secretary-General Luns on how American budget cuts impinged on NATO, "the cornerstone of Western defense."

Back at Staunton Hill, David and Nicky were left to sort out Sasha's estate. According to Marios, on Monday, November tenth, at nine in the morning, Ambassador Bruce's secretary called from Washington. Nick answered and was told to contact Wilmington Trust. The secretary called a second time. Nicky refused to discuss financial matters. "We've just buried my sister," he said. Later Mr. Hackman of Wilmington Trust called and spoke to David. Marios sensed conspiracy. The "old fox" must be worried, he thought. That night David flew to Seattle to collect some personal effects and tie up his affairs.

The following day, the eleventh, Marios drove to Lynchburg to do business at Anderson & Strudwick. He sold the two hundred shares of Northwest Airlines which Sasha had transferred to him in June. On November twelfth he called Leigh Middleditch for information about Sasha's trust. Middleditch told him he would have to speak to a Mr. Herdig at Wilmington Trust.

In London on the same day, von Kassel's solicitors withdrew their delaying summons, knowing Goodman, Derrick were now unable to declare von Kassel a bankrupt on Sasha's behalf. Only her estate could take action against him now.

When David returned from the West Coast on Wednesday, November thirteenth, Marios requested that he call Wilmington Trust on Mario's behalf. He didn't get along very well with the people there, and he wanted to know if he would succeed to Sasha's trust. David agreed and learned that Sasha's trust benefits would be divided equally between her two brothers.

Marios could scarcely conceal his surprise and dismay. He'd thought he was to be her beneficiary.

"There must be some mistake," he said.

David and Nicky were so impressed by his certainty that Sasha's trust would come to him as her sole heir that they too believed there must be some error.

"No, you can't play around with that kind of money," Marios concluded. Then he became bitter. "Now I've been left with nothing." He behaved as if this were the final blow. He had been drinking heavily of the Staunton Hill stock and made a great show of not eating; he seemed to subsist only on alcohol and cigarettes. Affecting a hangdog expression, according to David Surtees Bruce, he walked around with his head bowed in despair.

Stephen Massey called that week and wanted to know whether to go ahead with the sale of the rare books he had taken from Staunton Hill on November second. Keeping this call a secret from David and Nicky, Marios ordered him to go ahead with the auction. Massey was to ship the books to London where they would be sold. The proceeds were to be credited to Mario's account and deposited with his Zurich bank.

Meg Tibbs invited Marios, Nicky, and David over for a roast beef dinner. Not touching his food, Marios sat silently, lost in himself. But when Allen Tibbs said he had taken karate lessons, Marios revived and said he had studied karate in Japan under a famous instructor. Back at the Mansion House, Marios told David he had once tried to do business in Japan, but had failed. In Osaka he'd lost his composure and the deal had fallen through.

At home with his brothers-in-law Marios was the grieving husband, distraught and frequently raving. His large brown eyes sank deep into his head. He grew gaunt and was often drunk and incoherent. The dry, understated formal mode of discourse with which the Bruce brothers had grown up did not prepare them for the emotional effusions to which they were now subjected.

Marios called Sasha "the most beautiful thing in my life, and I didn't protect it, my little flower. It was perfect between us," he declared. "If I could have helped her, I would have been getting everything I wanted out of life. For a few seconds I had what I wanted.

"I thought with what we had, we could solve anything," he went on. "If there was love, that would heal everything. I thought the only answer was that. If she hadn't been in such pain, she couldn't have loved that much.

"She was convinced we would meet again someday," Marios told Sasha's brothers as they spent the weeks following her death alone together at Staunton Hill.

He too had thought of killing himself. "I should go with her," Marios whimpered. "What do I have to live for? My life is over, too."

According to Nicky, one night at one o'clock in the morning Marios asked him to go for a ride. Nicky thought his brother-in-law was bent on finding out what Sasha might have told him about their relationship. Nicky said he didn't feel like going. Later he would call Marios "paranoid."

People would wonder how Nicky could remain in that house with Marios. But Nicky had promised his beloved sister he would never breathe a word of what she told him about Marios to anyone, and certainly Nicky was immobilized by grief. Only in July 1977 would he tell Investigator John Mills that Sasha had told him that Marios beat and tortured her and threatened he could kill her and make it look like suicide. (His mother would tell the police that Nicky may have invented these things, that he was sometimes unable "to differentiate between reality and myth. And stories would get built up which had absolutely no foundation in fact.")

According to Marios, David and Nicky invited him to remain at Staunton Hill indefinitely, but he found it too painful, although he would have liked to be close to Sasha's grave. He had decided to return to Greece. Perhaps David and Nicky could visit him there—as his guests. At one point David asked him if he had ever been married before. "Yes, yes," Marios said. "I was married for some years in Tennessee to a woman, but it was something on paper, only a business relationship.''

Nicky, however, was aware of the ''other woman'' to whom, Sasha had told him, Marios was always threatening to return. He knew that Marios openly telephoned Mary from Staunton Hill, but he seems not to have confided any of these facts to David.

Marios knew David didn't like him, but he judged David was naive and ignorant of what a ''gold mine'' Staunton Hill was. At one level of his complex nature he was fond of Nicky and even Sasha had once complained to her mother about what a strong influence on her younger brother Marios was. Marios thought Nicky liked him. Incredulous, Marios noticed that although the Bruce brothers had grown up in fine houses surrounded by rare and beautiful objects, neither of them had much interest in the family china, silver, furniture or art. David would have preferred to live among things that had personal meaning for him, such as the Oriental art he collected. Nicky had no interest in objects at all.

Now negotiations between Marios and the brothers began. Marios proposed a deal based on the fact that as Sasha's heir he owned a third of the contents of the Mansion House. Moreover, Nicky had never recorded the deed by which Sasha sold him her share of the real estate. Believing the title of Staunton Hill was in doubt, and determined that the place should remain in the family, David decided to settle with Marios.

Marios reminded the boys that he was entitled to one third of furnishings which were now worth $1,163,976 and not the $120,000 he'd proposed paying for them only a week before. He would renounce all claims to Sasha's estate, they could be rid of him, for $600,000!

David made him a counteroffer: Marios could have $190,000 in cash, $100,000 from David and $90,000 from Nicky, since Nicky would pay off a Fidelity Bank loan of $10,000 which Sasha owed. With great alacrity, Marios agreed.

On November twentieth David, Nicky, and Marios drove together to Charlottesville to consult Leigh Middleditch on the form by which Marios should divest himself of Sasha's property. As part of the deal Nicky would file the deed so that the two brothers alone would legally own Staunton Hill.

Middleditch told David it would be all right if he wrote the text of the renouncement himself. Back at Staunton Hill, Marios, who had kept the deed in his possession, signed it and handed it over to Nicky to be recorded. Two renouncement forms would have to be drawn up because Marios was to give up not only his claim to the property, but also the rights of himself and his brother Eugenios to be Sasha's executors.

It was a straightforward arrangement. David wrote the renouncement of Marios's claim to Sasha's estate on plain Staunton Hill notepaper and dated it November twenty-second:

> I, the undersigned, Marios Michaelides, as executor of the last will and testament of Alexandra Bruce Michaelides, do hereby renounce my claim to the estate and property of my deceased wife Alexandra Bruce Michaelides, and leave all estate and property to the deceased's two surviving brothers, David Surtees Bruce and Nicholas Cabell Bruce.
>
> Yours,
> Marios Michaelides.

The checks made out to Marios were dated in 1976, David's on the fifteenth of January, to be drawn on the Fidelity National Bank in Lynchburg. Wilmington Trust needed time to cash in some of the brothers' assets. Marios later contended that he told the brothers, "Listen, you don't owe me anything," and they were said to have replied that he "deserved something," that the $190,000 was a gift.

For Sasha's funeral expenses, Marios took no responsibility. On November twenty-second David paid $1,672.80 to the Henderson Funeral Home in Brookneal.

On November twenty-third Leigh Middleditch received a letter from the Bruce brothers and Marios requesting that Sasha's will be sent to Staunton Hill. On the twenty-fifth the renouncement document was signed and notarized.

* * *

Marios now announced his departure. In the presence of the brothers, he went to the silver closet and took out the wooden case of heirloom wedding silver. There were tears in his eyes. The silver reminded him of Sasha, he said. But he took not only the wedding gift, but a few extra pieces as well. He told Nicky he was taking these because they, too, reminded him of his wife. Among them were pieces that had been buried on the Staunton Hill grounds at the end of the Civil War by Charles Bruce who shared his secret, according to Bruce family lore, only with Israel, a former slave, "coal-black, resolute, (and) sagacious."

Marios also took a few works of art out to his car. The brothers knew the silver was a wedding gift; Nicky himself had delivered it after the second wedding failed to take place in Washington. There was no reason, they thought at the time, why he shouldn't be entitled to it.

Marios told Sasha's brothers he would go to New York and then to Greece. But first he had to stop in Knoxville, Tennessee. "I have to talk to my friends there because they're the ones who encouraged me to marry Sasha," Marios said. He never mentioned Mary Lewis's name nor the town of Maryville. The father of his woman friend in Knoxville was a very important person, Marios said. At one time he had been the head of Levi Strauss!

After Marios had gone, Reginald Pettus drew up a document in which Marios would renounce his right to be Sasha's executor. It read:

> We, Marios Michaelides and Eugenios Michaelides, citizens of Greece, having been advised that in order to qualify as Executors of the estate of Alexandra Bruce Michaelides that we would have to come to America, post bond, and associate a resident of Virginia as Co-Executor, we therefore renounce our appointment as Executors under the will of Alexandra Bruce Michaelides and request the Clerk to appoint David S. Bruce.

David mailed the form to Athens, having decided that if either Pettus or Middleditch sent Marios the renouncement, he would become suspicious. Marios phoned David at once. "I'll sign this," he said. "But my brother Eugenios is very difficult and easily agitated. If he gets into this case, he'll get into it all the way and he'll become very difficult. Is it all right if I forge his signature?''

He sees conspiracies everywhere, David thought. Maybe Marios would enjoy forging his brother's signature. Maybe his brother would sign it and then Marios would say it was forged because that was the way his mind worked.

"Go ahead and sign it yourself," David told him.

Eugenios Michaelides, of course, had never heard of Sasha Bruce.

On December twenty-ninth David drove the seventeen miles between Staunton Hill and Charlotte Courthouse where before old Edwin Hoy, who had married Sasha and Marios, he posted a bond of eighty thousand dollars. Standing before the paintings of his great-grandfather Charles Bruce, his grandfather William Cabell Bruce, and his great-uncle, the Arthurian scholar Philip Alexander Bruce, he became his sister's executor, entering her will for probate. He offered to the court a document drawn up by Pettus removing Marios and his brother as Sasha's executors.

Yet, strangely, he also swore to the fact that Sasha's sole heir was "Marios Michaelides, thirty, Husband, Address: Meleagrou 11, Athens, Greece," in a document which began, "I do solemnly swear that I have made diligent inquiry as to the names, ages, and addresses of the heirs of the above-named decedent. . . ." It was as if Marios had never renounced his claim to Sasha's property! If the renouncement were valid, Marios's Athens lawyer, the fiery Panayotis Vrettos would declare three years later as he prepared to defend his client for Sasha's murder, "Why weren't David Surtees Bruce and Nicholas Cabell Bruce listed as Sasha's sole heirs?"

On that same December twenty-ninth, David also produced an Inventory and Appraisement of Sasha's estate. The three appraisers had been Marie Harper, Carroll Holt, the grocer, and Daphne Piester, whose father, Lee Bradley, had once managed Staunton Hill plantation.

The appraisal listed the value of Sasha's property as thirty-three thousand dollars, although when David and Marios visited Middleditch in Charlottesville on November twenty-second, the Arpad inventory had been mentioned and a Staunton Hill check had been used to pay Michael Arpad. Marios says he also gave David copies of the Arpad appraisal when he left Staunton Hill, cautioning him to "be careful because they could establish a tax fraud." In 1975 only estates worth more than sixty thousand dollars were subject to federal estate taxes.

It was not a question of his having appraised the property low, Carroll Holt chuckles. "That's the way they wanted it. It was cut and dried." Nick came over one day. He, Marie, and Daphne Piester went down to Staunton Hill and were told where to sign their names.

"I didn't know what I was doing," Marie remembered. "All I did was appraise the inside property, the sheets, silver, stuff like that. And heck, I didn't know what it was worth. I don't know why I was asked to do it. Actually I just went by and signed the papers."

"Do you want me to clean out Sasha's room?" Marie asked Nicky. He said he did. "Whom do you want to have it all?" was her next question.

"Anybody who can use it," Nick answered.

Marie was shocked to find that Sasha owned so little. There were eight pairs of jeans, a dozen shirts, a few dresses, a few pair of good boots. There was one book in her room—a volume of old drawings illustrating Christmas carols. The only item of any value was a pair of ruby earrings. Marie had them made into a ring for Paule d'Oberndorff, the cousin who was to have joined Sasha and her godmother at Staunton Hill on the weekend she was shot.

Marios did not return to his "flourishing" business in Greece, but remained in Maryville, Tennessee. This seems to have been his plan from that moment on the day of Sasha's death when Mary had issued her invitation. Mary promised not to ask too many questions; she wanted only for them to start life together again. She hoped the baby she was carrying would bring them close.

But when Marios came to Tennessee, his behavior was more erratic than even Mary had ever known it to be. He grew a beard and went around in ragged blue jeans. He was dirty and unkempt. He behaved as if he had no control over himself. And he lied continuously.

In Maryville, as in Charlotte County and Athens, Marios was a loner. He seemed fascinated by guns and talked about them constantly. He also kept in close touch with Anderson & Strudwick and steadily continued to filter money into his Zurich account. When he consented to meet the Lewis friends and neighbors, he made up stories about how wealthy he was. His conversation was endlessly about the stock market which he had learned, he said, to manipulate and control.

Mary found out about the one hundred ninety thousand dollars he'd gotten from the Bruces, but Marios said he had amassed this money by parlaying two thousand dollars, all the money he had in the world, on the stock market. Soon, he told her, he would be making millions. He invested most of the one hundred ninety thousand dollars in stocks and when people asked him how he earned his living, he said he supported himself from his investments. Soon his losses began to exceed his gains and the money dwindled away. Often he would talk about Niarchos, who had gained an empire by the sheer force of his will. He told Mary none of the circumstances of Sasha's death.

In February 1976, Marios returned to Staunton Hill. He told Nicky he wanted to pick up his mail and visit Sasha's grave. On February fourth he repaid the fifteen-thousand-dollar loan he had made from the Fidelity American Bank in Brookneal on the day before Sasha was shot. His stocks from Ford Motor, Strother Drug, and Hecks were returned to him.

While he was at Staunton Hill, Nicky had Marios act as witness to an agreement for the purchase of a piece of land belonging to a man named Puffenbarger.

In July David filed the inheritance tax return on Sasha's estate in Richmond. Her tangible property was listed as one third of the furniture, appliances, linen, and silver of Staunton Hill, valued again at $33,000. Her net worth minus deductions was a paltry $20,404.81. This time, however, her beneficiaries were listed as her two brothers. It developed that Wilmington Trust had needlessly paid more than $20,000 in 1975 taxes for Sasha, unaware that she had substantial losses to offset her income.

* * *

That summer of 1976 Marios paid still another visit to Staunton Hill. He told David he was coming to Lynchburg from an airport in North Carolina. There was a direct flight to Lynchburg from LaGuardia in New York and many flights from Washington. Why was he passing through North Carolina? David wondered.

David was at Staunton Hill alone. Saying nothing of Mary Lewis, Marios talked of his life in Knoxville. His "friend" advised him now not to go back into the family business, Marios confided, implying, David thought, that Marios's family was somehow responsible for Sasha's death. He was being advised to strike out on his own. He bragged about his life in Tennessee. He had been invited to join an exclusive social club, which was very costly. His Tennessee friends had taken him to Alaska to shoot bear.

He also had a new demand to make of the Bruce brothers. He wanted twenty thousand dollars a year from each of them for life! He would use this money to keep Sasha's memory alive by buying the apartment in Athens at Meleagrou 11 where he and Sasha had enjoyed so many happy times. This forty thousand a year would replace the trust money he felt he had been cheated out of. It was as if he had never been given the one hundred ninety thousand dollars.

The conversation turned to the fate of Staunton Hill. David admitted his doubts about whether he could manage the estate, even with Nicky paying half the costs. The upkeep will be astronomical, Marios told him. The heating system needed replacing; the tenant houses were in ruins; fuel costs were skyrocketing. Marios seemed to know what he was talking about. David became frightened.

Then Marios proposed that Staunton Hill be put on the market. The Bruce brothers could get rich by selling Staunton Hill! "A Texan would pay any amount of money for Staunton Hill," Marios declared. "A rich Texan would say 'You're buying history in Virginia!' A Texan would appreciate that death was associated with Staunton Hill. This would make it worth even more.

"You and Nick could sell me your shares of Staunton Hill for thirty-three thousand," Marios proposed. "I'll sell the property for four million dollars and put the difference in your name in a Swiss bank account so you wouldn't have to pay any taxes."

David evaded him and asked what happened to the twenty-five thousand dollars Sasha had borrowed from him in March 1975.

"It's best if you don't have a bankrupt estate because people will get suspicious," Marios advised. "If her estate were shown to be bankrupt with twenty-five thousand dollars claimed against it, the IRS might become suspicious. How could someone wealthy enough to maintain Staunton Hill have a bankrupt estate?"

David was angry. He knew he was being conned. But there didn't seem to be anything he could do. There was some truth in what Marios was saying.

Marios had still another surprise for David. Suddenly he produced a photograph of a baby. It was a little girl about five months old. David expressed admiration; Marios seemed so taken with this child.

"She comes from a very prominent American family," Marios said with pride. "I plan to adopt this baby in memory of Sasha." He said he even planned to name her Alexandra!

David felt uneasy as he examined the picture of the fair-skinned baby. The implication was that some of the profits from the four million dollars raised from the selling of Staunton Hill would go for paying the best Swiss governesses and for the education of this baby—all in Sasha's memory. How could her brother object to that?

The baby whose picture was shown to David Surtees Bruce that summer day in 1976 had, in fact, been born on March twentieth at 4:06 P.M. at the University of Tennessee Hospital in Knoxville to one Mary Rebecca Lewis Michaelides, aged thirty-three, and Marios G. Michaelides, aged thirty. She was christened Mary Alexandra Eugenia Michaelides, the "Alexandra" sandwiched in between the names of her two maternal grandmothers.

This, of course, had been Marios's idea. Mary wanted to refuse, but Marios had been so overwrought that she'd feared for him. And so she gave in. It was a nice thing to do for someone who had died like that. And perhaps the baby would help bring Marios back to life, release him from the gloom into which he had sunk.

Mary Alexandra Eugenia Michaelides was a beautiful child, her hair like spun gold, her skin pink and cream. By a strange conspiracy of nature she did not in the least resemble her dark, olive-skinned father. From the moment of her birth her cheeks had glowed with a blush of color, the tint of a rose.

"I shall call her Rosie," Mary decided. The name Rosie became her. And Mary couldn't bear to utter the names Alexandra or Sasha. Whenever Sasha's name was mentioned, Marios would stare off into space. Mary would have her way on this. Her daughter would never answer to the name Sasha.

Marios managed to wheedle an address for Nicky from David during that summer visit. If you ever come through Knoxville, you must look me up, he told David expansively. But although David asked where he might reach him, Marios managed to avoid answering. Marios's eye fell on a red vase. Could he have that? he asked David. It had sentimental value for him and Sasha. "Sure," David said. There were other objects, too, and books which reminded him of their time together.

Marios claims he paid David two hundred dollars for a Methuen edition of Oscar Wilde and for other things, a painting by Sully and a pair of K'ang Hsi vases—all at triple their value. But he never bothered to ask for receipts and paid in cash.

He had spent too long with his Tennessee friends, Marios told David as he was leaving. Now he planned to buy himself some property in Knoxville so that he wouldn't be a burden to them anymore.

On August sixth Marios purchased not the apartment overlooking the Royal Gardens in Athens in memory of Sasha, but a house at 5409 Riverbend Drive in Knoxville, Tennessee, for which he paid sixty-five thousand dollars. Title was conveyed to Mary Michaelides. The couple never actually occupied the property and it was put up for sale within the year.

Between March and October of 1976 the rare books and drawings, which included nine volumes of English caricatures, removed from Staunton Hill by Stephen Massey at the request of Marios and Sasha, were offered by Christie's in London. The Staunton Hill books and drawings were sold at six separate auctions. All the books found buyers with the exception of Elliot's *Birds of North America* and *Family of the Grouse*, together worth $15,500. In these cases the bidding did not reach the reserve and they were to be returned to Marios as their owner.

The proceeds of the rest amounted to $43,729.14. Christie's had been instructed to make payments to the Swiss Bank Corporation in Zurich into Marios's numbered account. David and Nicky still knew nothing of these sales of their books.

Late in 1976, Marie Harper was invited to visit the Bruces in Washington. She felt both honored and puzzled. Certainly she'd never thought she would find herself in this fabulous house with its pink-orange drawing room where the effect was of being inside a cantaloupe with the curtains the color of the rind.

On Saturday morning David Bruce took Marie aside. They should have investigated more after Sasha's death, he told her. His conscience bothered him. Marie thought Mr. Bruce seemed more interested in what Marios may have swindled from the family. He knew Marios was a shady fellow, but he didn't seem to believe Marios had killed Sasha.

The ambassador wanted to know about Marie's friendship with his daughter. Sasha was her best friend, Marie said. But the good times were possible only when Marios wasn't there. Yet Sasha loved that man, Marie told David Bruce. She wanted to please him. Mr. Bruce said he thought Sasha had killed herself, but that something had provoked her into it.

Mrs. Bruce didn't pay much attention to Marie. Marie tried not to show her discomfort but some of the guests made her feel more at home than Mrs. Bruce did. Marie chatted about Sasha's farming schemes and was surprised that Mrs. Bruce hadn't known about Sasha's course at the Virginia Polytechnic Institute.

"Sasha called me every day, but she had to do it collect," Evangeline Bruce told Marie.

Marie remembered Sasha calling her father on the telephone. She seemed always in search of a pretext to speak to her Daddy. David Bruce had left some of his possessions at Staunton Hill. Sasha would call and ask if he wanted his pipe stand. Did he want her to bring meat from the country to Washington?

Marie asked Mrs. Bruce why she thought Sasha would

have given away all her good clothes two weeks before she died.

"She was probably going to buy some new ones," Mrs. Bruce said.

But Marie knew Sasha never went shopping for clothes.

It was the weekend of Mrs. Bruce's birthday. Marie and Nicky went out to buy a present. When Mrs. Bruce opened the gift, she reportedly said to Marie, "He didn't pick this out. You did."

"No, ma'am," Marie answered to Mrs. Bruce's surprise.

As Marie was leaving, David Bruce whispered, "I left a note in your purse." The ambassador requested that Marie drive to Staunton Hill to check on a painting and the Bruce heirloom silver. He told Marie he had first asked Nicky to do him this favor, but Nicky had refused. Offended, his father told Marie he would not approach his son again on this subject.

Marie was instructed to search in the middle drawing room of the Mansion House for a portrait of Ambassador Bruce's grandmother, Sarah Seddon Bruce, painted by Thomas Sully. All he wanted to know was whether it was still there. Then Marie must look for the wedding silver. There would be twenty place settings in a big wooden box.

When Marie arrived back in Brookneal, she drove immediately to Staunton Hill. Then she called David Bruce in Washington. The picture was still there. David Bruce was relieved that Marios hadn't sold it.

She and Mike Carter had looked everywhere for the silver, Marie told the ambassador, but they couldn't find it.

Depression settled over Marie. One night she dreamt of a coffin with a hand hanging out. She put a glove on the hand and tried to stick it back into the coffin. But as soon as she pushed the hand back in, she spotted a foot creeping out. Then she tried to push that in, too.

On February 10, 1977, Marios made his final visit to Staunton Hill. Driving up in a new Lincoln automobile with Tennessee license plates, he picked up some mail and made a perfunctory visit to Sasha's grave. Then he pumped caretaker Mike Carter for information. Where were David and Nicky? Marios wanted to know. He seemed very nervous. Then he rented a trailer, filled it with valuable art, books, and furnishings from the Staunton Hill Mansion House, and drove away.

Downey Rice

The Staunton Hill bookplate exposed to some London acquaintances of the Bruces the source of those rare books auctioned off by Christie's during the summer of 1976. Mrs. Bruce now remembered Sasha's telling her, "I put all your family things together and nothing's gonna happen to them." Had her daughter been hinting that other items would soon be gone? But it remained astounding that these auctions were going on long after Sasha's death.

On October twenty-second Terry Graham, in Washington for the funeral of her father, was invited to tea by Mrs. Bruce. Only now did Mrs. Bruce ask Terry how she thought her friend had died.

"I think there was something very bad done," Terry told Evangeline Bruce. "I don't think this was a straightforward matter of suicide at all. If I were in your shoes, I would investigate what happened because I don't believe it was as simple as the authorities who took care of it said."

Terry heard herself growing shrill and agitated, not the way she ordinarily addressed Mrs. Bruce, who had been a formidable figure in her life. But she was very angry at the wrong she thought had been done to Sasha.

"I'd like you to talk to David," Mrs. Bruce said.

Terry had always been fond of David Bruce, whom she considered the epitome of the southern gentleman. He had always treated her as one of the family.

"We'd like to look into this, but how?" Bruce asked after Terry had described the weekend she had spent at Staunton Hill in the spring of 1974. "How do you get somebody to reopen a case?"

These two people who have lived such extraordinary lives, Terry thought, who know how to do everything in the political sphere—they don't know how to take care of their children. They're asking *me*!

Terry's father had known Charlie Bates, head of the FBI in San Francisco. At Dulles airport on her way home, in an astonishing coincidence, Terry heard Bates being paged. He recommended that she call an association of private investigators in New York. A woman answered in accents left over from the days of Al Capone. She suggested Downey Rice, who—coincidentally—was at the moment in San Diego where Terry lived.

Rice was both a southern gentleman himself and a tough old G-man who had joined the FBI in 1935. His conversation was sprinkled with references to "Mr. Hoover" and he talked like the thugs he tracked down. "The guy who will answer questions, who's a crook, he's my meat," Rice would say. He wiretapped and he "black-bagged," which meant breaking into people's offices and taking pictures of everything in their desks at four o'clock in the morning, as he himself proudly admitted. In Rice's day it was "the old steam kettle" that was used to read people's mail.

Rice had broken the case on which the movie *The House on Ninety-second Street* was based, capturing thirty-three German spies; after leaving the FBI in 1945 he became a counsel for the Kefauver Crime Commission. He was tall, courtly, and distinguished looking, a raconteur like David K. E. Bruce. He was also a lawyer. When Terry Graham called him in late 1976 he was sixty-three years old, still fond of calling himself "the Perry Mason of the East Coast."

In Washington Mrs. Bruce kept putting the telephone into her husband's hand and urging him to call Downey Rice. Before she left for Paris that fall, she pleaded, "Please do it before I leave. I just want to know it's been started." On November 8, 1976, almost a year to the day after Sasha's death, Evangeline again put the receiver in her husband's hand and this time dialed Downey Rice's number for him.

Escorted by Marie Harper, Rice arrived at Staunton Hill, making a beeline for the office, the small neo-Gothic building standing alongside the Mansion House. There he found old telephone bills, many recording mysterious calls to Maryville,

Tennessee, and collect calls from Haiti, too. And so Rice began.

Rice questioned David K. E. Bruce; why had he been neither alarmed nor surprised by Sasha's suicide? Journalist and family friend Tom Braden later staunchly declared that Bruce "never had any doubt" that his daughter was murdered . . . he was suspicious from the start. Bruce even knew there was "some sexual aberration" involved, according to Braden.

But this wasn't true. Lamely Bruce explained to Rice he hadn't wanted an autopsy and had arranged for so hasty a funeral because he had been told the autopsy would take three to four days and his schedule would not allow him to wait that long; he had an appointment with the President the next day. He had not been interviewed by the police investigators at the time because "again, it was the time element. I had to get back to Washington."

By February eleventh, Rice had a copy of the Haitian divorce decree, although the document was so vague and lacking in signatures that he wasn't sure who had gone to Haiti. Marios must have gone by himself and secretly divorced Mary in Haiti to marry Sasha, Rice concluded.

Rice decided to fly to Tennessee at once. If Marios had committed bigamy with Sasha, if they were never legally married, given the wording of her will, he could have no claim against her estate.

Rice arrived at the Lewis home on Mountain View Boulevard in the late afternoon of February seventeenth. Mary seemed to be alone. Rice introduced himself as a lawyer from Washington, without mentioning the Bruces. Mary said she couldn't talk to him. Her husband was in the hospital. He had stabbed himself while carving. But she invited Rice to come by the next morning.

Rice checked around the hospitals in the area—there were only two. No Michaelides was registered in either.

Promptly at ten the following morning, Rice reappeared at Mountain View Boulevard. This time Mary said her mother was home. If the matter was something private, it would be better if Rice would return in an hour when her mother would be gone.

At ten after eleven Rice at last found himself in the family room of the Lewis home—and received an unexpected boon as well. Seated in a corner with his leg propped up on a pillow sat Marios himself.

Rice saw "an intense, wiry, small person," so unprepossessing that Rice would wonder over his success with women. "We all wish we knew [his] secret," he would comment. The room was untidy with records strewn about. Rice positioned himself in the middle of it.

Smoothly, he handed Marios his card. He represented the Bruce family on "some matters that were of concern," Rice said. It was better that they all meet face-to-face to avoid "talk." "I've come in peace," he declared.

"Why has the Bruce family hired someone to make inquiries?" Marios, obviously agitated, wanted to know.

"We've got some problems," Rice answered. But he had come to Tennessee only because there were some unanswered questions concerned with the administering of Sasha's estate. He tried to calm Marios down.

Marios agreed to answer Rice's questions if in exchange he could be given the current address of Nicholas Bruce. He confided he had cut himself while carving. The injury wasn't serious, but it had required a number of stitches. Briefly sympathetic, Rice settled down to brass tacks.

"For instance, there was this business in Haiti," Rice said cryptically. He looked directly into Mary's eyes.

"Have you ever been to Haiti?" he asked her.

Mary looked over at Marios. Receiving a nod in the affirmative, she replied that she had.

Rice nearly fell off his seat. He had thought Mary didn't even know about the divorce!

"Can I tell him?" Mary asked Marios.

"Yeah, go ahead," Marios said.

"We had a secret divorce in Haiti. It was to please Marios."

Marios told Rice Sasha knew he was married as early as the second time he met her. When he and Sasha decided to marry, he and Mary had gone to a Knoxville lawyer for a divorce.

"What was his name?" Rice asked.

"I can't remember," Marios said. Mary didn't know the name either. This lawyer had concluded they had no grounds for divorce in Tennessee unless Sasha were named a corespondent—which Mary, fearing a scandal, did not wish to do. He had then urged them to try Haiti.

In Haiti, Mary said, she signed a petition alleging incompatibility. "But this was not true," she added. She had always been friendly with Marios. She explained how she showed her passport for identification and the divorce was immediately granted. Afterwards they returned to their hotel and Marios talked with Sasha on the telephone.

"It's strange," Rice pondered, "that you get divorced in July and in March of the next year have a baby."

"Can I tell him about the deal, Marios?"

And so Mary explained how she longed for a baby and had told Marios she would release him from their marriage only if he made her pregnant first.

Did her parents know about the divorce? Mary admitted they did not.

"Did Sasha know you were pregnant at the time of her death?" Rice asked Mary.

The two of them then spoke as if in unison.

"No," Mary said.

"Yes," Marios said.

Rice let that matter drop for the moment.

"Do you plan to remarry?" he asked the couple.

"No," Mary answered. She and Marios were "just friends." With this Marios agreed. Rice offered some grandfatherly advice. "You should, it would be good for the child," he said. "I'm not going to do it, but for other reasons," Marios told him. Rice speculated about whether the child was legitimate, but Mary said she had checked and if a child had been conceived prior to a divorce, it was. Rice wanted to know how the house on Riverbend Avenue in Knoxville could have passed to Mary if she maintained she was married, but was in fact single. They told Rice the house had been purchased for Mary and the child. But it was too large and too far from the center of town. Now Mary planned to move to Birmingham, Alabama, where her brother lived.

"Where do *you* intend to live?" Rice asked Marios.

"Athens," Marios said.

"At the same address where you had been?"

"No," Marios answered. But he wouldn't give a new address. Mail could be sent to him in care of Mary.

"What happened to the Jaguar bought at the time you and Sasha went to Greece?" Rice asked.

"I did wrong," Marios admitted. Although the Jaguar had been in Sasha's name, he had managed to sell it to an Athens dealer, pocketing the proceeds.

"Since it was in her name, how were you able to do this?"

Marios hinted he had bribed a customs official. But he would pay the money back. (Later Marios would say David gave him the Jaguar because David didn't consider that it belonged to the estate and so hadn't declared it on the inheritance tax return he filed in Richmond in July 1976. This was true. It was only on the September 26, 1978, accounting that the Jaguar appears as a $7,200 asset, sold by husband after decedent's death. "Michaelides is now a fugitive and claim is uncollectible," the revised accounting reads.)

"Who paid for the Jaguar originally?" Rice asked.

"I did," Marios said. "It was my money."

"My information is otherwise," Rice told him. "Sasha wrote the check."

"The Fidelity Bank in Brookneal could tell you it came from my brokerage account," Marios said testily.

Rice asked about the "Bruce family silver bearing the crest that was given to Sasha to be kept at Staunton Hill." Marios said he'd taken it to Greece because it reminded him of Sasha. If it was desirable, he would bring the silver back. But since he didn't declare the silver going into Greece, he would have trouble bringing it out.

"It would be a good idea to bring the silver back to the Bruces where it belongs," Rice said.

Rice found out many other things. He learned that Marios's visa had run out and was told Marios was in the business of exporting flour. Marios told him a man from Christie's had come to Staunton Hill and that Sasha had once attempted suicide by running her automobile into a piece of road equipment. Marios mentioned the May 1975 overdose. And it was Marios himself who revealed to Rice that Sasha had called Mary and asked her to take Marios and keep him in Knoxville "to settle him down," as if this detail would support a verdict of suicide rather than the reverse.

After Sasha's death, Marios said softly, he went back to Mary and Mary saved his life. She was his nurse. He buried his face in his hands and indulged in what Rice, unmoved, would later call "histrionics evidently designed to suggest that he was upset by talking about the great love of his life."

"Why would Sasha want to take her life?" Rice asked.

"She was unhappy."

"Why as a new bride was she unhappy?"

"She was happy on the outside but crying on the inside."

Rice turned to Marios's visit to Staunton Hill earlier that month.

"I just wanted to visit the grave of my love, pick up my mail, and ask where Nicky was," Marios said. "There's something I have to talk to Nick about and I don't know where to get in touch with him."

"You can reach him through me," Rice dryly told Marios.

"I hear you're interested in buying Staunton Hill," Rice said casually. "I would like to," Marios confided. "But I don't have the funds." In Marios's version of this conversation, Rice asked him, "What do you think will happen to that place? Do you want that place for yourself?"

Nearly two hours had passed. Mary nervously said her mother might come home any time now. She felt Rice's malicious intent and was frightened. He looked like an ambassador, so tall and dignified with his gray hair. But his manner had been heavy-handed. He was barely able to bring himself to be civil, she thought.

Rice thanked Mary and Marios for their candor. He hoped the lines of communication might be kept open. Then he asked to see their little girl.

"Why?" Marios asked, suspicious.

"The ambassador asked me to," Rice replied. "She has his daughter's name. Maybe he's planning to leave her something in his will."

Mary once more requested permission of Marios and after some hesitation Marios agreed. Rice was surprised to see that with her fair skin, blond hair, and blue eyes the child bore no resemblance whatsoever to the father he would soon be referring to as "the slimy Greek."

With some amusement Rice noted that Marios seemed to have forgotten that he was wounded and in great pain. By now he was up and walking around the house and it was Marios who saw Downey Rice to the door.

*   *   *

Rice set forth with the fervor of a trapper. In March he was at the offices of Anderson & Strudwick in Lynchburg. Overcoming problems of confidentiality, Rice managed to find out that Marios was still a customer. By March twenty-third he was anxious to brief Byron Keeling, the Charlotte County prosecutor, on the progress of his investigation. Meanwhile, Reginald Pettus sent Rice's growing file to Royston Jester III, longtime Lynchburg prosecutor and now a lawyer in private practice. Pettus was ready to argue that Sasha had died intestate given the circumstances surrounding the writing of her will; Marios had coerced her into that as into everything else. "In law," Pettus reminded David K. E. Bruce, "one may make certain allegations, even though one knows they may be incorrect."

Pettus feared, however, that the validity of the deed whereby Sasha transferred her interest in Staunton Hill to her brother Nick might also be questioned if they were contending that she had written her will under coercion. This might put a cloud over the title to the real estate of Staunton Hill which would prevent its sale. But David Surtees Bruce said he had decided not to part with Staunton Hill—yet.

Jester's opinion was that there was insufficient evidence to justify the expense of a prosecution of Michaelides on a charge of homicide. But he suggested that Sasha's body be exhumed and a complete autopsy be performed. Otherwise they couldn't even prove that the .22 Walther was the murder weapon. Jester wondered whether Sasha had been on drugs the day she was shot. He was unaware that the body had not been embalmed, making toxicology more than a year after her death all but impossible.

Pleased with Jester's suggestions, Pettus told him his letter "poignantly" displayed his talent for this sort of practice. He would recommend that Ambassador Bruce employ him. But, Pettus knew, Bruce was still disturbed by the publicity which would come to him as a result of pushing the case further. He was "terribly afraid of publicity." Even Pettus, who idolized the ambassador, had to admit it was "unusual" that Bruce still preferred at this late date to attribute Sasha's death to suicide rather than homicide. Bruce told Pettus he had refused an autopsy and had had Sasha buried so hastily because he wanted to get away as quickly as possible and felt completely helpless. He had been through a similar experience with his daughter Audrey and couldn't face another.

It was now April 1977. Bruce refused to request that the US Attorney General's Office investigate Sasha's death. He had no contact with Jimmy Carter's administration, he said. If his sons wanted to, they might look into it, but he was old. He could not bring Sasha back to life, and there was nothing he wanted to do about it.

Bruce did admit he was disturbed that his sons had continued to be friendly with Michaelides after Sasha's death. He couldn't understand this. He had heard that Nick had visited Staunton Hill, but his parents, who were in Washington, had no communication from him. Strange conduct, the ambassador thought. But he was worried about how the boys could give valid title to Staunton Hill under the circumstances.

Bruce revealed that the wedding silver had weighed eighty pounds and so it was unlikely that Marios had carted it to Greece in an airplane, as he had claimed. He must have sold it to some jeweler, Bruce figured. It was worth about forty thousand dollars.

Rice met with an FBI official in Washington in charge of the Fraud Division on April twentieth. By sending the rare books to New York, Michaelides had violated the federal statute prohibiting the interstate transportation of stolen property in an amount in excess of five thousand dollars. The FBI office in Richmond was handed the case. David K. E. Bruce expressed his pleasure that "the FBI is now proceeding to track that abominable rascal."

The Sasha Bruce House, a project organized by Mrs. Bruce as "a shelter for youths with problems," was opened in Washington on April twenty-eighth. The Brookneal *Union Star* described it as "a temporary refuge from emotional storms—family problems that drive kids out of their homes, troubles in school, brushes with the law, and the menaces that confront the young and troubled out on the streets." Sasha's neighbor Mary Morris was pained when she read that story; it seemed to describe Sasha's own life. Old friends like Wes

Profit hooted, poining out that, at Lyman, Sasha worked for
the dissolution of such institutions.

Julie Clark organized a memorial garden for Sasha, a place
where friends could pay their respects. The site was at Harvard,
not Radcliffe, as Julie had intended. A ceremony took place
on May first, which would have been Sasha's thirty-first
birthday. Attendance was sparse. Neither David nor Nicky
nor Terry Graham nor Wendy Wisner was there. Mrs. Bruce
came with Lavinia Currier. Jane ("Trickster") Frick also
turned up; soon she would commit suicide. The garden hadn't
yet bloomed and the little band of participants stood together
at a barren place. No one made a speech; no plaque was set
up. The event fell flat.

"If he made her miserable, it's irrelevant who pulled the
trigger," Mrs. Bruce told one of Sasha's friends.

Rice now arranged for a meeting of all the police authorities involved. The group gathered on July 6, 1977, at the
Virginia State Police headquarters in Richmond. O. T. Blalock
represented the FBI; several Virginia State Police agents had
been assigned to the case. The meeting lasted four hours. His
research had convinced him, Rice announced at once, that
Marios Michaelides had murdered Sasha Bruce.

The FBI had already decided that a murder indictment
should be pursued first. Only afterwards should the fraud
involving transportation of stolen property be taken up. Rice
was convinced the fraud charge could be "beefed up
substantially." "He knew damn well he wasn't entitled to
those books," Rice said. On the night following the shooting,
"he first said the library belonged to the three brothers and
then he said the two brothers and Sasha."

"He's got himself a fraud here now," Rice went on.
"He's represented that he owned these books, he didn't own
them. No way he could own them. He had just been dicker-
ing to buy the property from the brothers—he was drawing up
IOUs. He knew damn well he didn't own those things."

Sasha's complicity in the sale of the books was, of course,
obvious, but Rice argued that this did not exonerate Marios.
"It would be like saying that bank across the street is mine
and you know damn well it isn't. She can't give him title
where she doesn't have title and he knows she doesn't have

it. So, to me, it was an out-and-out fraud when he says to Stephen Massey of Christie's, these are my books.

"But still," Rice had to admit, "I'm not saying she's innocent. I think she was just as much a crook in this particular thing as he was. She was stealing from her brothers. They didn't know—they didn't authorize her. . . ."

Pervading Rice's presentation was his feeling that fair all-American girls had been dominated by a "slimy Greek." Stephen Massey, on the other hand, was described to the assembled police officers as "a nice young Englishman." Twigg, too, met with Rice's approval. "Both of these are nice English people," he said, "and English people are damn conservative when they come to telling you something."

Rice also planned to argue in court that the Haitian divorce was "collusive" and hence that Marios and Sasha had never been legally married. "It sure fooled the hell out of me!" Rice confessed.

"He's living with Mary now," Rice revealed. "As a lawyer, I'd say that's collusive, that's perjury."

Marios's admission that he "slung" Sasha generated some discussion. "Whatever the hell 'slung' means," Rice said, "but he had slung her and he slung her that night up there in Washington—up there at the house. I'd translate that saying he'd hit her or something."

"He might have picked her up and threw her," Blalock offered.

Rice spoke of the generation gap between the ambassador and his children. "If Sasha wanted something the brothers would strain to see it her way, to get it for her," Rice believed. "If she liked Marios, he was good enough for them."

"It's pointed out to me now by the ambassador that the younger fellows are somewhat dismayed and chagrined and upset and embarrassed by some of the revelations of what Marios did with the property . . . they feel like 'we blew this, we thought this fellow was all right. . . .' "

Marios was "a take-charge guy," Rice said, but "the fact of the matter was that he couldn't read a damn trust because if he had waited or she had waited or she had lived another couple of months she would have come into a very substantial amount of money." Rice had to admit, however, that he wasn't sure whether Marios ever had access to the trust agreement. He himself had been unable to locate a copy of Sasha's trust.

"The children didn't themselves have copies of their trusts," Rice had discovered. "It was pretty much oral what they understood. They did know that the trusts threw out somewhere between forty and eighty thousand dollars a year."

Together the group mistakenly figured out that Mary must have called Sasha on November sixth.

"Supposing this was a call from his wife in Tennessee, advising she was pregnant, this would have caused him to go into a tizzy at that point of time," Blalock reasoned.

"Absolutely," said Rice.

"It could have been a call from her putting on him to do something about. . . ."

Rice completed the thought. "Mary calls up and talks to somebody and it comes out that she is pregnant . . . a girl that he is supposed to have finished seeing, divorced and all that . . . somebody's going to go through the ceiling. And when you do go through the ceiling, who do you go after? Do you commit suicide or do you shoot the son-of-a-bitch or try to or what? Who shoots who at this point I don't know.

"It seems to me it's consistent with the possibility that when she learned that, Sasha, who had been using a .22, started after him, threatening. And he turned it around on her, grabbed it and turned it around on her. That's about as close as I come. It's nothing inconsistent with that in terms of how the weapon was found and what he did afterwards."

(Rice was founding much of his case for murder on Sasha's discovery of Mary's pregnancy on the day of the shooting. Yet in a shipboard note to her husband, Sasha had written of Marios's "secrets about Mary's baby"—this note came to the authorities only in the autumn of 1978, after Michaelides had already been indicted for Sasha's murder.)

With relish, Rice described his encounter with Marios in Tennessee: "Well, you know a lifetime of investigative work—you can get into some tough interviews. This was one of the tougher ones. Here's the guy sitting there and I wanted to talk to her, so I just ploughed into it.

"Well, he had the vapors and all that crap . . . and he was upset and excited and couldn't understand why the Bruce family was [making inquiries] and all that, and I said, 'come off of it, will you?' He told other people later on that whenever the Virginia State Police . . . would stop him for speeding—he's a notorious speeder—he would act like he couldn't speak the language and suggest that he was a diplomat and was leaving for Greece the next day and they would always let him go. So he's a big actor. So he tried all that crap. . . .

"He has never done a day's work in his life as far as a nine-to-five type operation is concerned," Rice added with disdain. "He is playing a role. He is obviously getting his kicks from dreaming up schemes and deals and things like that where we're thinking about baseball and how to dominate women.

"I'm sitting there in a room with a University of Tennessee graduate and a wholesome-looking American girl who has taken all of this garbage from this slimy Greek. . . . This is really mind-boggling, but he exercised . . . the same domination over this wealthy girl who ought to have had everything, but still she is totally subservient to the whims of this guy." Sasha "was a girl who could be dominated, although a good-looking girl, I understand," Rice said.

He paused over Marios's call to Anderson & Strudwick at 4:09 on the day of the shooting. "It sure intrigues me," Rice said. "If he knew at that time she was shot or after I don't know." Rice contended that Sasha's deportment "was not consistent with a person who is figuring to go out and kill herself that afternoon. She was making plans to go to Greece, she was making plans to receive the godparents and cooking things for them. . . ."

How the Bruce brothers could have given Marios one hundred ninety thousand dollars also required some explaining.

"Words will not describe these two boys," Rice told his fellow officers. "They're grown—one of them is thirty, thirty-one, or thirty-two and the other one is in his twenties. But *naive* is not a strong enough word. They are just unworldly. They have been raised with this money coming in and they have never been exposed to the rough and tumble—they don't understand values . . . in dealing with Michaelides they're dealing with the opposite end of the pole.

"Here's a fellow who translates everything into terms of money. His mind is like that—when it comes to the money angle. So he says, this is worth six hundred thousand dollars, so if you want me out, why don't you give me six hundred thousand. Well, he finally backs down to where he would take one hundred thousand dollars from each of them. They said to me, 'Well, that was a good deal because we reduced him from six hundred thousand to two hundred thousand dollars.'

"They are assuming at all times that his marriage to their sister was bona fide. I, of course, express my doubts. I think that the divorce being invalid would restore him as a husband of Mary and a marriage to Sasha would be bigamous."

Rice had learned that Marios forged his brother Eugenios's signature on the renouncement. "So far as I know, Eugenios has never been in the United States. How in the hell am I going to get specimens of his writing?" he worried. Rice was contemptuous of Marios's doubts about his being able to get the silver out of Greece: "You son-of-a-bitch, you got it in, get it out!"

"In a few months time he cleared pretty close to a half million," Rice concluded. "Now what's Mary Lewis's role in all this?"

Rice outlined the day of the shooting. He argued that Marios's behavior was "more consistent with a man who knew that she was shot than with a man who did not know what had happened to her. If she was just lying there, it seems to me your instincts in finding her would be to roll her over or do something, try to talk to her, but he seemed to know right away that she was shot. . . . He was thinking 'gun'—what made him think gun if he didn't really know what happened to her?" Rice pondered, recounting how Marios had admitted when he was in the house he looked immediately under the bed to see if the gun was there.

"That seemed to me to be a strange piece of business—looking under that bed for a gun when your wife is lying under the tree, you don't know, really, don't know what's the matter with her. He's running all around doing that."

Rice revealed that Marios had telephoned Stephen Massey from Greece about the three volumes not sold at the London auctions. Massey had told him they were still in England, but if they were sent over, they might be sold in the States. But Marios had told Massey he was returning to America via London and would pick up the books himself. By the time Rice was on his trail, Marios had the books in his possession.

Marios's whereabouts were a matter of concern. Rice thought

his own visit to Tennessee wouldn't do anything to help Marios's peace of mind. "He's timid, he's sensitive," Rice assessed correctly. "He could be a runner!"

Rice had tried not to scare him off. "With his investments here," Rice speculated, "he'll be coming back from time to time. I can't conceive of him spending full-time over there in Tennessee because this is a modest home in a small town and they've just got the upstairs part for him and his wife and baby. And this fellow has been staying at the Savoy and St. Regency and got this couple hundred thousand and driving his Lincoln. He's a CB man, got a CB in that Lincoln he's driving."

As they began to close in on Michaelides, Rice outlined the next steps he thought should be taken. He wrote them down "just like Bureau leads, the way I used to."

Rice wanted the Fidelity Bank records in Brookneal. In Richmond he thought they might find a photograph issued with Marios's pilot's license or driver's license. "No one has ever seen a photograph of this guy," Rice noted. "No wedding pictures, there are no nothings." In Maryville the newspaper said they had a picture with every announcement except Mary's; in the story they ran only the bride was shown.

All the banks, including the one in Keysville where Marios had tried to borrow two hundred fifty thousand dollars, would have personal files. Rice wanted the Lewis home in Maryville checked to see if any valuables from Staunton Hill had been moved there; he wanted the Lewis phone records for the fall of 1975. Rice thought Marios's safe-deposit box at the Fidelity American Bank in Lynchburg might contain some of his "ill-gotten gains." The same Greek who had told David about Marios's having beat up a woman in Athens would be asked somehow to obtain a sample of Eugenios's writing. Anderson & Strudwick would be requested to reveal their records and so would Master Charge. The hotel in Haiti would be checked to see if Mary and Marios had occupied the same room.

Rice considered trying to interview Mary alone. "Well, I tell you what I was going to do," Rice admitted. "I was gonna go down and see her mother. I'd say 'Ma, what the hell is going on?' My wife said if it's the last thing you do, you have got to tell that woman what's been going on—what her daughter is married to, because she may be in a vulnerable position.''

FBI agent Blalock urged, ''We've got to be very careful.''

Rice understood. ''All right. Suppose he finds a new pigeon. The only place he is going to find a new pigeon is in the States. So he is going to be around here looking for one. He may decide Mary is expendable.''

''Not so long as she cooperates,'' Boone of the State Police said.

John E. Mills of the Virginia State Police now took over from Rice, scrupulously interviewing everyone connected with Sasha's death. There were so few witnesses that Mills's patience gave way at times. ''Are you saying that you believe that he actually pulled the trigger or are you saying that he drove her to it?'' he demanded of Buss Baker. ''I ain't going to answer that,'' was Buss's reply.

Trying to communicate with John LeGrand, whose English was half Cajun, on the question of Sasha's black eye, Mills snapped, ''Just don't care one way or the other, huh?''

Meg Tibbs had understood Sasha's typical emotional pattern: ''Whenever I saw her she was always happy and very full of life. She was either covering up her problems or wishing them away.'' But Tibbs would not confirm Marios's saying Sasha had been *shot* when he came to her door after finding the body. ''I really don't think he said she shot herself,'' Meg told Mills. ''I think he said she killed herself, she's dying. . . .'' Stephen Massey had been ordered by Christie's not to discuss the matter with anyone and Priscilla Jaretzki suddenly revealed that she hadn't wanted Rainer Esslen to drive Marios back to Staunton Hill the night Sasha was shot because she was afraid that Marios was a cold-blooded murderer.

On August second Marios phoned Downey Rice and said he had a portion of the silver. He would either return it to Staunton Hill in person or mail it. He promised to return the remainder at a later date.

Two weeks later, on August seventeenth, Marios telephoned Mike Carter, the Staunton Hill caretaker. He was planning to mail the silverware back to Staunton Hill, Marios said. He gave Carter the registration number of the package. The next day a small box wrapped in brown paper and addressed to Mr. Mike Carter arrived. Inside were one hundred and two of the two hundred pieces of silver Marios had taken. The return address read: "Marios Michaelides, 3600 Haven View Circle, Birmingham, Alabama."

Rice wrote to Marios on August thirtieth in Birmingham thanking him for the silver and asking when the balance might be expected. It was silver given to David Bruce by his mother, Rice pointed out, and was "a part of Staunton Hill." In the same letter he requested a check for the Jaguar in the amount of 4,734 pounds to be made payable to David Surtees Bruce as executor.

Sasha may have taken her own life, Mike Carter told John Mills on August thirty-first, but Marios drove her to it. She was "a dumb kid who had climbed a tree and couldn't figure out how to get down."

At the scene of the shooting on September second Mills found three 22-caliber shell casings. By October fifth he knew they had all been fired from the Walther pistol.

By November 1977, Ambassador Bruce was convinced that Marios should be tried for bigamy and fraud and then kicked out of the country and not be allowed ever to return. If some of the money and things he stole could be returned, fine, Bruce said, but he was not concerned about that. Regarding the murder charge, Bruce said, "Oh, yes, that too. If it could be proved."

On November ninth David K. E. Bruce was driven to the Clark Brothers Gun Shop to identify the L. C. Smith shotgun Marios had sold. Bruce told Mills he didn't have the serial number, but was certain he could identify the gun. When Clark got up and went into a back room to fetch it, Mills followed and requested that he show the ambassador a similiar one. Clark handed the ambassador a 10-gauge L. C. Smith instead of the 8-gauge one from Staunton Hill. Bruce took the gun and examined it. "Yep, this is the gun that my old grandpappy gave me," he said. "This is my gun."

* * *

"Would the family object to an autopsy?" Mills asked Bruce.

"Was she not cremated?" her father replied.

Bruce thought the bigamy charge was the easiest route since it would be difficult to convict Marios of stealing from Staunton Hill since his daughter was an accomplice. But he agreed now to testify in court. Rice planned to use the bigamy charge to destroy Michaelides's stance as Sasha's surviving husband. Then they could go after him in civil court to recover the assets he "grabbed from the estate." The bigamy conviction would also set Michaelides up for deportation since bigamy could be considered a crime involving "moral turpitude."

The bigamy case Rice worked up was founded on a 1921 Virginia decision, *L. G. Corvin* v. *Commonwealth of Virginia*, in which a man named Corvin moved to West Virginia expressly for the purpose of getting a divorce and so was judged guilty of bad faith and fraud in a conviction later upheld by the Virginia Supreme Court of Appeals. Mary and Marios, who remained intimate, even bed partners, at the moment of the Haitian divorce, which had been granted on the ground of "incompatibility," had also obtained their decree by false representations in which they had "colluded." The jurisdiction for the bigamy charge could be the place of the second marriage, Virginia. The Corvin decision concluded that Virginia will not recognize a divorce secured in another state "upon false testimony as to domicile and cause for divorce."

The Haitian divorce was "patently preposterous," Rice said. Mary had admitted to him how she and Marios were "still friends." Now he had to convince Byron Keeling, Charlotte County commonwealth attorney, that Marios's wedding to Sasha represented a criminal act of bigamy in Virginia. Keeling wondered whether Marios could have obtained a divorce in Tennessee, a question an irritated Rice found "irrelevant, speculative, and procrastination." He explained to Keeling that "incompatibility" was not a ground for absolute divorce in Tennessee. Mary could have obtained an absolute divorce only if she had charged Marios with adultery and named Sasha as corespondent.

*   *   *

On November twenty-eighth Judge J. R. Snoddy, Jr., of Charlotte County signed the court order to exhume Sasha's body for the purpose of an autopsy.

Having been stricken by a heart attack, David K. E. Bruce died on December fifth at Georgetown University Hospital. He was seventy-nine years old.

Dr. David Oxley performed the autopsy on December nineteenth in Roanoke. He was instructed to offer his conclusion on the basis of forensic and other evidence as to the probable cause of death. Sasha's body was in so advanced a state of decomposition that it was impossible to do any toxicology. It was too late to determine whether there had been a contact ring around the wound; this would have resulted if the muzzle of the gun had been moved slightly off the skin. It was too late to look for powder residue inside the path of the wound.

Oxley removed the bullet, a .22 Remington-Long Rifle. It was so mutilated and corroded that it was impossible to determine the lands and grooves that would have matched it with any particular weapon. The skull fracture indicated it had been a contact or near-contact wound. There were no other fractures, no other bullets. The soft tissue was gone.

With this slim evidence, Oxley confirmed the original verdict of suicide. Sasha's remains were cremated and transported to Oak Hill Cemetery in Maryland where she would be buried beside her father.

Negotiations between Marios and Downey Rice continued as Marios sought to extricate himself from the growing case against him by appeasing the adversaries he grossly underestimated, having believed the whole matter would blow over sooner or later. "Looking at Sasha's checking account as well as mine," Marios wrote to Rice on December twenty-first, "it becomes obvious to me that my memory had deceived me." Sasha had indeed paid for the Jaguar. Marios was ready, he told Rice, "to settle our differences."

Using a *Wall Street Journal* exchange rate for December fourteenth, Marios wanted to pay $1.79 to the pound, or $8,433.36 for the Jaguar. In exchange he expected a statement that neither the executor of Sasha's will nor "anybody else" will make further demands on him regarding this subject.

Keeping the lines of communication open, Rice questioned why they should use the exchange rate of December fourteenth.

By February first, Marios had hired a Birmingham lawyer named Virginia Emerson to deal with the claims being made against him. Rice treated her with sarcasm. "It is nice to know that Marios Michaelides has asked you to represent him," he said. Rice first told Emerson that only the Jaguar was at issue. "It is simply a question of reimbursing David S. Bruce, executor of his sister's estate, for the car," he said.

On the same day Rice wrote to Royston Jester, who had been advising him. A former agent friend in Alabama had sent information about Maurice Bell, the correspondent lawyer in Alabama who had arranged the Haitian divorce. After the Bar Association cracked down on lawyers handling quickie divorces, Bell had left Montgomery and gone first to Tijuana and then to Haiti. He returned to Montgomery in the mid-seventies.

Rice was now having Mary and Marios watched closely. His strategy was to maintain an unhurried and low-key dialogue with Marios while hastening to consolidate his cases against him for bigamy, grand larceny, embezzlement, and murder.

By February twenty-eighth Virginia Emerson had discovered that in Rice's letters to Marios he mentioned other items in addition to the Jaguar. Now she requested a complete list of all the claims being made against her client.

Rice flew to London in February where he chatted with Patrick Swafler of Goodman, Derrick. He wondered whether there had been a conspiracy between von Kassel and Michaelides. Perhaps von Kassel knew the end had come and so Sasha got handed on at the right time and place to someone with the right sympathies. Rice wasn't sure.

Rice informed Royston Jester on March second that with the information he had obtained from Christie's on his London trip he now had Michaelides on two state violations and one federal violation. He had larceny or larceny after trust from the Bruce brothers. And he had concealment of an asset from Sasha's estate with the Jaguar. He also had his illegal transportation of property in excess of five thousand dollars across state lines. A new US attorney was about to be appointed in Virginia and Rice hoped for additional help from the FBI.

If an outstanding bigamy warrant would lead to federal help under the unlawful flight to avoid prosecution statute, the FBI could simply arrest Marios in Alabama, Mills thought. Meanwhile as Rice kept up his correspondence with Virginia Emerson, copies were going to David Surtees Bruce, Reginald Pettus, John Mills, and Royston Jester III.

"As to other 'claims,' " Rice wrote Emerson disingenuously, on March eighth, "I am afraid that we are getting into something that sounds like an adversary relationship when, in fact, we have simply been getting some information and guidance from your client." Now Rice did admit to Emerson that he had been asking Marios about various Bruce family heirlooms, including silverware and a ring which was stolen on their honeymoon.

As far as Emerson knew, none of the crested silverware was in the United States. She raised a question regarding whose law would pertain with regard to the Jaguar which had never entered the United States; Greek law might apply, she thought. Marios had believed his dealings with Rice had "remained on a merely informational and nonadversary level," she argued. And once more she offered that Marios pay for the Jaguar in exchange for "a complete release of any and all claims of the estate against him."

Revealing nothing to Emerson, Rice and Mills now looked forward to indictments and a trial. Mills would arrange for the shotgun to be collected from the Clark Brothers so that it could be used as evidence in court. Concerned that Marios not be alerted to the seriousness of the charges against him, he trusted the Clark Brothers not to contact him.

Rice's contempt for Emerson grew. "I never did get along very well with lady lawyers, and my guess is that this one would be no exception," he said, calling her arguments "preposterous." How could it be illegal for Michaelides to bring the Bruce silver back from Greece when he had already returned some of it? And how could Greek law control a

Jaguar bought by Sasha in her maiden name as an individual in Switzerland through a British dealer?

Still, Rice replied on March 31, 1978, "we are not anxious to get into litigation either." He suggested that the silver be presented to the American Embassy in Athens and said he expected $9,988.74 and not $8,433,36 for the Jaguar. "Of course Mr. Michaelides would expect a release when these matters are behind us," he concluded vaguely. He said nothing about further claims the estate might have.

Emerson replied, now offering $7,200, the amount for which she revealed Marios had sold the Jaguar in Athens. Such a figure "would neither enrich nor penalize Mr. Michaelides for his efforts in having the by-then-used car released from impoundment at the customs office and sold." She was not convinced the Jaguar was even legally an asset of Sasha's estate. Certainly the silver was questionably so. "Can you steal your own wedding gift?" Marios said. "And why did they ask for the silver to be mailed to Staunton Hill if David Bruce wanted it for sentimental value? He never went there."

Emerson was adamant. Her client could not remove the silverware from Greece without facing criminal charges under Greek law. The US Embassy is not legally Greek soil and so it would be just as illegal for Michaelides to take it there as outside Greece, she reasoned. He would need a special exemption from Greek law to make a return of the silver to the United States legally possible. "We feel certain," she told Rice acidly, "that Mr. Bruce does not seek to induce Mr. Michaelides to commit any crime."

Emerson concluded with a veiled threat, a reference to the Arpad inventory which would "show the good faith of Marios's efforts." Michaelides knew of course that Sasha's third of the Staunton Hill furnishings had been grossly undervalued in the accounting of her estate. He was preparing his defense.

Rice read this final letter from "Michaelides's Portia" to David Surtees Bruce over the telephone. The game plan that called for stringing Michaelides along at a casual pace had outlived its usefulness. On March twenty-second Royston Jester and John Mills had met with Commonwealth Attorney Keeling. By May third arrest warrants charging Michaelides with bigamy and grand larceny of the rare books were in Mills's possession.

The Case Against
Marios Michaelides

On May 8, 1978, from Royston Jester's Lynchburg office, Downey Rice phoned his Birmingham contact, John Pope, to find out if Marios was at home. Calling back ten minutes later, Pope reported that Marios was indeed in Birmingham.

On the tenth, Pope affirmed again that Marios was home. Virginia State Police investigator John Mills then boarded a police airplane with two Virginia agents and flew to Birmingham. Ezra H. Vogel of the Alabama Bureau of Investigation, who met them at the airport at eleven thirty, said Marios actually lived in a small city outside Birmingham called Hoover. At the Jefferson County Administration Building, Alabama arrest warrants were issued.

By the time they reached the Michaelides apartment at 3600 Haven View Circle, the group had swelled to seven and included two deputy sheriffs from Jefferson County and one Hoover police sergeant. A knock at the front door produced no response. After pounding for ten minutes, one of the officers heard a baby crying inside. One of the deputies renewed his knocking with greater vigor. Finally Mary opened the door.

Mills told her he had warrants for the arrest of Marios as "a fugitive from justice from the State of Virginia, charged by the State of Virginia with the offenses of bigamy and embezzlement." He did not reveal that he himself had come from Virginia. Confused, Mary thought he said "indictments." She told Mills that Marios had gone to Greece on April twenty-third to visit his family. He had been scheduled to return to Birmingham today, the tenth; a bad cold had led him to postpone his return for one day.

With no intention of taking Mary's word for this, the gang of officers now made their way into the apartment in search of Marios. Would you consent to be interviewed? Mills meanwhile asked Mary. Still believing he was an Alabama investigator, she agreed. The baby began to cry again and so Mary picked her up and held her on her lap throughout the interview. Feeling as if she had been captured by the entire United States Cavalry, she was in a state of near-hysteria.

Her first thought was that it might not be wise to answer any of Mills's questions.

"I should call a lawyer," Mary began.

"Why don't you wait," Mills urged smoothly. "There are just a few things I should ask you."

"I'd like a fair exchange of information," Mary countered, abandoning her original instinct that she needed and had a right to legal advice.

Marios had told her almost nothing about his relationship with Sasha and the Bruce brothers. She still didn't know whether or not Sasha had been told about Rosie.

"We'll get to that," Mills promised.

Mary did not object when Mills turned on a tape recorder. He told her none of her rights and insisted that she remain downstairs. Meanwhile the police went over the upper floor untroubled by the fact that no search warrant had been issued.

The apartment was filthy and in disarray. There was an arsenal of guns. On one wall were pasted graphs, lines going up and down, every which way. Books and papers scattered about also pointed to someone's obsession with the stock market. The furniture was a cheap five-and-dime variety. Three large and obviously expensive bird books were sitting on the floor of one room. The inordinate amount of silver seemed out of place in these shabby surroundings.

Terrified and increasingly disoriented, Mary submitted to Mills's questions. He asked her husband's name and she began "Marios Michaeli—" only to correct herself. "No, I'm sorry. I'm not married."

Mary explained that she had gotten a divorce in Haiti to avoid a scandal: "That was the medium out of this kind of an ugly thing," she said. When Mills asked her why she wanted a divorce, she replied, "My husband was in love with another woman, and I gave him the divorce in return that he would give me a child, and that was our deal."

"Isn't this a little unusual, Mrs. Michaelides?" Mills baited her.

"I was fearful that I'd never remarry and never be able to

get a chance for a family," Mary explained. Although her husband was unfaithful, she hadn't lost her feelings of friendship for him "because in Greece very often men are unfaithful and it's kind of like the social circle." She admitted that Marios had been unfaithful many times before; she had been conditioned to accept it.

Mills asked if she had ever intended to use the child to win Marios back.

"Maybe initially I did," Mary admitted, "but by the time she was conceived, I no longer had feelings of that nature because I knew the other woman that was involved was a very unstable, very unhappy individual and was going through great emotional stress and trauma."

Mary admitted truthfully that she had agreed to the divorce before she conceived Rosie; she had decided after Sasha's May suicide attempt "that if I didn't conceive this last time that I would give him the divorce anyway, because she in the meantime had tried to commit suicide." Mary thought Sasha had tried suicide because the marriage to Marios had been delayed and there had been so much difficulty because he was still married. "If nothing happens, let's just call it quits and wash our hands," Mary said she told Marios that last time they slept together in June 1975 in Tennessee.

Mills embarrassed Mary by asking if Marios ever struck her.

"No, he's never struck me," Mary replied evenly.

She had no idea where Marios had met Sasha and she had never heard the name Anton von Kassel. Mills returned to the trip to Haiti, beginning with simple questions about where they stayed and then working up to the point as he attempted to reinforce the bigamy case developed by Downey Rice.

"Okay, being there approximately three or four days, did you and Mr. Michaelides share the same room while you were there?"

"Yes, we did."

"Now, after the divorce was final? Did you still share the same room?"

"Well, that was just one more day," Mary went on, obviously unaware of the direction of the argument. "Yes, we did. I became violently ill and first of all he was taking care of me because I had gotten that Montezuma's Revenge from the water."

Mary found out she was pregnant only a few weeks after the divorce. When he returned from his honeymoon with Sasha in Greece, Marios came back to Tennessee for a four- or five-day visit to set the stage to show Mary's parents that their marriage was disintegrating, "in order to psychologically and emotionally prepare them . . . this was the reason for the return visit." But they did not share the same room. Sasha died soon after and Marios came back.

"So what you are telling me now is that your parents to this date do not know that you and Marios Michaelides went to Haiti for a divorce and that he supposedly married Alexandra Bruce?"

"No, they don't know," Mary confessed, in her confusion failing to pick up on Mills's "supposedly."

Mary said she and Marios were not now living as man and wife. "We're just friends really, we're just cohabiting under the same roof . . . we are here because of the child. We're trying to make a home for her. We have a platonic relationship; we've had one since Alexandra died, and since the time that Rosie was conceived, really."

During the three months Marios was married to Sasha they'd never discussed getting back together.

She had never met Sasha, Mary told Mills, although she had talked to her on the telephone, both in Greece and when Marios made his visit to Tennessee. And then there was a call on Sunday November second, early in the morning, when Sasha asked Mary to invite Marios back to Tennessee for an indeterminable stay.

"She didn't say what the trouble was then. I don't to this day really know what was the problem," Mary said. "I don't know because Marios has never talked to me about it." After Sasha's death Marios said, "If you'll stay with me, if you accept the terms of just living under the same roof together, and providing a home for the child . . . I have to have something to live for now."

"I felt so sorry for him, too," Mary remembered. "He was absolutely crushed, he was torn up, and I guess I still was feeling sorry for myself a little bit, too."

She couldn't understand where the bigamy charge came from. "You know, we were honorably divorced in order that he honorably marry her. I don't see how they can present grounds for bigamy. What's their case?"

Mills told her it was based on there being a lack of grounds in Tennessee: "If there were no grounds for divorce in Tennessee, then how could there be grounds for divorce in Haiti?"

Mary immediately recognized the fallaciousness of such reasoning. "That was the reason we didn't get the divorce in Tennessee," she told her adversary. Not about to explain the Corvin decision to Mary, let alone the issue of "collusion," Mills quickly changed the subject. Did Mary think Marios married Sasha for her money or "Do you think it was true love?"

"No," Mary said staunchly, "because Marios had had opportunities to marry a lot of richer women than Sasha." When he married her, he was "asset rich and capital poor." He came from a very wealthy family in Greece, Mary said loyally. "They are a manufacturing family and he had a very similar background to Alexandra. He did not marry her for her money. I know that because he could have married a lot of richer women than she ever thought about being and didn't."

"Financially, is he caring for you now?" Mills asked her.

Mary said he brought money from abroad and played the stock market. But she admitted things had become "kind of frayed" and she had discussed dissolving their connection. Marios would return by himself to Greece and she would remain in America.

"It was an honorable effort," Mary told Mills, "but it really hasn't been satisfactory to either one of us."

Did Mary know of any property that Marios might have removed from Staunton Hill when he came back to her? "Silver, this type thing?"

"Oh, no," Mary said.

"Statues? paintings? books?"

The silver was given to Marios by David Bruce, Mary said.

"Where is the silver now?" Mills asked.

"Well, most of it, there's some of it that's here," Mary admitted. "And some of it is in Greece." The lawyer who asked for the silver back made Marios angry because he also asked for the car; Marios had decided he wasn't going to return the remainder until they got that straightened out. The part that was in Greece was taken there "by him and Alexandra."

"Do his parents know about the marriage to Sasha?" Mills asked cleverly.

"Yes, they do," Mary said, lying.

But when Mills asked whether the Michaelides family knew of Mary's present status with Marios, she had to admit, "As far as I know, they do. See, I haven't—" (She did not complete that sentence, did not admit she had never met them.) "I don't really . . . I mean, I assume they do."

"When do you expect him back?" Mills of course wanted to know.

"He's coming back tomorrow."

"How?"

"He's coming back on a TWA flight."

By now Mills had alarmed Mary sufficiently for her to take some action. "I want to," she stammered, "I'm going to call him and tell him, now I want to be advised on this, because I'm interested in his welfare and if you . . . I should also contact my lawyer, right?"

"We will, we'll discuss it," Mills evaded. "Mrs. Michaelides, I certainly want to thank you for this interview and we apologize for having to come in like this, but we had no choice."

"I understand," Mary said, seemingly submissive. "If only you hadn't brought that uniformed man."

"Well, sometimes that's necessary in cases like this."

Mills asked if he could see the books. "I'd rather you wouldn't since Marios is not at home," Mary told him. Then, pulling herself together and with considerable spunk, in an apartment crawling with police officers, Mary followed her instincts, picked up the telephone, and dialed Athens. Luckily, Marios answered. She told him what had happened while Mills stood there helplessly, unable even to threaten her with punishment for helping a fugitive evade justice. She was free to make that call, Mary felt. There was no warrant for *her* arrest.

Putting down the receiver, Mary gave Mills a message from Marios. He had decided to remain in Greece until he had time to do some investigating of his own.

*   *   *

The next morning Mills and Vogel returned to the Jefferson County Administration Building where a deputy district attorney drew up an affidavit from Mills. This time Vogel was issued a search warrant. Back they went to Haven View Circle where they served Mary with the warrant and entered the apartment unchallenged. The silver and books listed in the warrant were photographed and removed. The police carried away the two-volume *Birds of North America* and the *Family of the Grouse*. The confiscated silver included six goblets, an ashtray, a candle holder and snuffer, a jewelry box, a platter, and an inkstand—all with the Bruce crest picturing a lion with its head raised and its tail extended. A silver compote bore the initials D. B. The wooden silver chest, also with the family crest pictured on it, now contained thirty knives, thirty-four forks, and thirty-five spoons.

Mills noticed a few other items which he thought might have come from Staunton Hill because they seemed very old and out of place in that apartment. Hanging on the living room walls were a painting depicting prancing horses by Edouard Swebach, another called "Italian Water Girl" by Thomas Sully, and still another entitled "Battle of Waterloo." In that room were also two bronze figurines of horses and a blue and white vase with pine trees and deer. A colorful blue vase with a hole drilled for a lamp cord seemed suspicious, as did a drum table with a leather top. At least two hundred books seemed to Mills to be similar to those he had observed in the Staunton Hill library. One set containing forty-three volumes was on a sporting subject. The police finally departed at 6:05 P.M.

By Monday, May fifteenth, all the articles seized from Mary's apartment were safely stored in an evidence locker at the State Police headquarters in Appomattox, Virginia.

Mary knew, of course, that those other objects and books Mills noticed but did not remove also came from Staunton Hill. Frightened, she telephoned Marios's attorney, Virginia Emerson. Could you mail Marios the things from Staunton Hill which are still in the apartment? Mary pleaded. Emerson refused. All summer Mary wondered what to do about those objects.

* * *

By May twenty-third Mills knew that Marios had closed out his account at Anderson & Strudwick.

As soon as he returned to Virginia, Mills contacted David Surtees Bruce about the other items he suspected had been stolen from Staunton Hill. On May twenty-fourth Mills made copies of the Staunton Hill identification plate so he could recover the remaining rare books. David was ordered to make another survey of the Mansion House to determine whether any other articles were missing. With the Arpad inventory as his guide, he came up with a second list which included paintings by Swebach and Sully and a print of "The Battle of Waterloo" by Heath. There was a bronze figure of a stallion stamped Barye, and a bronze figure of a prancing horse, as well as a baluster-shaped vase from the K'ang Hsi period with pine trees and deer and flying birds, two baluster-shaped eighteenth-century vases, and two more K'ang Hsi blue and white bases made into lamps. There was also a set of leather-bound books called *Sporting Magazine*, a forty-three volume set of books entitled *Badminton Magazine*, and a drum table in the Georgian style valued at twenty-two hundred dollars.

By May twenty-ninth Marios had closed out both his account with the Fidelity Bank in Brookneal and his safe-deposit box. The money was wired to Alabama. Mary then sent it to Switzerland.

Downey Rice made one last visit to Tennessee. This time he told Mary's mother that he wanted to talk to her in order to "help Marios." Mrs. Lewis shut the door in his face. "There was something about that man I didn't like," she said later.

Hearing the story in Athens, Marios wondered. Had Rice come to make a deal? Was he ready to ask Marios to agree that his marriage to Sasha was invalid in exchange for dropping the murder charge? Was he there to ask Marios to sign a new renouncement? Or was "I think I can help Marios" just a ploy to get inside?

Marios would not return, Mills and Rice knew. On June seventh Mills consulted the FBI. Could they assist in having Marios returned to the United States from Greece to face the bigamy and embezzlement charges by issuing "unlawful flight warrants?'' On June fifteenth Royston Jester told Mills he had discovered that the United States did enjoy extradition privileges with Greece for charges of bigamy and embezzlement provided there was a grand jury indictment. It would appear that he hadn't consulted a standard treaty book.

Believing Jester knew what he was talking about and Marios could be extradited, the Charlotte County group now proceeded to obtain those indictments for bigamy and embezzlement. Rice had long been dissatisfied with the alcoholic prosecutor, Byron Keeling, whom he had accused of procrastinating. An unexpected boon now occurred. Keeling died suddenly, removing a significant obstacle from the case. An arsenal of weapons was found mysteriously locked in his desk.

On June twenty-seventh Edwin B. Baker, a country lawyer, was appointed to fill Keeling's term as commonwealth attorney. A thirty-six-year-old poker-playing amateur actor fresh from the tobacco fields of Charlotte County, Baker had once clerked in Reginald Pettus's office.

A week later, a special grand jury of inquest was called and on July fifth, Charlotte County indicted Marios Michaelides for ''feloniously and unlawfully'' marrying Alexandra Bruce and for ''feloniously, unlawfully, wrongfully, and fraudulently'' disposing of certain items of personal property belonging to ''the estate of Alexandra Bruce Michaelides, David S. Bruce, and Nicholas C. Bruce.'' A list of the books sold by Christie's appeared on this indictment, along with the recovered *Birds of North America* and *Family of the Grouse*.

Although he had advised the Bruces on the case, Charlotte County appointed Royston Jester III as special prosecutor ''to aid and assist the commonwealth in the prosecution of certain criminal indictments issued against the defendant Marios Michaelides.'' This was also accomplished on July fifth.

Would the prosecution be hurt by a statute of limitations? Rice wondered. He hoped to be able to use the date the fraud was *discovered* to give them ample time to recover the art stolen from Staunton Hill. A civil action would of course result in unwelcome publicity, and any judgment against Michaelides might never be collected since he was probably out of the country for good. Yet, Rice speculated, a judgment might keep him permanently out of the United States, make life miserable for him in Greece, and serve as the basis for a claim against his Swiss bank account. They could also seize any Staunton Hill property stored in Maryville or elsewhere. Unsatisfied judgments against Marios might also support tax deductions for the Bruce brothers. Mary could be a defendant, a coconspirator in the bigamy who had since enjoyed the fruits of Marios's treachery.

After the May eleventh raid, Mary moved to an apartment in Vestavia, also in Jefferson County. That summer she had her furnishings crated and readied for shipment to Athens where she now planned to join Marios with the baby, Rosie. She made a visit to Greece, returning to Alabama on August eleventh. Meanwhile she had hired a lawyer named J. Ray Knopf to represent her.

Marios continued to deposit all the money he could get his hands on in his Swiss bank account.

With the two indictments in hand, Jester urged the FBI to issue those unlawful flight warrants and began to draw up documents to be sent to the State Department for the extradition of Marios from Greece.

On August twenty-fifth Mary asked Knopf to draw up her will. She was planning to leave for Athens on September fifteenth.

"I wanted to believe I wasn't so stupid," Mary says, explaining why she felt she had to go back to Greece that September. "I wanted to believe I hadn't been wrong about him." It seemed impossible still that she had been so completely mesmerized, so entirely taken in by this clever, witty, passionate man. As Sasha had learned, the truth could be discovered only in Greece. Mary began her preparations for this final pilgrimage. On September first she left Birmingham, arranging for eight hundred dollars owed to her to be forwarded to her parents in Maryville.

*   *   *

The Charlotte County Special Grand Jury of Inquest convened again on September fifth and three days later charged that "on or about the seventh day of November, 1975, in the County of Charlotte, Marios Michaelides did feloniously kill and murder Alexandra Bruce Michaelides." The report of the Roanoke deputy chief medical examiner, Dr. David W. Oxley, was made available to the grand jury, but he was not invited personally to appear, no doubt because he thought Sasha had committed suicide. David Surtees Bruce testified that he was ninety percent certain that Marios Michaelides had murdered his sister.

On the trail of the remaining Staunton Hill property taken by Michaelides, Mills went to Maryville on September twentieth. He hoped for an interview with Mary before she departed for Greece. But Mrs. Lewis told Mills that her daughter had left on September seventeenth. Having consulted an attorney, this time Mrs. Lewis agreed to be interviewed.

Mary had told her about the divorce before leaving for Greece, she said. Mary had sold the Lincoln which had been in both her own and Marios's names. She had ordered her mother to tell no one her address in Greece, but Mrs. Lewis told Mills that Mary had called her on the nineteenth and was at the Atergi Hotel in Athens. Mills showed her the list of items missing from Staunton Hill. Yes, Mrs. Lewis admitted, Mary had told her there were things stored in "that warehouse" that Marios had taken from the Bruces. Mary had said she didn't like that type of furniture and wished the police had taken all of it. Mrs. Lewis confided she feared for her daughter's life in Greece. She was frightened that the Greeks would take her grandchild from her and she would never see little Rosie again.

All the Michaelideses' possessions were still in Alabama awaiting shipment. This time Mills was not too late. Obviously eager to cooperate, Mrs. Lewis phoned her son, David P. Lewis, in Birmingham. Lewis had often gone sailing with Marios and had almost been taken in by one of Marios's schemes. Marios had told him he was making millions on his stock deals because he had figured out a computer system to break the stock market. He had invited David Lewis to go into a consulting business with him. So successfully did

Marios convince this professor of economics of his expertise that, after the raids, David told Mary he wanted to save the system Marios had developed. He asked her permission and entered Marios's study. There he found that all Marios had were graphs he had copied out of a book!

Cooperating with the police now was "a point of honor" for Lewis. Mary's possessions were at the Finch Warehouse in Birmingham, he told Mills.

Mills flew back to Birmingham on September twenty-sixth. The DA had already obtained a manifest of the items stored at the Finch Warehouse in the name Mary Lewis Michaelides. Mills compared his stolen property list with the manifest and found that nearly every item appeared on both.

Mills got a search warrant and at 10:40 A.M. the next day a party, which included J. Ray Knopf and Mary's sister-in-law as well as a battalion of police, descended upon the Finch Warehouse. The recovered property included the Sully and the Swebach paintings, Heath's "Battle of Waterloo," the K'ang Hsi vases, a bronze horse, and many books. When Knopf produced a receipt for a drum table which Mary had purchased in Birmingham, it was not seized. An antique derringer pistol with four revolving barrels and a white handle was engraved "Charles Bruce."

The raid on the warehouse lasted until 4:45 P.M.

The recovered property was locked into a garage at State Police headquarters in Birmingham. Back in Virginia it was stored "under lock and key" at Mills's home until October third, when it was transported back to Staunton Hill. There it was locked into a vault in the basement of the Mansion House. The only two keys were placed in the custody of David Surtees Bruce.

The garrulous Knopf spoke without hesitation to Mills. He revealed he had recommended to Mary that she get a "divorce by proclamation" to be certain Rosie was legitimate. In July Marios had convinced Mary to come to Greece for two weeks so he could see Rosie. When she returned and told Knopf she was planning to move to Greece permanently, he had tried to talk her out of it. Mary might be well-educated, Knopf volunteered, "but she is very vulnerable and insecure."

What business is Marios in? Mills asked Knopf.

He and his brother Eugenios manufacture perfume by removing water from the Red Sea, Knopf said.

Knopf offered to come to Virginia to work out a solution so Mary and Marios could return to the United States together. But Marios would not return voluntarily to face criminal charges. Mills saw no point in informing Knopf that Marios had been indicted for Sasha's murder on September eighth.

I wish I knew more about Marios, Knopf mused. "I don't know if Marios had anything to do with Sasha's death or not, but I ask myself this question. 'Why did he settle for approximately one hundred thousand when he could have let her live and stayed with her and had a million?' "

Although Marios doesn't wish to return to the United States at present, Knopf concluded, "He might in the future. If he doesn't kick Mary out."

A final accounting of Sasha's estate was made in September 1978. By now everyone knew of the Arpad inventory; the question arose as to whether Sasha's one-third share of the furnishings of Staunton Hill should be changed from $33,000 to $200,000. There would be tax penalties on both state and federal taxes. Rice decided to stay with the $33,000 figure, invoking, if necessary, David Bruce's original $100,000 valuation made in 1970 and the appraisal by Marie Harper, Carroll Holt, and Daphne Piester made right after Sasha's death.

Still unaware that a murder indictment had been handed down against him, from Greece Marios instructed J. Ray Knopf to forward a selection of Sasha's letters to him to Edwin Baker, the Charlotte County prosecutor. Anxious to get his hands on these documents, Baker told Knopf they would certainly wait on any further indictments until they considered this new evidence.

"Don't worry. They have a very thin case," Knopf reassured Marios. Knopf then chose the letters he thought would help Marios and mailed them to Virginia.

On October fifth Marios wrote a letter of his own to Baker. He denied that he killed Sasha and demanded "truth and justice." He also threatened to furnish evidence to the newspapers that would "destroy the false image of the family" should justice not be accorded him. The IRS might like to know "about a multimillion dollar tax evasion," Marios said. According to Marios, these alleged tax evasions, rather than the circumstances of Sasha's death, explained the motivation of the Bruces in pursuing him so unfairly.

Attempting to put the bigamy charge to rest, Marios argued that Haitian divorces were accepted by all states, in contrast to those obtained in Mexico. Couples flew to Haiti for divorces in order to avoid having to file joint tax returns, Marios pointed out. If the IRS accepted the validity of those divorces, he didn't understand why his was in question. He didn't use the word "collusion," but the point was well taken since divorces for tax purposes were obviously collusive.

He had stolen nothing from Staunton Hill, Marios insisted. "Everything that was found on my hands was either given to me by my wife or her brothers or it was bought by me from her brothers after her death." He did not have receipts because he paid cash, he argued slyly, "since my wife's brothers were afraid to create evidence for an IRS investigation since the whole estate had been grossly undervalued."

"Until today," Marios wrote in his letter to Baker, "I thought that all of us, and I mean my wife's family and myself, would have had the time to evaluate the amount of responsibility each has had for her death. Unfortunately it seems to me that her loss has not changed the destructiveness that her family has performed upon her and upon her two brothers or their mentality which seeks to blame others for their actions."

Nicholas Bruce would support him in describing the unhappy family lives of the Bruce children, Marios claimed. "Specifically ask him if it is true or not that he left his family's home a long time ago after witnessing a vicious and dehumanizing verbal assault upon his sister after which he said, 'First you attack my brother David in this way and he is gone. Now it is Alexandra's turn. Well, I'm not waiting around for you to do it to me.' "

David Bruce Jr., Marios claimed in a story denied much later by the family, cut off his mother's head from every picture in which she appeared in his personal photograph album. "Whenever he hears or thinks about his mother, he has a noticeable emotional reaction." Nicholas gave away his wealth to a religious organization "to detach himself from the ties of his family"; David lives in Taiwan "simply to be separated from his family 'by two continents and two oceans,' as he put it.''

Marios then described the abortive Washington wedding which he saw as the immediate cause of Sasha's suicide. Her aunt had written that Sasha "was nothing more than a common whore." "Shortly thereafter," Marios said, "my wife, who never recovered from that experience, which represented the final straw in an insupportable burden of similar events, took her life.

"Nick will remember that in talking about his own mother he criticized her as a very sick and dangerous woman," Marios added. Sasha herself was not "an emotionally unbalanced person. She was a criminally mistreated and unhappy person."

If he had killed her, if he were a thief of property, why had he chosen the United States as his place of residence? Marios demanded. Even after Rice threatened him, he didn't move his property back to Greece: "I knew my innocence and could not conceive that any sort of criminal proceedings could possibly be instituted against me."

He would not return to the United States to defend himself now, Marios said, "because of the fear that I am facing very powerful and dangerous people who do not know to put a limit anywhere." But neither did he wish to live with a stigma he didn't deserve.

His only recourse was to seek publicity by furnishing that evidence of a "multimillion dollar tax evasion" to the newspapers. He volunteered to take a polygraph test provided his accusers did as well.

"Ending my letter," Marios wrote, "I would like to emphasize that my goal is restoration of my name and the return of the objects taken from me and permanent disassociation from the pure maliciousness that prompted the accusations against me."

In late September Edwin Baker met with Tom Ramsey, the legal assistance officer who handled extradition treaties for the State Department. On September twenty-eighth they had received a telegram from Athens. The Greek government wouldn't place Michaelides under provisional arrest, as the State Department wanted. Nor would they consider extradition back to the United States; a 1931 treaty with the United States absolutely and clearly forbade the extradition of Greek citizens, provided they were citizens before the crime was committed, for any offense. Rice, Jester, and Baker had not done their homework.

But the Greek authorities would entertain a request to try Marios in Athens; their civil law system, unlike the Anglo-Saxon, allowed an individual to be tried outside the jurisdiction in which the crime was committed.

Unwilling to forward any documentation to Greece, Baker proposed a meeting in Athens between officials of their Ministry of Justice and representatives from Virginia. "To have this bunch come over, it would be a first," a Charlotte County observer laughed. Greece said no. Michaelides was placed under surveillance in Athens and his right to leave Greece was revoked. But the Greek Ministry of Justice would go no further without seeing the evidence against him.

Well into October 1978 a blackout prevailed over the news that indictments had been handed down against Ambassador Bruce's Greek son-in-law. This should not have been surprising for tiny Charlotte County where, it is said, "the old courthouse runs everything, who gets appointed, who gets elected, everything" and David Bruce is considered "a little god. You don't say anything bad about the Bruces."

Back in June, John Clement, a reporter for the Richmond *Times-Dispatch* covering Southside Virginia, had been informed by one of his sources that "a real good story" was brewing in Charlotte County. "What could be happening in Charlotte County?" Clement wondered. Sufficiently intrigued, he scoured the tiny clerk's office in Charlotte Courthouse, but could find nothing. Then Clement interviewed Ed Baker, who he knew was considered by the courthouse crowd to be "a good old boy from way back."

"You're not going to find any documents in the courthouse. You're not going to find anything. You don't know anything," Baker told Clement in September when from his source Clement already knew that a special grand jury of inquest had met twice and had handed down three indictments.

"I don't know what you're looking for," Stuart Fallen, the clerk of the court who had replaced Edwin Hoy and who was a man in his mid-twenties, told Clement as he searched through the court diaries.

Finally Clement went back to Baker and threatened a suit in which he would charge Baker with a violation of the Freedom of Information Act of Virginia which specifies that documents "made and received in pursuance of law by public officers" had to be made available to both the press and citizens of the state. By now Clement knew that the State Department was in on the case. He was ready to break the story no matter what.

"Yes, there were indictments," Baker now admitted to Clement. "I think you'll find them if you go down to the courthouse."

By the time Clement had driven the twenty minutes from Baker's office in Keysville to Charlotte Courthouse the indictments had miraculously appeared.

"I just came from the court and they're in my docket," Fallen, all innocence, told Clement. He had been carrying the indictments around on his person. Technically they had been in the courthouse!

The Sunday before his copyrighted article was to appear, Clement drove to Staunton Hill to offer David Surtees Bruce the opportunity to respond. Clement left his card. That night David left town.

The State Police in Birmingham told Clement as he worked on a follow-up to his original story of October twenty-second, "Oh Lord, we can't talk to you. That judge up there has put a gag order on it!" Clement printed that Judge Snoddy had ordered Baker not to discuss the case. Later Snoddy admitted to Clement that there had been no gag order issued by the court. He had simply told Baker to keep his mouth shut. Baker confided to the *Life* reporter covering the story that there had never been a gag order. He had called Judge Snoddy and asked how he might avoid carnivorous reporters. "Tell them 'no comment,' " he said the judge told him. So he began replying, "I talked to Judge Snoddy and must say 'no comment.' " It was not Baker's fault if this was mistakenly interpreted by reporters as a ruling from on high.

In the sensationalized accounts of Sasha's death which flooded the papers, Marios became "the secretive, unctuous Greek . . . a tall, slender, dark-haired Greek-looking charmer— the kind one would find roaming at late-night hours around the Constitution Square in Athens, trying to pick up lonely tourists.'' When Sasha's baby brother lost a shoe, someone wrote, a butler retrieved it on a silver tray. Staunton Hill became a ''ghostly Scottish castle,'' the tree a ''fifty-foot Magnolia,'' and the silver discovered in a ''deserted'' apartment in Birmingham. Rosie was repeatedly referred to as ''Alexandra'' or ''Sasha.'' *Life* hired a helicopter to fly over Staunton Hill so its photographer could take pictures of the real thing.

''If he was out to kill her, why didn't he make sure she was dead before calling for help?'' a local was reported as reasoning. The most outlandish and gratuitous comment came in *Life*, which printed that in the 1920s Mrs. Bruce's father, drunk, fell down the steps of the residence in Peking and broke his neck, while it was whispered that his wife had actually pushed him. When I asked him if there was any basis of truth in this story, David Surtees Bruce denied it vociferously: ''My grandmother never killed my grandfather.'' And much was made over the ''mystifying'' series of ''untimely'' deaths which followed Sasha's; by now Elizabeth Hamlett, Buss Baker, Byron Keeling, and David K. E. Bruce were gone. Downey Rice had a routine gall bladder operation in November of 1978 after which he immediately went back to work on the Michaelides case. On December 3 he died suddenly of an apparent heart attack.

Persisting in his refusal to send any evidence to Greece, Baker announced he didn't consider it his legal right to request a trial in Greece and would not do it. He knew that the Greeks had to come to him for the evidence. They had not done so, he claimed, and he doubted that they would. ''They'd have had a hell of a time getting witnesses from Charlotte County,'' Baker said. His hope was to negotiate with Michaelides's American lawyer, John Lowe of Charlottesville, who would later represent Private Garwood. Baker was determined that Marios stand trial in Charlotte County.

Bewildered by the silence from Virginia, but anxious to show good faith, the Athens public prosecutor, Alexander Metaxas, on October twenty-fifth ordered Michaelides to appear before a magistrate on charges of willful manslaughter, bigamy, and vagrancy. Should Michaelides fail to appear at this hearing, Metaxas said, the prosecutor's office would immediately order his arrest.

Denying all the charges against him, Marios angrily used the Greek press to accuse the Bruces of framing him so that he would be ineligible for what in private he called his "true inheritance." "My wife's family persecutes me because I know a secret that can send them to jail," he claimed. As soon as he cleared his name, he would sue the Bruces for what was rightfully his. Since he had renounced his rights to Sasha's estate, he couldn't have murdered her for gain. "Had she lived," he said, "I would have had the advantage of sharing her large income from a huge trust."

"If one is interested in money," Michaelides's lawyer Panayotis Vrettos cried, "then he does not give up 1.5 million dollars for a mere two hundred thousand." Marios's "secret" was a tax evasion which would land the Bruces in jail. "It's millions of dollars we're talking about," Vrettos exclaimed, "and, yes, that includes undervaluing their property in Virginia."

The $190,000 was given to him as a gift by Sasha's brothers "as a show of sympathy and liking," Marios insisted. The renouncement was dated November 1975, the checks for $100,000 and $90,000, January 1976. Didn't this fact alone prove his point?

The last of the four indictments against Marios Michaelides was handed down on November eighth. It accused him of "unlawfully and feloniously steal(ing) certain items of personal property." Affixed to the indictment was a long list that ranged from the silver confiscated on May eleventh to the works of art and books removed from the Finch Warehouse in September. Included as well was the L. C. Smith 8-gauge shotgun for which Marios had received four hundred dollars but which was valued at six thousand dollars. Today it would be worth thirty thousand dollars.

John Lowe, Marios's new lawyer, announced that Marios would return to the United States to stand trial provided polygraph tests to be taken by himself and the Bruces be made admissible in court proceedings. Should Marios "pass" the lie detector test, Virginia would agree to drop all charges.

On November eleventh, Duncan Spencer of *The Washington Star* called Evangeline Bruce and told her of Marios's challenge. Mrs. Bruce replied that she and her two sons would be willing to take lie detector tests if it would help the case. On Monday the thirteenth her secretary, Robin Young, denied that Mrs. Bruce had ever made such an offer. "She definitely has not made any statement to the press and she has no idea where it came from," ran the *Washington Post* story.

Lowe also insisted upon a change of venue to Richmond or northern Virginia because of the influence of the Bruces in Charlotte County. Should Marios return, Virginia would also decline to seek a trial in Greece. He said he feared Marios might be framed. Someone might suddenly appear and claim Marios had confessed to him. An eyewitness might mysteriously turn up. "It's troublesome when a family hires a hard-pressing lawyer, like a hired gun," Lowe said. "When you hire a private detective and throw money around, there's room to cloud the truth."

The motive of the Bruces was to protect their property, Lowe claimed. Because of improprieties in taxation, they were ready to destroy a man's reputation vindictively. They were simply trying to prevent Marios from returning to the United States to exert his legitimate claim to his wife's estate. The murder charge was "an absolute fabrication, a fantasy." But Lowe couldn't go into court and offer a motion to quash the murder indictment on the ground of insufficient evidence because Marios had never been served by the court. Technically it had no power over him.

Lowe also believed he could contest the validity of the document of renouncement in court. It may have been because the renouncement was illegal, Lowe thought, that in December 1975 David had listed Marios as Sasha's "sole inheritor" in the Charlotte County Book of Records. Did David know then that the disclaimer was invalid? Did David and Nicholas not wish to appear as the beneficiaries of a falsely appraised estate? Or did they fear that the heir was liable to the claims of Mark's Trust? Virginia law indeed outlines that for a disclaimer to be valid it must describe the property disclaimed and be executed in the manner of a deed of real estate. David's paper fulfills none of the requirements.

With the threat of Marios's inheriting Sasha's property, Lowe asserted, he had to be gotten out of the way. As a bigamist, he would have been ineligible to inherit under the terms of her will; as a murderer he could not lay claim to the estate of a murdered spouse in Virginia.

"If I killed her as the product of a fight, or as a result of her finding out about the baby, it would not have been premeditated," Marios began saying. "I knew Priscilla was coming. How could the crime have been premeditated?" Under Greek law the punishment for murder in the first degree could be death by firing squad provided the crime was committed under "repulsive circumstances." The death penalty in Virginia is reserved for "willful, deliberated, and premeditated killing" under circumstances which seem not to apply to that altercation between husband and wife at Staunton Hill on November seventh.

"It was not premeditated," David Surtees Bruce agreed. "His mind snapped."

"Over trusts people get indicted," Marios said. "They indict someone down there for not liking fried chicken!" And didn't they go for the murder charge only when they found bigamy and grand larceny were not extraditable, but murder might be? "If someone had hurt my child, I'd go straight for murder. If murder had come first, it would look entirely different. It would look as if they were interested in whether I hurt her or not."

John Lowe telephoned Wilmington Trust and asked if Marios retained any rights to Sasha's trust. "We're not going to tell you anything," was the reply. "You have a moral obligation to answer," Lowe said. Why didn't they just say "No, he has no rights," Lowe wondered later.

Marios was now convinced that either he—or Rosie—might be in line either for Sasha's or part of David K. E. Bruce's trusts. If he were guilty of murder, he would be effectively barred from participating in those trusts. And he knew title would not clear on Staunton Hill if there were doubt about the legality of the renouncement. The Bruces couldn't imagine that he would sign another renouncement, Marios scoffed. "Half of Staunton Hill was Ailsa's. Did David K. E. Bruce turn it back? He wouldn't renounce so he couldn't imagine anyone else would!"

Marios was certain he could beat the bigamy charge. "How could I have known I was not legally married to Sasha and also have killed her to inherit her estate?" he reasoned. There could be no bigamy conviction in Greece where civil marriages were not recognized.

Meanwhile the statute of limitations was running out on the grand larceny charge in both countries. In Greece it was only three months if the crime was committed abroad; in Virginia they had five years to recover personal property and three years to recover "money paid under fraud." There was also sufficient ambiguity regarding what David and Nicky had permitted Marios to take and what he had stolen. He and Sasha had brought one of the bronze horses to Athens together, Marios claimed. Later he brought it back to Birmingham "for sentimental reasons." In his first affidavit David had accused him of stealing a bronze horse by Barye which Sasha herself had sold to Arpad for eighteen hundred dollars to help pay for the inventory; there is in fact a letter addressed to Sasha from Michael Arpad dated July 26, 1975, which refers to his getting a price of fifteen hundred dollars for what he calls "a group of the tartar on the horse."

The silver inkstand had been a gift from Sasha to Marios. Other pieces of silver he had purchased himself, Marios said. Some of the books listed by David, like a Franklin Mint Shakespeare, he had bought. And of those with the Staunton Hill bookplate—how did they know Sasha had not given them to him? He ignored the fact that they were not hers to give. Nor did he attempt to justify having sold the rare books through Christie's after her death.

Behind it all, Marios asserted, was David's listing of Sasha's share of the Staunton Hill furnishings as $33,000, although Rice had used the Arpad evaluation during the Alabama raids as a means of identifying Staunton Hill property. If the correct appraisal were invoked, what would that do to the gift tax Bruce paid in 1970 when he gave his children the contents?

In using that $33,000 figure, David had profited twice. Neither the estate nor his share of Sasha's one third had been appropriately taxed.

And wasn't it at least a conflict of interest—if not strictly against the law—for Royston Jester, who had worked for the Bruces on this case, to be made special prosecutor?

"Just because you're a bastard," Marios said sardonically, "doesn't mean you're a killer."

"I'm not wrong about him," David Surtees Bruce said from Virginia with a vehemence belying worries about back taxes or clear title to his house. "I wouldn't expect any remorse. He's the kind you have to wipe off the street. When you're dealing with certain kinds of psychopaths, they don't consider they did wrong in the first place."

The Greeks had made their formal request for the evidence against Michaelides through the State Department only to be rewarded by silence. The Governor's office in Richmond took the position that the decision had to be Baker's; neither the governor nor the state attorney general had authority over local commonwealth attorneys in Virginia. Only Judge Snoddy could rule over Baker's conduct.

Meanwhile Baker still pretended he was eager for a trial in Greece, on one occasion even pulling a United States passport from his desk drawer, proof that he was ready to go. The State Department was giving him a "run-around" he declared. He complained that the six-hundred-dollar bill Charlotte County received from the State Department to cover the cost of translating the indictments into Greek was too high and delayed paying it.

Baker next sent the State Department a series of questions about Greek law and judicial procedure. "Would I be required to go to Greece?" he wanted to know. "Would I participate?"

In mid-March 1979, Baker got his answers. In Athens the only role for Baker and Jester would be as witnesses. Baker said he and Jester would decide either to forward the evidence or to drop the case. Two more months passed.

* * *

Baker had also asked the State Department whether Marios would have an opportunity to see the evidence should he send it over. According to the Greek system, the accused is permitted to respond to the evidence marshaled against him prior to the decision regarding whether to indict, unlike the Anglo-Saxon where grand jury proceedings are sealed and indictment precedes accessibility of the evidence provided the accused has not already been arrested and charged.

One State Department lawyer joked, "The Greeks can't convene a trial on the basis of an indictment that's one and a half lines long!" They had gone quite far in charging Michaelides without possessing any of the evidence. Why was Baker so anxious that Michaelides not see it? He would have access to it soon enough once the Greek Ministry of Justice began proceedings against him.

If Michaelides saw the evidence and there was no trial, Baker asserted, he would never return to Charlotte County, so strong was the case against him.

"Won't you at least give us some of the evidence?" the State Department wearily requested.

"Well, no," Baker replied.

Since June 1978 Baker had lost eighty pounds, forty at the Duke University reducing clinic. His hair turned from black to white. "In the movie version of this case," joked Frederick Gray, Jr., commonwealth secretary now handling the liaison between Baker and the Governor's office, "you'll have to be played by two actors!"

Baker returned to his old demand for a meeting in Athens with the Greek officials. If they would assure him that they would indict and try Michaelides after an oral rendition of the evidence, he would send over the complete file.

In May 1979 John Mills called Mrs. Lewis and asked if Mary would not be willing to testify against Marios. He was told she would not.

In a federal court where a speedy trial was in effect, Baker would have been in trouble, State Department lawyers thought. A prosecutor had to show he had made expeditious efforts to get the man back for trial. But the courts in Virginia were under no such restriction. Baker must have concluded he could sit on the evidence forever. In July 1979 John N. Dalton, Governor of Virginia, announced to the press that his office was trying to convince Baker to cooperate with the State Department. "Why is it so difficult to give the evidence?" Frederick Gray still asked. "You're not going to get Marios back to America unless he's scared. It's his home, so why should he leave? Send the evidence!"

"Why doesn't the American system of justice *force* Baker to send the evidence to Greece given the extradition law and that the Greek Ministry of Justice is willing to try him?" demanded Marios's flamboyant lawyer in Greece, Panayotis Vrettos.

Still Baker tried to negotiate with John Lowe for Michaelides's return to Virginia. Well into the summer of 1979 talks continued. Baker balked on the issue of change of venue. "The funny thing about this whole case," he would confide in his best homespun manner, "is that everywhere within the English-speaking world, this case has received more publicity and more talk than it has right here in Charlotte County. I'm sure that probably ninety percent of the people in this county don't even know about it . . . if you summoned a jury panel, you'd hardly find two or three who heard anything about the case." Although by law Baker could have tried the case himself in the new jurisdiction, he may have felt he had the best chance of winning a murder conviction on his home ground.

Baker told Lowe that in Greece there were fewer restrictions on hearsay and circumstantial evidence. With the judge retaining the most substantial role, nothing was inadmissible. Decisions were made by a trained jurist who knew what evidence was. Marios would be better off if he came back.

In September 1979 the Charlotte County Board of Supervisors expressed extreme reluctance to pay the cost of sending witnesses to a trial in Greece. Baker's salary was around twelve thousand dollars a year and there was a dispute about raising it to fourteen thousand. The Greek government was accustomed to paying for the transportation of witnesses by the kilometer. But the Bruce family told Gray they would be willing to contribute. In Greece this would not be viewed as undue influence.

David Surtees Bruce contends that by September 1979 Baker and Jester had agreed to both the polygraph and the change of venue. They balked only at the removal of Jester. According to Lowe, there was no agreement that members of the Bruce family would take the polygraph and no agreement as to change of venue. Negotiations between Lowe and Baker for Marios's return just petered out.

That December Baker confided to the press that "several reliable sources" had suggested that the CIA had played a role in Sasha's murder. The American government had made "deliberate attempts" to hush up the issue and the second [sic] autopsy "confirmed some suspicions" he had. The State Department was delaying action on attempts to extradite Michaelides, Baker repeated. The Secretary of State himself was personally involved in the obstruction of justice.

A few days later Baker issued a retraction. He now denied accusing the CIA of involvement in Sasha's death or stating that Michaelides may have had CIA connections prior to the slaying. What he had meant was only that "several people," still nameless, had suggested to him some past involvement or connection between the agency and Michaelides.

"Turn off the recorder," Prosecutor Baker had whispered to me in his Keysville office on May 2, 1979. "I've been waiting for someone like you to come down. There's a great story here!" He patted the two fat files on his desk possessively. And then he proposed collaboration on a book about Sasha's murder.

Baker said he was certain Michaelides would never return to the United States to stand trial. All he had to do now was ask Judge Snoddy to close the case and the project could proceed. "There's a lot of money in this," Baker said. "Maybe half a million." He would do none of the actual writing himself, although his name would appear as coauthor. His contribution would be the files he was pulling closer to him. An old army buddy of his who lived in Pennsylvania, now a lawyer, would represent Baker in the negotiations with New York publishers.

Meanwhile it was urgent that the writing begin. Baker could be consulted in June at the Duke University reducing clinic; Judge Snoddy's permission would easily be obtained later. "No information until we make a deal!" Baker said next. And that was that.

"Solicitation of a bribe!" decided a Virginia deputy attorney general when he found out. "That isn't a crime, is it?" Edward Bennett Williams would later wonder, referring to Baker's overture. "If a commonwealth attorney says, 'drop the case,'" Gray of the Governor's office worried, "a judge will accept his view that the evidence—or the circumstances—have made it impossible to proceed." Meanwhile Baker had requested from Royston Jester documents and evidence that Baker said were missing from his own set of files.

Shortly after Baker ran unopposed for reelection as commonwealth attorney in November 1979, a meeting was held at the courthouse in Farmville. Present were the deputy attorney general, Judge Snoddy, the ubiquitous Jester, Gray, David Surtees Bruce, and Baker. Judge Snoddy told Baker he would do well to remove himself from the Michaelides case quietly and this time without resorting to the press. The short, amateur actor, now white-haired and slim, had played out his hand. At last he relinquished to the State Department his heavy file folders composed of the Rice and Mills investigations.

"Welcome!" Marios had cried that summer of 1979, an elegant Athens businessman in a tan suit and light blue shirt carrying an attaché case. Behind the omnipresent sunglasses stood a short, dapper young man with a curly brown mustache, dark olive skin, and irregular teeth. "You've come to save my life, you've come to rescue me!" he announced dramatically in minimally accented English, belying those natives of Charlotte County who said they could scarcely understand him. He presented himself as the helpless victim of powerful people from the Bruces to State Department lackeys and bought prosecutors. If he did pull that trigger on November 7, 1975, it seemed by now he had convinced himself that he hadn't done it.

"I read every day in *The Herald Tribune* of people with tax evasions of five thousand, eight thousand dollars who end up behind bars," he argued passionately. "Those people can do whatever they like. Who dares touch them? If there is any bloody justice in this life, Baker and the Bruces should go to

the electric chair! This is not a district attorney! This is a
gangster! Crime is crime everywhere. He could bring the case
here and chop my head off. But his power is only in Lynchburg,
Virginia, where he can force people to testify to lies, where
he can shut me up before I even go to trial. I can't come back
and defend myself because I am going in a place where they
have sent a lynching party!''

A Greek journalist in Washington had intimated that Marios may have been an officer of the LOK, the Greek Special
Forces, who one day had been observed visiting Anton von
Kassel in London. But no such mysterious figure out of a
paramilitary conspiracy greeted the visitor to Athens.

''The CIA terrifies me,'' he confessed, lighting what must
have been his tenth cigarette, and laughing off the thought of
an intrigue embracing Greek colonels, intelligence agencies,
the Bruces, and himself. ''They want a James Bond story.''
But Marios and his family were ''peaceful people.'' He did
have powerful friends, however, who had offered ''to take
care of the Virginia situation for him.''

''You should pursue the story of Audrey and Stephen
Currier,'' he advised, lapsing into his nonaggressive, self-
pitying mode, ''and leave this one that the filthy Greek did
it.'' Still later he would play the sardonic social critic whose
satiric bent enabled him to penetrate the follies of others.
''There is nothing more dangerous than a Virginian with his
feelings hurt,'' he reflected. His own merchant origins
notwithstanding, patrician aspirations surfaced as he attacked
mercantile Greeks like Niarchos. ''Once a merchant,'' Marios declared, ''you'd sell your mother's bed to make a
profit.''

Sasha's death ruined his life, he claimed. Since Downey
Rice had begun hounding him, he hadn't slept with a woman
and had lost so much weight that he looked like a different
person. He didn't want a trial not because he feared for
himself—his life was over anyway—but because he wished to
protect Sasha's reputation. He called her ''my little girl'' and
repeated ''my wife was not crazy'' several times. He had
turned down book and television rights to his story, so repelled was he by the thought of profiting from Sasha's death.

''Do you find me weak?'' he asked disingenuously. He
cast his eyes up at the cathedral ceiling of the lobby of the
Grande Bretagne Hotel. ''Is somebody up there loving me or

hating me?'' he intoned. ''I'm only a human being. Give me a break!''

''Do you think this could all be theater?'' he challenged.

His brother Eugenios had urged him to be cautious about what he told me. ''How come she came here alone and wasn't frightened to meet a criminal?'' Eugenios demanded. ''How do we know she hasn't come from Baker's office?'' Nonetheless Marios introduced me to Mary and Rosie, who were living with him in a modest but modern apartment adjacent to a polluted section of the Aegean. Mary wore matronly suburbanite clothes—a brown chino skirt, checked blouse, and sensible brown stacked-heel shoes with rubber soles. She had gray hair cut short and was overweight. All exuberance, Rosie danced about in a red dress and red sandals, her blond hair caught by a barrette. The apartment was crowded with heavy new furniture, a powder blue crushed-velvet couch, glass tables, and a very elaborate tape-recorder/record-player system. Nothing in that apartment indicated that the scene was taking place in Greece.

Mary wanted to return to Tennessee but was afraid of being charged as an accessory. Could she be extradited to Virginia? she wondered. She said she was convinced of Marios's innocence. Nor could she blame him even if he had married Sasha for her money. ''Didn't David Bruce once do the same thing?'' Mary asked. ''It's condoned as far as he's concerned!''

''My nerves are shot!'' Marios apologized after harsh words to Mary who wanted to go out for lunch on this suffocatingly hot day when the temperature had already climbed to 106 degrees (the apartment was not air-conditioned). ''Is your stomach hurting you, Marios?'' Mary inquired solicitously as Marios elaborately winced, then reached for the Pepto-Bismol.

Casually I asked to see an example of the Bruce crested silver. ''Do you have any of it?''

''Yes,'' Mary said and rose to fetch it from the kitchen.

''No,'' Marios said simultaneously.

Mary sat back down.

''Would Rosie be better off without a father or with a father accused of murder?'' Marios wanted to know.

''Don't wait to call home until your body is chopped up into pieces and shipped home in a trunk,'' he advised me another day. Solicitous, he discouraged pursuit of the Byzantine icon smuggling angle of Sasha's story. ''I wouldn't want to be in your shoes!'' he pronounced. Passing a shop window filled with magnificent icons, he affected a shiver of revulsion. He himself was the victim of a racist frame-up engineered by very powerful people. ''For David Bruce Senior I was a Greek. I was expendable. Imagine if I were from Argentina. Then the tango would be thrown in!''

Marios couldn't understand why Bruce hadn't taken ''one of his kids and put it on the path he was on . . . leave something behind him, a dynasty. He never took an interest in shaping one of them.'' He returned to his romantic musing. He had a mole on his right hand. Sasha developed one just like it on her left. They would place these moles together when they went to sleep at night, so perfect was their love. Abruptly the conversation would suddenly turn to the Bruce trusts. ''If Nick and David don't have children . . . how is that crazy thing set?'' Marios wondered. ''If I only knew the rules of that damn thing. . . .

''All the drugs, icons, gigolos,'' Marios said, ''none of it was a real rebellion.'' His lawyer Vrettos would bring psychiatrists to any trial to analyze Sasha's character. But he was certain he had ''zero chance'' if he stood trial in the United States. If the ''old fox'' had lived, he murmured, ''things would never have gone this far. The old fox, an expert negotiator, would have known when to compromise.''

But Nick might help him now, Marios thought. If only he could smoke Nick out. ''Nick wouldn't lie,'' Marios was certain. ''I don't believe Nick would lie under any circumstances. He's a person of real integrity. I believe he's a good, decent person. Instinctively he must understand that his family has the power to present things differently from what they really were, about that Nick has no illusions.'' (At that moment during the summer of 1979, Marios did not yet know about Nicky's testimony to John Mills in which he had revealed that Sasha confided in him about how Marios had tortured her, that ''he knew every way to inflict pain,'' and that after her May overdose he had threatened, ''I could kill you and make it look like suicide.'')

''If you are ever in trouble,'' Marios told the departing visitor, ''you should take the next plane to Greece and knock on my door. You don't even have to send me a cable. I'll know.''

*   *   *

Nicholas Bruce was living in a run-down converted brownstone in a semi-industrial neighborhood bordering Center City, Philadelphia. He appeared, a tall, gangling boy in glasses, exceedingly skinny with unwashed brown hair hanging limply in his eyes. Unshaven, he wore an old violet T-shirt and blue jeans. With a sweet vulnerable smile he said he would not talk about his family. "Between those two," Nick stated, referring to his mother and brother, "you should have all you need."

Impervious to Michaelides's allegations about gift taxes and tax evasions, David Surtees Bruce now began to pursue the case in earnest. According to the Greek code, relatives of a victim may file a criminal complaint in Greece, even if the crime were committed in America.

"Revenge is a dish best savored cold," David said. "Most people tell me to lay off, but if he didn't do it, he drove her to it. If you felt even one percent sure he killed her, you have a moral obligation to find out."

David believed Michaelides would confess under the pressure of testifying in a courtroom. "His personality is such that under the right kind of pressure questioning, he'd break down and tell the truth. The very day of the incident was the one on which he would have been exposed," David said, placing a great emphasis on the importance to Sasha of Priscilla's visit.

In Greece a judge does the investigation carried on in America by a grand jury. The actual indictment is then handed down by a three-judge panel presided over by the original investigating magistrate. Circumventing the state of Virginia, David Surtees Bruce organized a petition to an investigating magistrate in Athens.

Early in 1980 David invited George Mangakis, a well-known Greek lawyer, to Staunton Hill to advise him on whether it was really worthwhile to pursue the case in Greece. Sharing an interest in the writers of the Frankfurt School, they got along well. Mangakis had a Ph.D. from a German university and was a professor of criminal law at Athens University. He was also a figure of moral stature in Greece; a leader of the resistance against the junta, he had been tortured and jailed for two years. As in the French system, Mangakis would be the "civil prosecutor" whose function was to aid and supervise the work of the district attorney, or "state prosecutor." Mangakis agreed to take the case.

Around the same time that Mangakis was visiting Staunton Hill, in Athens Mary found a book about the fate of foreign women in Greece. Becoming alarmed, she decided to return to Tennessee, this time for good, and, despite Marios's objections, taking Rosie with her. "I don't care if you go to the ends of the earth," Marios had yelled the day she left. "If Mommy goes to the ends of the earth, I want to go with her," Rosie now three years old piped up.

In the spring of 1980 the State Department formally transmitted the file of evidence against Marios Michaelides through the diplomatic pouch to the American Embassy in Athens. The translations into Greek now took six months to complete. Mangakis's own translation was not accepted by Vrettos or Michaelides's other lawyer, Nicholas Androulakis, also a professor at Athens University. The American Embassy took the position that if the Greeks decided to prosecute, they should pay for the witnesses to come to Greece. On October eighth the file, now in Greek, was transmitted to the Ministry of Foreign Affairs of Greece at the request of Professor Mangakis, representing "the David Bruce family."

By the time the Greek authorities were ready to examine Marios, it was March 1981. As Downey Rice had predicted, Marios had indeed found himself "a new pigeon." He was now living with a pretty, blue-eyed Englishwoman with creamy white skin in her late thirties named Shirley Corderoy, whose Greek husband had run away with his eighteen-year-old secretary. With his typical humor, Marios told me I was soon to meet his "third victim."

Together they ran the Power Investment Trust, Inc., a brokerage outfit affiliated with E. F. Hutton, speculating in currency, and grossing, Marios claimed, four thousand dollars a day. Video machines hooked up to the world's stock exchanges flashed prices around the clock. These cost E. F.

Hutton twenty-five thousand dollars a month, Marios proudly told me.

He and Shirley were investing their own money in platinum. "With your partner you must be totally open, totally honest," Marios said of his new relationship.

"All these years he idealized Sasha," Shirley said. "He made a myth of her."

"That's over now," Marios promised. He planned to make all that up to her. When Shirley asked him why he needed to corner the cotton market, he said he would be doing it for her.

Shirley feared Marios's life would be ruined by this case being brought against him: "He'll lose his work, he'll lose everything." Even if he were cleared, he would no longer be trusted with other people's money.

Marios was with her nearly every minute of the day. He commented on her new pink blouse. "Handsome," he pronounced. Her stockings were correctly pale. They were "rebels," he declared, boring into the stock market from within, having fun.

The investigating magistrate who would determine whether Marios Michaelides was to be indicted in Greece for Sasha's murder was Spiro Tsiros, a religious man, tall and fat and rumpled with gold teeth, thinning hair, and horn-rimmed glasses, a man with a strong moral sense and a scrupulous regard for the law.

On March thirtieth Tsiros was ready to hear Marios's side; murder would be the only one of the charges the Greeks were prepared to consider. Tsiros's first task was to decide whether to jail Marios pending the outcome of his investigation. With murder charges, the defendant was customarily jailed without bail until the court reached its decision, although some cases dragged on for months before an indictment was handed down.

"Between two Greeks the case would go in the garbage can in a second," Marios pronounced after reading the state of Virginia's evidence. "No one in the file actually says I did it!" According to the Greek system, Michaelides would be granted an opportunity to respond to the file with no penalty of perjury; he would not be under oath and could say anything he wanted. Mangakis, the Bruces' lawyer, would not be present.

Dressed in a blue suit, white shirt, and royal blue paisley tie, Michaelides entered the magistrate's office accompanied by Vrettos and Androulakis. A secretary sat at an antiquated manual typewriter, two fingers poised to take down what Marios said. Behind Tsiros's desk was an iconlike painting of Christ. Another hung on the wall behind the couch on which Marios sat. Only the presence of a uniformed policeman outside the door indicated that this was criminal court.

Taking the offensive, Michaelides began to point out inaccuracies in the translation of the file. Meg Tibbs's account of what Marios had told her in Greek read "she shot herself" as if Marios already knew the details of the shooting. Her qualifications, "I'm not sure, I don't remember," had been omitted.

"Why didn't Tibbs hear the gunshots?" Tsiros asked.

"It was winter," Marios said.

Tsiros wasn't concerned about the silver, the rare books, or the Jaguar. Only the issue of murder interested him.

"Why did Mary come here?" he wanted to know.

Marios told him he'd wanted to see his child.

Tsiros turned to Nicholas Bruce's testimony, the most damaging in the file.

"He states you said you could kill her one day and make it look like suicide," the magistrate noted.

"Why did he wait two and a half years to come up with that when he was acting as my friend and I was advising him," Marios rejoined, obviously ready for this question, if exaggerating by nearly a year. He instructed Tsiros to reread the interview with Mrs. Bruce where she comments on her younger son's penchant for fantasy, his inability to distinguish the real from the make-believe.

"If you saw Nick, you would understand his credibility," Marios told Tsiros.

"Why?"

"He's on drugs," Marios replied.

Then Marios had a question of his own. How did the magistrate explain that Nick remained his friend for so long a period of time if Nick believed he had killed Sasha?

"You had control over him," Tsiros told Marios.

"Did you know von Kassel?" Tsiros asked.

And this time Marios had to reply, "Yes, I did."

"How was your relationship with Sasha?"

"Perfect."

"Did you beat her with your fist?"

"In moments of hysteria I slapped her."

"What do you mean by hysteria?"

"Trying to cut her veins with a razor blade."

At one point Marios objected to the whole file. "Those testimonies weren't taken under oath," he complained. "They didn't bring anyone here. What about *their* credibility? Who are those people?"

Marios said pieces of his interview with the police on November eighth, including comments about the Washington wedding, hadn't been transcribed. And only interviews conducted more than a year later, not those made the weekend of the incident, had been sent to Greece. "Shouldn't we be able to compare the two sets?" he wanted to know.

"She made thirty suicide attempts," Vrettos declared. "Don't you want to hear?"

"When was the last time you saw the gun?" Tsiros asked.

This time Marios said it was ten days prior to Sasha's death that he put it under the bed.

"Why did you do that?"

"She was so disturbed. I didn't want her to have direct access to the gun."

Vrettos directed Tsiros's attention to Rice's phrase "the slimy Greek."

Marios flushed with anger. Always it rankled that he be thought inferior—Mediterranean, dark—not Anglo-Saxon, not "white."

"I noticed it. I noticed it," Tsiros said.

Androulakis asked how he visualized the practicalities of such a trial. But Tsiros was concerned only with determining whether or not to indict the man before him for murder. He refused to accept into evidence a copy of the Arpad inventory because it was in English. Nor was he interested in a Chamber of Commerce "stamp book" Marios had brought along as proof that he had been a respectable businessman since 1969. "You can bring it to me some other time," Tsiros said.

Nearly four hours had passed. Finally Tsiros left the room to consult with the district attorney. He was gone a half hour.

When he returned, he could not conceal his repugnance for the whole story.

"Divorce, a child with the first woman. You marry, then go back to her," Tsiros began. "Deep inside me, deep in my heart, I feel that you did it."

"But we'll let you go for the moment," Tsiros added. Marios could remain free pending his decision. "This way we satisfy both sides." He had seen Marios around the courthouse, he had a job, he had been back in Greece for two years. The magistrate was confident he wouldn't run away. Now Tsiros would take the case to the Judicial Council.

"No, I have not done it," Marios answered. "You can criticize my morality, but that you wouldn't consider me the most straight person doesn't make me a criminal. Whatever I did, I did in the open."

"I will be very pleased to find out you didn't do it because here we are not for chopping off heads, we are for justice," Tsiros replied. "I will be very pleased to find out you are innocent." He shook hands with Marios. Marios thanked him.

"Don't thank me," Tsiros said.

Outside, Marios despaired. "He was prejudiced against me, he was definitely prejudiced against me," he wailed. "He's the harshest of the whole group of magistrates. He was antagonistic; he was not objective."

What made Tsiros so rigid, one of Marios's friends speculated, was a scandal in his own family. When Tsiros's brother was in law school, he was accused of throwing his girl friend, an agricultural engineer, out a window. The coroner later ruled the woman had not died of the fall, but of suffocation during the sexual act. This brother had never practiced law, but the incident made Tsiros himself all the more unbending.

"He didn't believe me, he didn't believe me," Marios cried.

I traveled to Greece again in late March 1981 when Michaelides requested that I appear before Spiro Tsiros. Curiosity, access to these court proceedings, and the fact that any testimony would in all likelihood be more damaging than helpful to the defendant governed the decision to return to Athens. The same testimony would have been offered had either side requested it; it seemed reasonable for a private citizen to satisfy either side's request for information at this unlikely trial outside the jurisdiction in which the crime was allegedly committed and with practicalities making it difficult for closer observers to attend. A return to Athens also provided the opportunity to demand from Michaelides explanations for the discrepancies in his story.

"Sasha never lied to me!" he shouted when told Terry Graham denied approving of his isolation of Sasha at Staunton Hill. "Massey's afraid of losing his job!" he accused when told the rare book expert had denied witnessing a suicide attempt on the first weekend of November. He could not deny lying to David about Rosie's picture. Could *this* be David's motive in pursuing the case against him so relentlessly?

"You don't use a hydrogen bomb to kill a mosquito!" Marios scoffed. "Why didn't he just punch me in the nose?"

I informed the State Department and requested advice about this paid invitation by the defense in which a writer was to be a witness in a capital case in a foreign court. "We're afraid of slander and libel being printed about Sasha," David's attorney complained when I telephoned. "You're only calling me because the State Department already has!" He had no sympathy with the rights of a defendant being tried in Greece for a crime committed in America. "Let him come back to Virginia," David's lawyer threatened. "We'll give him a trial there!"

The day I testified in Athens to my astonishment Shirley Corderoy was permitted to interpret. Tsiros knew only enough English to enjoy helping; delightedly he came up with the Greek word for "obsession."

"What about Marios makes you think he's not a murderer?" Tsiros wanted to know. "Do you know anything about the way the body was found that would absolve Marios?" Shirley grew increasingly uncomfortable as I told Tsiros of John LeGrand's statement that Marios had told him, "I bet she killed herself."

"Who made her feel bad about herself?" Tsiros asked, introducing the issue of Sasha's November second plea that Mary take Marios off her hands.

"Why did she want to settle him down?"

And now both he and Shirley had to hear, for the first

time, that Marios had convinced Sasha she must "purify herself" to become worthy of him, and how miserable she had become under the enforced isolation he demanded at Staunton Hill.

"How was she to purify herself?" Tsiros wondered.

It was difficult to translate the word "purify" into Greek, especially since Shirley was now close to hysteria, so close to tears that it was virtually impossible for her to continue. She was hearing too many things about Sasha for the first time. She hadn't wanted to interpret, but the court had provided no alternative.

Tsiros held his horn-rimmed glasses in one hand while he donned another pair to read over the statement. He was clearly repelled by the story. Shirley had to be prevented from amending "she was unhappy" to "both she and he were unhappy."

Then, incredibly, Tsiros called in Marios who had been pacing nervously in the corridor the whole time. He was to read back the Greek translation into English so that its accuracy could be testified to! Perhaps Tsiros had intended this as a test for the defendant. Had Marios omitted the damaging passages, and been called on it, this would be further circumstantial evidence of his guilt. But the magistrate's enlisting the defendant as the final arbiter of the accuracy of the translation seemed highly irregular.

And so Marios sat down and read out the entire statement in English. He passed the discussion of Sasha's history of suicide attempts. At the part describing how he had ordered her to purify herself, how unhappy she was with him and how the last week of her life she had attempted to get rid of him and failed, he turned white and his voice trembled. But he swallowed hard and read on to the end.

Outside in the soft Athens springtime Marios said, "That was okay because it was what Sasha thought. And the statement shouldn't be completely positive!"

"David got that money!" he said angrily, referring to the fortune due Sasha on her thirtieth birthday. "He profited by his sister's death." The implication was that the money should have come to him.

"If the renouncement is found to be not legal," he announced, "I will give my share of Staunton Hill to charity!"

Who pulled the trigger of that .22 Walther? Why did Sasha choose first Anton and then Marios to be agents of her destruction? Why did Marios so allow himself to lose control of the situation that events would dramatically suggest that Sasha felt pushed into shooting herself? Or, worse, they would convince many who knew them both that he shot her, although greed dictated that he should have held out a while longer? Marios offered no illumination.

He laughed darkly. "Well, you go on trial for murder and I'll write the book."

Back in Maryville, Tennessee, furious with herself at having been taken in for so long by her former husband, Mary declared she was now willing to testify for the state of Virginia if it came to that. In August 1981 the Tennessee Bureau of Investigation called with a message. John Mills wished to see her. It was a bolt out of the blue. Mary wavered. Rosie's welfare was her first concern and she wished only to get on with her life. "I have nothing to say," she told the investigator.

In October the Greeks threw out the case against Marios on the ground of insufficient evidence. Waiting out the period during which David Surtees Bruce had to decide whether he would appeal the decision handed down by Tsiros and the consulting magistrates, Marios asserted indignantly that he was now ready to hire lawyers in the United States to have the charges against him in Virginia dropped. He knew that even if he had been tried and acquitted in Athens, he could still go on trial for murder if he ever returned to the United States; double jeopardy would not apply.

As this is written, the Virginia indictment for murder against Marios still stands. Under the immutable presumption of American constitutional law, he is innocent. That presumption could be overcome, and his guilt established, only if he returned to face trial and was convicted.

Fearing that he might have designs on their daughter, Mary trembled at the thought of Marios's return.

Angrier than ever at having been deceived and humiliated by his clever brother-in-law, and having long since persuaded himself of Marios's guilt, David chose to proceed to the

Court of Appeals of Athens. In January 1982 the Athens
Court of Appeals confirmed the ruling of the Criminal Court:
Virginia had presented insufficient evidence to indict Marios
Michaelides for the murder of Sasha Bruce.

Still David went on, taking the case to the Supreme Court,
although it was empowered to examine only the legalities of
the first two proceedings.

Meanwhile E. F. Hutton had removed Marios and Shirley
from their Athens brokerage operation. Americans were sent
in their place and all their funds were impounded. Under the
new socialist government of Andreas Papandreou, George
Mangakis became Greece's Minister of Justice.

By now David Surtees Bruce had settled permanently at
Staunton Hill. "It matters that it's been in the family all this
time," he said. "The incident has changed me inside. You
feel you're carrying on the torch. My brother has decided
Staunton Hill is not the place for him and doesn't want
anything to do with it. But my sister really loved this place
and I'm taking up where she left off.

"I despise large occasions, but I associate with local
individuals. I don't worry about the differences because here
I'm accepted because of family tradition. I like to be part of
the larger local life, although it took some reading of family
history. I'm happy being that way. I fit into all that. I'm not
an interloper. If they saw you as an interloper, they'd want to
know something more about you. But I'm accepted by the
local people and they don't come barging in. I'm pretty much
left alone and that suits me fine.

"Americans have no sense of where they come from. I'm a
deracinated person. If I had settled down someplace and set
down roots, it might have helped. But not having done so
made it imperative for me to have this place—a place I could
come home to, a place I could focus on with some family
tradition behind it. I could shake it off, but I would still feel
it's part of my heritage."

Evangeline Bruce called me on the telephone several times.
Once she quoted to me something Nicky had said that day.
"We were too happy, too lucky." It was as if the whole
family had been in a grand touring car, traveling along quite

happily. Then suddenly "there was a terrible accident. And this set off a chain reaction of accidents and pile-ups. And then the car was buried by dirt."

She spoke of the companionship she shared with her daughter. Sasha had once written a little biography of Evangeline Bruce. And Mrs. Bruce said she was planning to publish a volume of letters between herself and Sasha. Her daughter gained her sense of public spirit from her Bruce grandmother, Mrs. Bruce revealed. But the case was "David's case." She had considered suing *Life* magazine for what they had written about her, but her lawyer, Edward Bennett Williams, had dissuaded her.

In one of these telephone conversations, her mother outlined Sasha's best qualities: her irrepressible spirits, her dancing, how "merry" she was, her passionate love, her music, her political passions—but, above all, her "moral courage." She did choose the wrong men. But "Don't we all?" her mother reflected. Mrs. Bruce was sympathetic even with the obsessive quality of Sasha's relationships with her two Greeks. "Isn't that the way it always is?" she asked rhetorically. "Sasha didn't think men found her beautiful," her mother remembered fondly.

Sasha had been in touch with her up to two weeks before her death through reverse charge calls so Marios wouldn't know. Yet she had encouraged the marriage to Marios, Mrs. Bruce admitted. She wanted to be supportive of Sasha in whatever she decided to do. Her daughter needed that.

For Evangeline Bruce, Sasha, no less than her father, embodied the spirit of their family. "I see the lives of David and Sasha as triumphant," she pronounced.

Sensational Crime Stories from SIGNET and MENTOR